LEAD TO BEAT

As a leader, unique thinker, relentless achiever, and entrepreneur, Jonathan Escobar Marin has spent years changing the way companies operate, focusing on objectives that set the pace for organizations and professionals. His proven methods are catalysts for radical change, helping to redesign the architecture that defines the dynamics of priority management in organizations. In his book, *Lead to Beat*, Jonathan brilliantly underscores the absolute truths that generate profound insights: the need to be disproportionately focused on what's important, the connection between vision and execution, leadership as a synergetic force, the difference between doing and impacting, disciplined rhythm as a lever for agility and alignment, the mutual reinforcement generated by a culture of performance and development, and more. Jonathan explains like no one else how to move your organization toward success, so that you can truly realize your company's ultimate purpose. This book is a must-read for anyone who wants to understand or change the way the heart of their company beats!"

—David Payeras Bailly, chief people officer, MANGO

Lead to Beat is ultimately a needed reappraisal of effective leadership in a faster-than-ever changing environment, encapsulated in four key drivers. The book is grounded in pragmatism and actionability, a testament to its author, a former executive who knows and understands the challenges leaders face on a daily basis. The book is courageous enough to challenge some of the status quo mantras that hold organizations back from thriving. *Lead to Beat* tells you what you need to lead successfully. Are you ready to deliver what is needed to achieve it?"

—Pol Coding, general manager of food ventures, PepsiCo

Many seek the recipe for creating a high-performance team and generating value for their customers or consumers. Jonathan not only found that recipe but also shares it with the world. With the experience of having successfully transformed hundreds of companies over the years and knowing what gets results and what doesn't, Jonathan helps the companies he works with set a crucial drumbeat to pace themselves and compete in a changing environment where you either shift up two gears or fall behind. But Jonathan doesn't propose doing more but rather doing better—always thinking about the impact.

Jonathan implements working methods that leave out the embellishments, focusing only on what generates value. Against all odds, his strategy is so straightforward to apply once you learn it that it's impossible to go back once you try. The metamorphosis he achieves in companies is such that there's no turning back after experiencing the new ways of working.

But don't be fooled by its simplicity; these ways of working are only suitable for the brave, those who not only want to challenge their company's status quo but also themselves. People who are willing to question not only what they do but how they do it. Forget everything you know because what works for you today won't serve you tomorrow. *Lead to Beat* is more than just a working method; it's a mindset that will always keep you a step ahead, adapting to every unforeseen event with agility and without losing focus. If you're ready to play to win, you can't miss this book."

> **—Arantxa García,** global culture and talent acquisition director, Danone

Jonathan Escobar Marin captures with precision the pulse of modern leadership—where clarity, distributed empowerment, and execution discipline are no longer optional but essential. His book is not just timely; it's transformational for anyone navigating the new rhythm of change."

> **—Alfonso Gómez,** CEO, BBVA Switzerland

Jonathan is a remarkable professional whose true strength lies in his ability to help businesses focus on fewer, but truly impactful priorities. He is passionately committed to impact and focus. With his pragmatic approach, he simplifies the path to real, measurable results. Working with him for the last six years in two global organizations has meant cutting through the noise and moving straight forward to success. *Lead to Beat* is a must-read."

—**Jerome du Chaffaut,** CEO, Altadis
general manager Iberia cluster, Imperial Brands PLC

I am terribly humbled to be asked to write a review for Jonathan Escobar Marin's first book, *Lead to Beat*. Apart from being an amazing human being, Jonathan is also a visionary and a great leader. Since I met him I have done nothing but learn and live an extraordinary change journey that has impacted and changed the organization I worked with in an incredible and irreversible way.

Lead to Beat is a powerful and timely exploration of what it means to lead with purpose, clarity, and courage in a world that is more complex today than we could have ever imagined and changes from one day to another. Today, all industries and all players are exposed and can see their positions change overnight. With four simple yet powerful drivers Jonathan offers a compelling yet simple strategy to shake your business and make it become a high-performing organization.

Jonathan has changed hundreds of organizations and continues to do so. Once you start working with him and 'moving the needle,' there is absolutely no way back. This is not a book for the shy or the fearful; this is for the courageous leaders that want to challenge their organizations, challenge their ways of working, put their talents to work, and break the status quo. Any CEO that wants to beat the odds of today's world must read *Lead to Beat*."

—**Belén Moreu,** head of human resources Americas, Schindler

The best endorsement of *Lead to Beat* is the impact it had on me, and on my business. As a leader, I learned to cut through the noise with brutal honesty, prioritize what truly mattered in complex settings, and build a culture where impact outweighed activity. Our business unit rose to become one of the top performers in the division. Distributed leadership, radical clarity, and the discipline of execution—even when painful—created not just results, but real flexibility, interdependence, and empowerment. That progress showed up week after week, like a drumbeat. Jonathan was by my side throughout: supportive, passionate, and always willing to challenge the status quo. This book isn't just about getting organized; it's a leadership philosophy. And yes, it's a must-read."

—**Regina Kuzmina,** executive vice president and general manager for beauty and wellbeing, Unilever

Lead to Beat is an essential read for every business leader navigating today's fast-paced and ever-changing market landscape. This insightful book delves into the profound impact of technological advancements and shifting consumer behaviors on traditional business models. It offers practical and visionary strategies for success, including brutal focus, distributed leadership, impact over activity, and disciplined execution. Jonathan's views on fostering a culture of speed, flexibility, and continuous learning are particularly relevant in today's environment. The importance of organizational culture in driving performance and impact is a crucial reminder for leaders aiming to create lasting legacies. Overall, *Lead to Beat* is a valuable resource for any business leader looking to adapt, innovate, and thrive in the complexities of modern markets. Highly recommended!"

—**Brian Guy,** president and chief commercial officer, Breckenridge Pharmaceutical, Inc.

working with Jonathan was a turning point in my professional journey. His expertise, distilled in *Lead to Beat*, does not just offer impactful tools; it fosters a strong sense of urgency and a mindset shift: from processes to impact obsession, from hierarchy to leadership, from generic goals to specific and measurable results, from intention to disciplined execution. Communication, transparency, accountability, focus, and rhythm became my new way of leading. *Lead to Beat* also emphasizes the importance of staying humble, open to feedback, and ready to adjust, adapt, or transform because the environment changes rapidly, and as leaders, we must sharpen our senses, stay alert, and never sit still. For those who are driven to win, ready to evolve, and bold enough to lead with humility, *Lead to Beat* is a must-read."

—**Gerardo Tufano,** CEO, Cosmetix West

Jonathan has deeply transformed our approach to leadership and our ability to execute. He has enabled us to create a long-term vision while at the same time implementing, step by step, in an unquestionable way the basics, the fundamentals, to get the teams on board. This way of working is also in his *Lead to Beat* book: the leadership and development of skills at all levels to create teams that win."

—**Christophe Gehl,** CEO, HARTMANN France

Collaborating with Jonathan has been one of the most transformative experiences of my professional journey. His relentless focus on action over overthinking and on impact over activity challenged not only how I led but how my entire organization operated. Through the PEAK way of working, which we implemented and evolved together, we shifted from inertia and complexity to clarity and execution. The results were profound—both in terms of performance and culture. Jonathan doesn't just offer expertise; he stands with you, drives momentum, and builds the discipline to turn strategy into measurable change. *Lead to Beat* captures that energy and clarity. It's not just a book—it's a playbook for transformation."

—**Giannpaolo Santorsola,** CEO, Davante

Jonathan's practical wisdom transforms complex organizational change into accessible, actionable steps. This essential guide offers leaders both the framework and tools to create lasting cultural transformation—precisely what today's organizations need to thrive in uncertain times."

—Christine Doig-Cardet, director of product, personalization, Spotify

Lead to Beat is not just a business book; it's a wake-up call. What stays with you is its urgency, the sense that leading today means choosing discomfort over complacency, action over excuses. Bold, sharp, and refreshingly honest, it challenges you to rethink your role as a leader and invites you to lead with courage, clarity, and purpose. It leaves you with a clear question: What kind of leader do you want to be? A powerful and necessary read for anyone serious about real change."

—Judith Gonzalez, general manager, Danone

Working with Jonathan was a turning point for our company. He helped us fundamentally change how we organized ourselves to achieve our goals. He transformed how we worked—driving brutal focus on what truly matters, aligning teams around clear objectives, and instilling a culture of ownership and execution. The clarity and rhythm we gained under his guidance not only boosted performance but also triggered a profound cultural shift—elevating our leadership maturity and strengthening how we operate as a team. Lead to Beat captures that same clarity and intensity. It's not a theory—it's a proven, practical approach to driving results through focus, discipline, and empowered teams. If you're serious about leading with impact, you should read this book."

—Ariel Cilento, CTO and cofounder, Simplestate

is a tech executive, I'm constantly searching for voices that truly understand how global enterprises operate, not just at the surface level but deep within the systems that drive transformation and scale. Jonathan has done the heavy lifting. He has dissected the mechanics of how large organizations move, adapt, and grow, and this book is a masterclass in that understanding.

This isn't a book for the complacent. It's for the curious, the brave, and the leaders who are ready to lift the hood and see how things really work. Like a marathoner fine-tuning each detail to gain that next edge, readers will find both big shifts and micro-adjustments that can unlock growth. But the real risk is staying the same. Too many do. If you're someone who wakes up each day wanting to serve better, lead with more clarity, and make meaningful change, this book is for you. Jonathan's contribution to the enterprise world is profound, and by extension, so is his impact on society. This is the book for leaders who stand at the crossroads of something that needs to change. Read it. Use it. And keep evolving."

—**Anna N Schlegel,** president, Women in Localization
founder, Universalization.a

Lead to Beat delivers a disciplined, real-world approach for delivering results in a world defined by speed and uncertainty. As leaders, we often spend too much time debating the *why* and the *what*, and stumble through the *how* with trial and error. While many strategy frameworks look good in PowerPoint, few survive the leap into execution. This book closes that gap by distilling what Jonathan Escobar Marín calls 'common sense with uncommon discipline.'

Jonathan is not an academic theorist—he's a practitioner who has dedicated his career to building and refining a leadership rhythm that empowers teams, aligns priorities, and drives sustainable impact. Read this book not just for inspiration, but for implementation. Understand the principles. Apply the rhythm. Create the beat that transforms your organization."

—**Ovidiu Solomonov,** chief operating officer, AVIV Group

In my work at the intersection of health and business performance, I've consistently observed that the most successful organizations don't view care for people and business results as competing priorities. Rather, they recognize these elements as mutually reinforcing. *Lead to Beat* masterfully articulates this symbiotic relationship, offering a practical framework where performance and wellbeing build upon each other.

What makes Jonathan Escobar Marin's approach so relevant is how it creates clarity and structure. By establishing sharp focus and a transparent drumbeat of execution and evolution, team members experience the satisfaction of working on what truly drives impact. Research has consistently shown that high-performing teams thrive when they have clarity of purpose, well-defined roles, transparent goals, and the courage to contribute across traditional boundaries.

Lead to Beat is a comprehensive approach to building organizations where people and performance flourish together. I've witnessed firsthand, at global scale, how these principles transform not just business outcomes but also the lived experience of the people driving those outcomes."

—**Diana Han,** chief health and wellbeing officer, Unilever

Lead to Beat draws from real experience and simple truths—the same ones Jonathan has used to shape world-class organizations, coach leaders, and change how I lead every day. This isn't about quick wins or fleeting trends—it's about leadership that lasts. This book delivers enduring value. You'll come away stronger—and so will those you lead."

—**Jordan Cristillo,** director HR strategy, Magna International

EAD TO BEAT ➡ LEAD

TO BEAT ➡ LEAD TO B

EAD TO BEAT ➡ LEAD

TO BEAT ➡ LEAD TO B

LEAD TO BEAT ➡ LEAD

TO BEAT ➡ LEAD TO B

LEAD TO BEAT ➡ LEAD

TO BEAT ➡ LEAD TO B

LEAD TO BEAT

LEAD TO BEAT

LEAD TO BEAT

LEAD TO BEAT

LEAD TO BEAT

LEAD TO BEAT

LEAD TO BEAT

LEAD TO BEAT

LEAD TO
BEAT

The Leadership Rhythm
That Shapes Tomorrow

JONATHAN ESCOBAR MARIN

FC

**FAST
COMPANY**
Press

Fast Company Press
New York, New York
www.fastcompanypress.com

This work is being published under the Fast Company Press imprint by an exclusive arrangement with *Fast Company*. *Fast Company* and the *Fast Company* logo are registered trademarks of Mansueto Ventures, LLC. The Fast Company Press logo is a wholly owned trademark of Mansueto Ventures, LLC.

Distributed by Greenleaf Book Group

For ordering information or special discounts for bulk purchases, please contact Greenleaf Book Group at PO Box 91869, Austin, TX 78709, 512.891.6100.

Design and composition by Greenleaf Book Group
Creative direction by Carla Serena, Serena Studio
Author photograph by Joan Manuel Ramos Fernández

Publisher's Cataloging-in-Publication data is available.

Print ISBN: 978-1-63908-148-6

eBook ISBN: 978-1-63908-149-3

To offset the number of trees consumed in the printing of our books, Greenleaf donates a portion of the proceeds from each printing to the Arbor Day Foundation. Greenleaf Book Group has replaced over 50,000 trees since 2007.

Printed in Canada on acid-free paper

25 26 27 28 29 30 31   10 9 8 7 6 5 4 3 2 1

First Edition

CONTENTS

Introduction   1

1. Brutal Focus   43

2. Distributed Leadership   105

3. Impact over Activity   167

4. A Disciplined Drumbeat   221

What Is Needed   281

Notes   323

Index   329

About the Author   341

THE RHYTHM OF CHANGE

UNPREDICTABILITY IS THE ONLY STABILITY.

Even the most sophisticated boardrooms face a stark new reality: Markets now transform faster than traditional planning cycles can anticipate. A single event can reshape category economics overnight. A new trend can make decades of consumer behavior obsolete by sunrise. Supply chains built over generations can be outmaneuvered by a new platform ecosystem in weeks.

Even AI systems considered cutting-edge become baseline capabilities within months as the progression from generative AI to agentic

AI accelerates, while physical AI transforms how we interact with the material world. Platforms disrupt themselves faster than competitors can react, and ecosystems that once seemed unshakable are redefined by the next breakthrough in personalization, recommendation engines, or real-time data processing. While some enter into debate about the impact of AGI (artificial general intelligence), quantum computing, humanoid robots, AI-powered autonomy, or any other form of agentic or physical AI, market leadership is already being redefined by these forces and others more immediate and merciless: consumer expectations that evolve at the speed of social media, value chains that fragment and reassemble with algorithmic precision, and competition that emerges from blind spots to capture billions in market value before traditional radar even registers their presence. We are no longer in an era of disruption. We've entered an age of unprecedented and continuous metamorphosis.

The physics of business have fundamentally changed. Market power no longer flows from size but from speed. Brand loyalty doesn't erode gradually; it pivots instantly. Distribution advantages don't decay; they invert. Algorithms driving user engagement today can become tomorrow's bottlenecks. Decentralized protocols can siphon users away from centralized platforms, challenging the very foundation of well-established business models. A single quantum breakthrough could rewrite many tech standards overnight. Premium positions don't slowly commoditize; they collapse between quarterly earnings calls.

Today's advantage is tomorrow's anchor. Yesterday's competitive moat is today's prison. Last quarter's winning formula is this quarter's recipe for irrelevance. As AI evolves from perception and generation to autonomous action, organizations that fail to evolve their ways of working and organizational structures to integrate both agentic and physical AI capabilities risk rapid obsolescence. Yet in this maelstrom lies unprecedented opportunity. The same forces that destroy established positions create openings for explosive growth. The same forces that threaten to disrupt a traditional supply chain can turn a digital marketplace into a global hub for new behaviors, services, and monetization

JONATHAN ESCOBAR MARIN

MARKET POWER NO LONGER FLOWS FROM SIZE BUT FROM SPEED.

models—if leaders are prepared to lead. Subscription models that dominate today may be overtaken by AI-driven pay-per-value systems, where users are charged dynamically based on engagement, outcomes, or even emotions. The same dynamics that shatter traditional barriers enable rapid scale. The same currents that sweep away the unprepared carry the prepared to beat market dominance—if they lead to beat with discipline and foresight.

Surviving this metamorphosis isn't about predicting the future. The only certainty is unpredictability, and today's leaders must build organizations that thrive on uncertainty, that turn volatility into velocity, that convert unpredictability from threat to weapon. Your mission isn't to weather this storm. It's to become it.

Welcome to the age where rigid systems are a liability, where speed, flexibility, dynamism, and agility spring from a strategic, disciplined, stable rhythm of execution and evolution, and where market dominance comes from mastering this powerful paradox. The question isn't whether your market will transform; it's whether you'll be the transformer or the transformed.

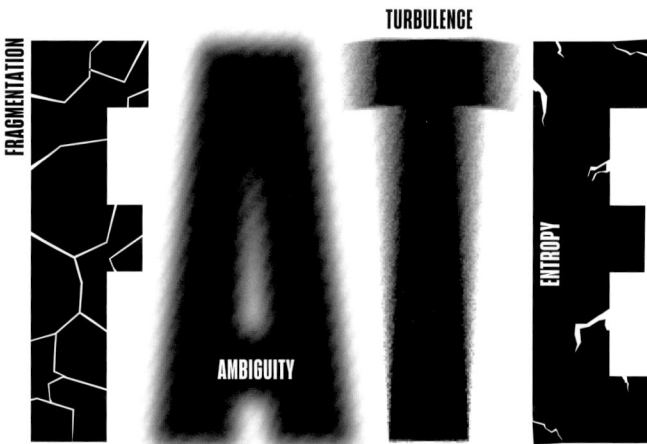

Image 0.1: The four forces of FATE—fragmentation, ambiguity, turbulence, and entropy—driving continuous metamorphosis in the business landscape
© 2025, Jonathan Escobar Marin

JONATHAN ESCOBAR MARIN

THE ONLY CERTAINTY IS UNPREDICTABILITY.

Four elements—fragmentation, ambiguity, turbulence, and entropy—combine to form a powerful force—FATE—that permeates every aspect of this ever-changing reality, and they are especially prevalent in the business world. Much like its namesake, FATE is inevitable; it exists all the time, and how your organization's beat matches its rhythm will determine whether you win. It is a complex and ever-evolving amalgamation of pressure points, born from the collision of exponentially advancing technologies, social upheavals, economic disruptions, geopolitical tensions, and environmental crises. The emergence of AI systems that combine autonomous reasoning and planning with physical world engagement adds another dimension to this complexity, fundamentally altering how organizations operate and compete. With all this, fragmentation shatters traditional models, ambiguity fuels confusion and indecision, turbulence tests resilience, and entropy seeks to break down virtually fortified systems.

But among these challenges lies opportunity for those who are brave enough to embrace the rhythm of these changes and evolve with them. To thrive in this world, you must learn to recognize and anticipate exponential change. Go-to-market playbooks and seemingly invincible flywheel business models are always one disruption away from obsolescence. Sophisticated business frameworks—from platform economics to network effects—are outdated before they are put into action. You cannot trust any product, platform, service, market, ecosystem, or channel to drive your business forever. Survival belongs to those who beat change before it beats them, who find its rhythm of execution and evolution and keep it, with a disciplined drumbeat.

FINDING YOUR RHYTHM

To face your FATE, you will need to harness the power of anticipation, to bridge the vast chasm between lofty strategies, compelling visions, and desired results. You'll need to close the gap between PowerPoint illusions and tangible outcomes for your customers, focusing on the brutally important goals to achieve what is needed to win.

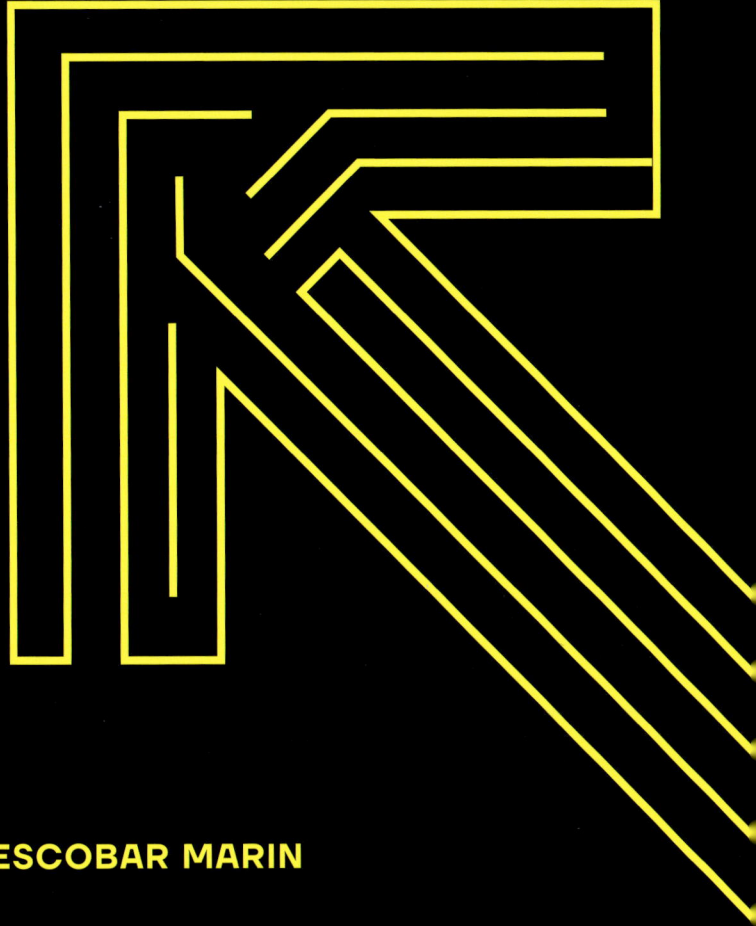

JONATHAN ESCOBAR MARIN

You cannot trust any product, platform, service, market, ecosystem, or channel to drive your business forever.

The very forces that upend the status quo also create a rhythm of urgency, innovation, and transformation, fueled by a scrappy, entrepreneurial spirit. This rhythm can mean the difference between leading the next wave of innovation or being overtaken by a new AI disruptor. It's about finding the balance between experimentation and performance, between speed and long-term vision. Winners seizing this rhythm consistently exhibit four relentless drivers: brutal focus, distributed leadership, impact over activity, and a disciplined drumbeat that creates their organization's beat, syncing it to crush FATE. These four drivers, working in concert, provide a powerful antidote to the challenges posed by FATE. They enable organizations to cut through the noise, beat change in real time, and continuously reinvent themselves to shape tomorrow and stay ahead of the curve. These drivers set the transformative rhythm that lets organizations not only survive change, but lead to beat it as well.

Take the modern workforce, which is fragmented across remote, hybrid, and physical settings. To survive—let alone thrive—in this environment, organizations need brutal focus on what is needed: They must set clear priorities and align their efforts with what truly moves the needle. They need to empower distributed leadership, fostering a culture where leadership is not confined to a title but distributed across individuals and teams. Organizations need to accelerate the impact of their execution, shifting from overactivity to outcomes by streamlining efforts toward what drives real results. This means leveraging data for clarity, aligning resources with the most impactful initiatives, and eliminating distractions that dilute focus. And they need to forge a rhythm of continuous learning and evolution through their drumbeat. With AI-driven insights and real-time analytics, organizations can empower decisive action at speed and scale, ensuring each effort contributes directly to meaningful results. Rather than simply acting fast, the emphasis is on acting purposefully fast to achieve meaningful impact.

The challenges we face are immense, but through brutal focus, unleashed talent, impact obsession, and relentless evolution driven by a disciplined drumbeat, you set your organization's beat—the rhythm that rules tomorrow. That beat pulses as culture, surging through every decision, action, and interaction, defining who you are and how you win. By embracing this rhythm of change with passion and rigor, your organization can do more than just survive against FATE; you can harness its energy to fuel transformative growth and impact. The maelstrom is always upon us, but within its churning currents lies the possibility of renewal, reinvention, and unparalleled achievement. Let's look at each of those drivers and how they each address an element of FATE.

Brutal Focus

In a world where attention is the scarcest resource, fragmentation has become an existential threat to organizational success—making brutal focus the ultimate antidote. A product category that once had three dominant players now faces thirty microbrands, each targeting ever-narrower customer segments. What was once a simple brand presence now requires orchestrating hundreds of touchpoints across customers, consumers, and users, each demanding unique content, pricing, and engagement strategies.

The splintering is relentless. Global brands must now navigate a maze of local preferences: Consumers in the same region, same age group, and same income bracket increasingly demand dramatically different product variations. Distribution channels that once served millions now splinter into thousands of microchannels, each requiring distinct positioning, pricing, and go-to-market strategies. Operations must stay ahead of increasingly fragmented demand patterns and compressed delivery timelines, while marketing teams struggle to maintain brand coherence across an evolving mix of physical and digital touchpoints. In this hybrid reality, the savage speed of customer response has become as critical as the quality of execution.

Consider how a single product category now fragments into dozens of subsegments—premium, super premium, mass, value, natural, synthetic, sustainable, indulgent, functional, traditional, modern, fusion—each demanding its own value-delivery ecosystem, marketing approach, and innovation pipeline. What was once a straightforward path to market now resembles a complex web of fulfillment systems, subscription services, and on-demand delivery platforms.

The challenge isn't just external. Organizations themselves are fragmenting as they try to serve these splintered markets. R&D teams split between immediate improvements and long-term innovations; supply chains fragment among speed, agility, efficiency, and resilience; and marketing teams divide between brand building and performance optimization. The pressure to be everything to everyone while maintaining operational efficiency has never been more intense. And in this fragmented landscape, the winners aren't those who can serve every microsegment but those who know exactly which fragments to ignore. For those who haven't yet felt the full force of fragmentation in their markets, brace for impact. No industry, regardless of its size or reach, will remain immune to the great splintering ahead.

But brutal focus conquers shattered landscapes. To thrive among this fragmentation, organizations need to have brutal focus on what is needed—to zero in on the bets that truly matter and pursue them with singular clarity and conviction. This means more than simply setting priorities; it means ruthlessly deprioritizing everything else. It means having the courage to say no to the myriad distractions and the discipline to channel all efforts toward following a singular target with a unique rhythm.

This philosophy isn't limited to one company's success story. It's also about understanding that, in today's world, the ability to concentrate on your core, to innovate relentlessly, and to lead with paranoid obsession on your must-win battles forms the backbone of any enduring success. Whether it's embracing a "day one" mentality, where every day is approached with the freshness and urgency of a startup, or simply ensuring that every decision aligns with the ultimate goal of serving the customer better, the principle remains the same: Brutal focus is your most potent strategy in the age of fragmentation.

BRUTAL FOCUS MEANS MORE THAN SIMPLY SETTING PRIORITIES; IT MEANS RUTHLESSLY DEPRIORITIZING EVERYTHING ELSE.

Distributed Leadership

Ambiguity is the water in which businesses swim. From the blurring of industry boundaries to the fluidity of customer expectations, organizations find themselves adrift in a sea of unknowns. The dissolution of traditional industry boundaries has birthed bewildering new realities: Tech platforms now function as financial service providers for millions, while electric vehicle manufacturers quietly revolutionize home energy storage and the robotics that will become our everyday assistants. Social media platforms and digital marketplaces have morphed into retail powerhouses, while traditional retailers have become sophisticated data companies through their consumer platforms. The mutations continue: Gaming companies now host luxury fashion shows in virtual worlds, and hardware manufacturers have transformed into content production studios. Business models themselves are shifting shape; everything from cars to wardrobes is becoming subscription-based, physical products are evolving into data-driven service platforms, and direct-to-consumer companies are building distribution networks that would make last century's industry giants envious. These transformations are not isolated; they are the symptoms of dissolving boundaries between industries, where the undefined and untagged are becoming the new normal.

Meanwhile, customers present us with fascinating paradoxes that only deepen the ambiguity organizations must navigate: They demand hyperpersonalization while fiercely guarding their privacy; seek luxurious offerings while protecting the planet; and expect seamless, instant service while insisting on responsible, transparent supply chains. In this landscape, technology acts not as a mere enabler but as a force multiplier of ambiguity. AI systems simultaneously manage value creation, delivery networks, and customer engagement; digital twins bridge physical and virtual experiences; and augmented reality erases the distinction between online and offline shopping interactions. These aren't merely changes; they represent a continuous and undefined rewiring of how value is created, captured, and delivered in the new economy.

In this relentless landscape of ambiguity, the question is no longer whether organizational designs must change but how. To own the unknown, leaders must dismantle rigid determinism and overcome the organizational structures that hinder collective intelligence. This doesn't mean flattening hierarchies in pursuit of an idealized horizontality. Rather, it means first transforming how departments function—evolving from isolated units into centers of excellence and talent pools where specialists maintain functional discipline while flowing to cross-functional missions—and second, evolving management from self-power and control to distributed power and enablement. When verticality connects people and amplifies collective intelligence rather than creating artificial separations between organizational strata, it becomes a strength rather than a liability.

Organizations must recognize that those closest to emerging realities are often the first to detect crucial shifts in the business landscape. Embracing ambiguity requires organizations to empower teams with both the proximity to real-time data and market signals, and the autonomy, skills, and agentic and physical AI resources to act decisively on the ground-level intelligence they gather.

This approach goes beyond merely delegating decision-making; it involves creating an ecosystem where cross-functional, cross-hierarchical teams can rapidly detect, understand, and respond to emerging patterns, enabled by unprecedented clarity about accountability, collaboration, co-learning, and shared goals. It's about distributed leadership. To own the unknown, multiply leaders. To multiply leaders, rewire your organization. This rewiring turns ambiguity into a strategic advantage. This shift unleashes the collective capacity to thrive amid ambiguity.

Imagine your organization as a constellation of AI-augmented microenterprises, each pulsing with the spirit and autonomy of a startup. These units seamlessly blend human creativity, expertise, and emotional intelligence with AI capabilities to deliver unprecedented results. Yet they move in perfect synchronization, creating a dynamic network where each node amplifies the organization's overarching purpose

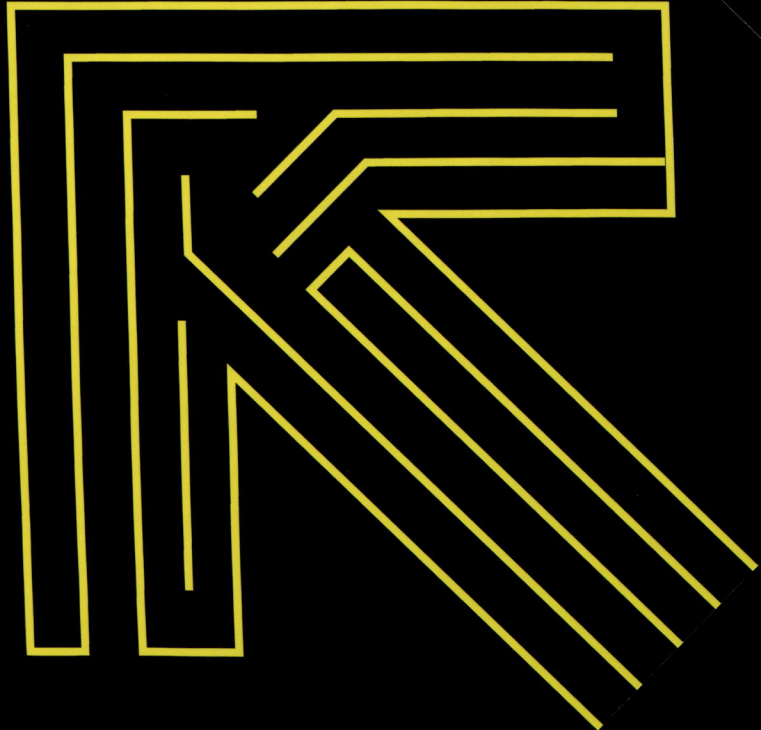

JONATHAN ESCOBAR M

To own the unkno
multiply Leaders.
To multiply Leaders,
rewire your organization.

and brutal focus. This is distributed leadership—not merely delegating authority but creating an ecosystem of augmented intelligence where every intersection becomes a catalyst for innovation and impact.

The challenge lies not in adopting technology but in reimagining organizational design for this new reality. As Brandt Allen warned, "Old Organization + New Technology = Expensive Old Organization."[1] This truth becomes even more critical in the age of AI superintelligence—simply layering new technologies onto outdated structures creates expensive inefficiency rather than transformative capability.

Technology alone cannot transform an organization. To succeed, we must go beyond technology and create a new organizational ecosystem capable of thriving in this rewired reality. This transformation doesn't happen by chance; it requires dismantling rigid hierarchies, breaking silos, and empowering leaders at every level. The results you achieve are not defined by the tools you implement but by the organization you design to use them.

By rewiring traditional structures into an ecosystem of AI-powered cross-functional teams driven by brutal focus and equipped with the authority to act on frontline insights, companies tap into the collective intelligence and entrepreneurial spirit of their workforce, turning ambiguity into a strategic advantage. This approach ensures that organizations can detect and respond to untagged market shifts far earlier than traditional structures would allow, beating the pace in a perpetually ambiguous and undefined business landscape.

Impact over Activity

Turbulence is the very fabric of today's business environment. A single TikTok trend can deplete global inventory of any product within hours, while a production disruption in Taiwan can paralyze production across continents. Market dynamics shift at bewildering speeds: Premium providers suddenly find themselves competing with value players, while budget offerings unexpectedly capture luxury market share.

Consider how a teenager's viral product review can overwhelm exceptionally advanced demand forecasting systems or how a single supply chain disruption can trigger a cascade of shortages across seemingly unrelated categories. We've witnessed entire distribution networks reconfigure overnight as consumers abruptly shift between physical and digital channels, leaving billions in infrastructure either obsolete or suddenly insufficient.

The velocity of change is unprecedented: Customer preferences morph before development cycles are complete, brand loyalty evaporates and resurges for reasons that defy traditional marketing metrics, and pricing algorithms engage in split-second wars that reshape entire market segments. A minor innovation by a niche player can trigger industry-wide transformations, while a single regulatory announcement in a distant market can force global changes worth billions.

These turbulent forces don't only create chaos; they breed opportunity as well. When a three-person startup can capture market share from century-old brands through algorithmic optimization, when direct-to-consumer upstarts can scale from zero to market leadership in months rather than decades, and when local innovations can rapidly globalize, we're operating in a business environment where turbulence itself becomes a source of competitive advantage. And if you don't find yourself there yet, it will come. Turbulence will hit each industry, no matter how established or regulated it is.

In order for you to flow with this turbulence, your execution must achieve impact at the speed of abrupt disruption—and be seamlessly integrated at all levels. Success belongs to those who dare to learn faster than the rest. Your speed of learning determines your speed of winning, both in the short and long term. Organizations need to enhance their capability to achieve results fast, faster, at light speed, while building sustainable competitive advantages. We must accelerate execution and decision-making, leverage AI insights, empower judgment, and take swift, decisive action in the face of the unexpected. This means more than simply reacting faster; it means proactively sensing and anticipating emerging threats and opportunities. It means building resilience in

Old Organization +
New Technology =
Expensive Old
Organization."

—Brandt Allen

JONATHAN ESCOBAR MARIN

Technology alone cannot transform an organization. The results you achieve are not defined by the tools you implement but by the organization you design to use them.

the way of working to absorb shocks and pivoting with speed in real time, establishing patterns that strengthen over weeks and quarters. When disruption moves at light speed, your impact must outrace it, building lasting advantage with every move—creating both immediate victories and long-term superiority. This is not about activity—which leads nowhere—but about *swift* activity to make an impact and win. Winning isn't merely an option; it's everything. Activity without impact or learning is waste.

This ethos of swift, data-informed decision-making and empowering teams with the autonomy to act with dynamism and speed has proven to be a cornerstone for companies seeing meteoric rises, and sustaining their success over time. Through disciplined synchronization rhythms, teams stay aligned and focused while maintaining the agility to beat market dynamics, creating enduring competitive positions. By harnessing real-time data, AI, and cross-silo intelligence, teams are given the environment to navigate challenges with agility, turning potential setbacks into opportunities for growth.

True resilience transcends mere adaptability; it embodies antifragility—the capacity to not only withstand but to thrive from disorder as well. This means building organizational muscle to execute faster, learn faster, and deliver impact faster with each iteration. True resilience is about making every team leaner, stronger, and better equipped to seize opportunities. Challenges are inevitable, yet it's the approach to overcoming these adversities that distinguishes the exceptional from the average. Rather than just bouncing back, resilient organizations accelerate forward, using each challenge as a catalyst to strengthen their execution capabilities. The strategy isn't merely to endure disruptions but to leverage them as catalysts for innovation and growth. This involves fostering an environment where a transparent ritual of connection between teams and leaders ensures obstacles are tackled efficiently and decisions flow naturally.

Impact over activity is an active force for acceleration—not only the ability to withstand shocks, but also the capacity to emerge stronger, faster, and more impactful after each challenge. In this era of relentless change, the goal is to cultivate an organizational culture where agility and innovation are not only responses to adversity, but also are pro-active elements of the business strategy. Here, every disruption is a dance, every challenge a chance to demonstrate the power of honoring impact over being comfortable with activity, and every team member a potential leader ready to steer the company through any storm with confidence and ingenuity.

A Disciplined Drumbeat

Entropy is the ultimate enemy of organizational survival. AI tools become obsolete within weeks, while carefully constructed value chains unravel in months. Market leadership that took decades to build can dissolve in quarters as new consumption patterns emerge faster than traditional planning cycles can adapt.

The decay is merciless and accelerating. Premium offerings become commoditized before their marketing campaigns conclude. Distribution networks optimized for efficiency crumble under demands for sustain-ability. Operational excellence built over generations becomes a liability when flexibility trumps size. Brand equity, once measured in decades, now requires constant regeneration as customer loyalty shifts with dig-ital immediacy.

Consider how development life cycles have compressed from years to months: Solutions must be continuously updated, offerings must evolve before production runs complete, and innovation pipe-lines must deliver in weeks rather than quarters. Market intelligence becomes stale before reports can be finalized, while competitive advantages erode before they can be fully exploited. The half-life of success grows shorter by the day.

The challenge extends beyond products and markets. Organizational capabilities decay at an unprecedented rate: Today's core competencies become tomorrow's anchors, carefully built systems ossify into barriers,

ACTIVITY WITHOUT IMPACT OR LEARNING IS WASTE.

TRANSFORM BEFORE YOU ARE MADE OBSOLETE.

and accumulated knowledge transforms into dangerous assumptions. What worked last quarter may not only be ineffective but actively harmful this quarter. Sales strategies that drove growth last season create resistance in the next, while distribution models optimized for one reality become bottlenecks in another. Those who haven't yet felt entropy's corrosive touch, take note: In tomorrow's business landscape, even the mightiest fortresses will crumble without constant reconstruction.

You must transform before you are made obsolete, and that requires a rigorous adherence to the organizational rhythm of change. You do that by creating a disciplined drumbeat. Your drumbeat is a kind of meta driver that powers and refines all the others, systematically transforming long-term aspirations into reality through disciplined cycles of repetition, experimentation, learning, and improvement. It's what makes you put your choices for brutal focus, your distributed leadership, and your learnings from your obsession with impact under review. Those choices, like anything in the world, are subject to unpredictable entropy, and rhythmic, repeated review will keep you evolving to meet emergent challenges.

The drumbeat creates clarity and focus. It eliminates ambiguity by defining when actions will happen, who will be involved, and what outcomes are expected. It enables you as a leader to connect the dots between business and culture—seamlessly linking focus, leadership, talent, results, learning, and evolution. It's where your organization's values stop being words and start being actions.

The drumbeat ensures that prioritization is not just a buzzword, silos are dismantled, talent empowerment translates into real human power, and progress is deliberate—measured by its impact on customers rather than in creating PowerPoints or delivering polished speeches. It ensures that innovation, both at the business and cultural level, remains continuous. In essence, the drumbeat demonstrates (or not) the behaviors your culture claims to uphold—not on posters, but throughout the organization.

Again, we must all transform before we are made obsolete. To thrive within entropy, organizations need to hardwire a rhythm of continuous reinvention—their drumbeat—into their very cultural DNA. This means more than embracing change; it means actively leading to beat it. It means institutionalizing a culture of relentless experimentation, learning, and reinvention. It means treating innovation not as a one-off event or an only-for-product mindset but as an ongoing, all-encompassing process that involves continuous renewal of all that integrates the business. Innovation isn't a project; it's the beat of survival. Either your entire business learns to evolve, or evolution will select you out of existence.

Your drumbeat provides the structure that makes business and cultural innovation a rhythmic beat, not a sporadic pulse. It creates the cadence that turns values and strategic transformation into operational reality. The drumbeat is where a culture of learning and innovation becomes measurable—in the rhythmic practices that either amplify or diminish your organization's potential. It ensures that learning becomes innovation, and innovation becomes results.

This ethos of rhythmic transformation has been the key to most companies' remarkable resurgence and turnarounds under brave, inspiring leaders. By instilling a growth mindset and a learning culture and by continuously evolving their focus on products, customers, business models, management systems, and capabilities, companies from different sectors have been able to not only weather the entropy of the digital age, but to also thrive in it, reclaiming their positions as some of the world's most valuable and impactful entities. That continuous evolution is not only a part of how leading companies beat change; it *is* their drumbeat as well—the meta-driver propelling the other drivers and the organization forward.

Table 0.1 presents the challenges of FATE and the transformative power of the rhythmic drivers to inspire and motivate organizations to rise above the challenges of the modern business landscape. By embracing the drivers with passion and determination, our organizations can unlock their full potential and create a powerful, lasting impact.

JONATHAN ESCOBAR MARIN

The drumbeat demonstrates (or not) the behaviors your culture claims to uphold—not only on posters, but also throughout the organization.

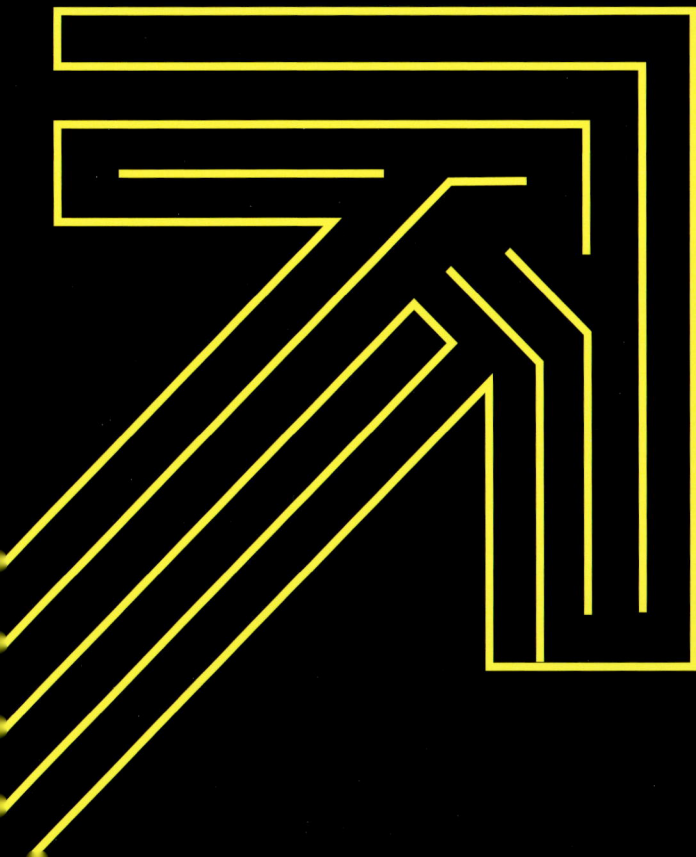

JONATHAN ESCOBAR MARIN

Innovation isn't a project; it's the beat of survival. Either your entire business learns to evolve, or evolution will select you out of existence.

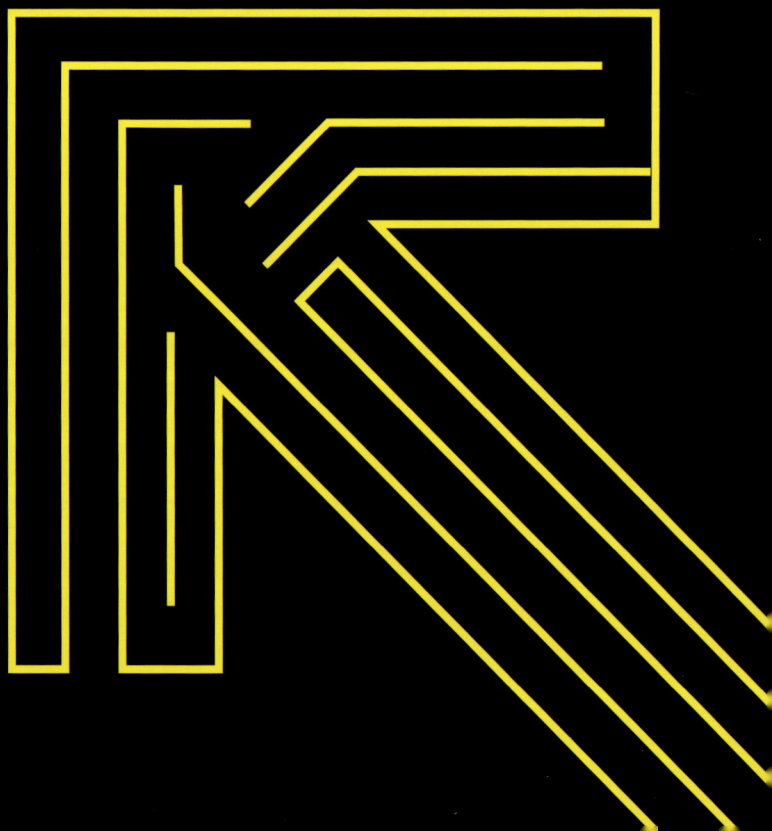

TABLE 0.1. BEATING FATE: YOUR LEADERSHIP RHYTHM

FATE	The Challenge	The Driver	The Rhythm
Fragmentation	Navigating complex markets, diverse customer needs, and competing technologies.	**Brutal focus:** Choose your battlefield and win big in a few areas instead of losing slowly everywhere.	Ignite a laser-sharp focus on what truly matters, conquer complexity, cut the crap, and drive clear choices in your organization to outmaneuver competition through cross-company missions with unambiguous targets, dates, and staffing.
Ambiguity	Mastering the dissolving boundaries of industries while the undefined and untagged become the new normal.	**Distributed leadership:** Foster a culture of unstoppable leadership across hierarchies and silos to master ambiguity.	Harness the collective genius of your teams, discover hidden talent and superior team players who can lead, and overcome the undefined with confidence.
Turbulence	Facing continuous waves of relentless disruption and unprecedented change that reshape your entire business operations overnight.	**Impact over activity:** Stop confusing motion with progress by ruthlessly pursuing measurable impact at lightning speed.	Speed up execution and make agile, data-informed decisions to seize opportunities, overcome adversities, redefine the rules, and stay ahead of the curve, ensuring every action drives concrete results.
Entropy	Preventing stagnation and decline in the face of rapid industry transformation, where today's competitive advantage becomes tomorrow's liability at unprecedented speed.	**A disciplined drumbeat:** Make your plans and strategies obsolete before the market makes them obsolete.	Forge an unstoppable learning culture; continually reinvent, innovate, and evolve, ensuring your organization's enduring success and legacy.

LEAD TO BEAT

Make your plans and strategies obsolete before the market makes them obsolete. The challenges posed by the four fingers of FATE are daunting, but they are not insurmountable. By mastering the rhythm of change—by building brutal focus, empowering distributed leadership, prioritizing impact over activity, and practicing disciplined adherence to your drumbeat—you will lead to beat the maelstrom, outpace your competitors, and win with your desired customers. In a world where stability is an illusion, your drumbeat becomes your greatest reality. Your drumbeat turns daunting challenges into the rhythm of relentless triumph.

Remember, this is not a deterministic road map. It's a synthesis of patterns I've validated through more than twenty years of evolving organizations across five continents and multiple industries. It's a distillation of what I've seen consistently drive results in practice, proven through hundreds of leaders and teams who have achieved breakthrough impact and performance while growing as professionals. It's the conclusion that what separates winning cultures from the rest isn't their stated values; it's their drumbeat—the consistent, practical rhythm that leads them to beat intentions with impact.

Andreas Joehle, partner at Ufenau Capital Partners and CEO of HARTMANN GROUP by the time Jonathan was a director there, puts it succinctly: "What Jonathan is describing—brutal focus on what matters the most, building a network of A-players distributed across the organization, shaping a culture obsessed with impacting, winning, not doing, and shaping a disciplined leadership rhythm to raise the bar quarter per quarter—is the 'simple' key to success, which most people have at least heard about, but don't know how to turn the key to open the door, and many simply don't want to turn it—even worse!"[2]

This insight from Andreas gets to the heart of the challenge. The principles themselves aren't complex secrets, but their disciplined execution separates extraordinary organizations from the mediocre. Many leaders intellectually understand these concepts, yet struggle to

JONATHAN ESCOBAR MARIN

STOP CONFUSING MOTION WITH PROGRESS BY RUTHLESSLY PURSUING MEASURABLE IMPACT AT LIGHTNING SPEED.

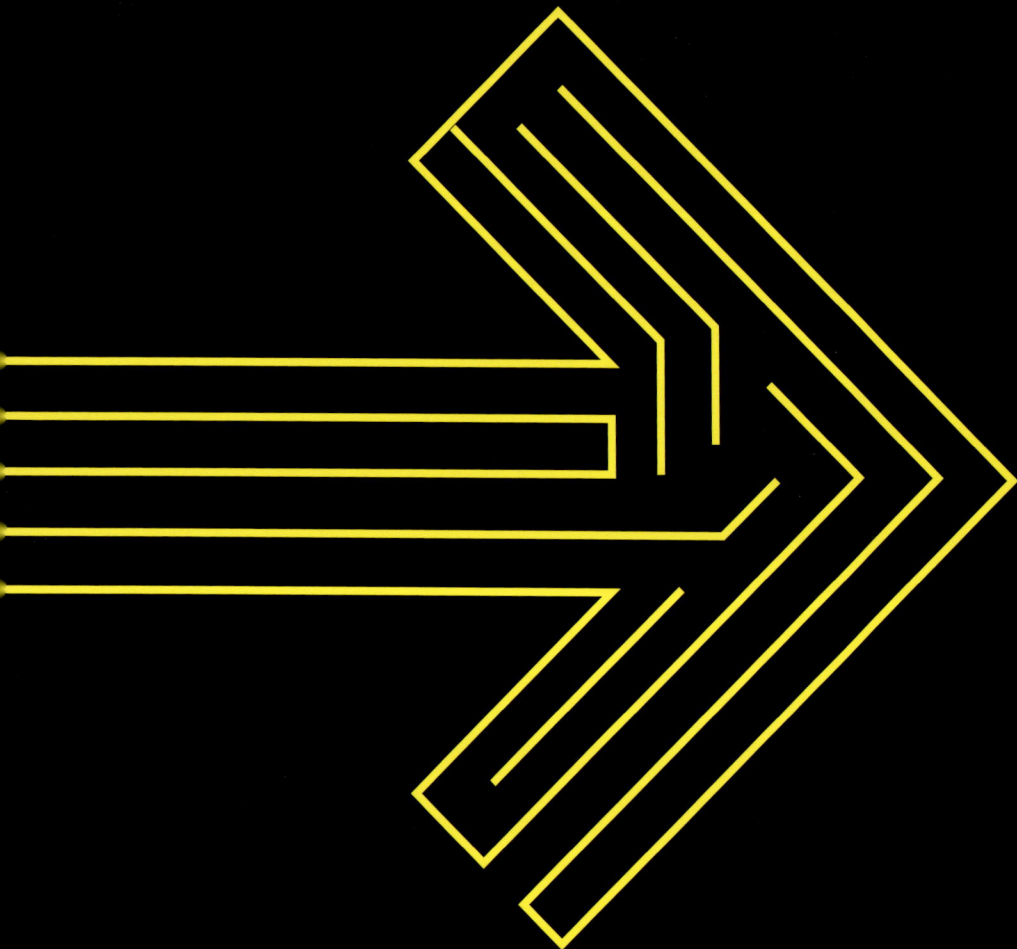

JONATHAN ESCOBAR MARIN

In a world where stability is an illusion, your drumbeat becomes your greatest reality.

operationalize them or resist the discipline required to make them work. What follows is an actionable set of practices for turning that key, opening the door to organizational greatness, and sustaining the journey toward becoming truly exceptional.

Central to these practices is the recognition that culture isn't fluffy values or empty hype; it's the beat your drumbeat forges through raw, pragmatic action. It's the beat of behaviors your drumbeat hammers into reality. For culture to stick, its practices must be both memorable and repeatable. Brutal focus, multiplied ownership, impact obsession, and continuous evolution aren't merely ideals; they emerge when leaders and teams together live and breathe the beat of their organization's culture, turning intention into action and action into impact.

Because culture drives business, these four drivers orchestrated by the drumbeat shape the underlying cultural system of any high-performing, high-impact organization—more specifically any unit with a leadership team owning a profit and loss—where you find accelerated market share capture, margin expansion, brand value appreciation, consumer advocacy driving organic growth, rapid penetration across new consumer segments, and unprecedented talent magnetism. These drivers manifest in the ability to command value premiums while expanding scale, to launch innovations that create entirely new market opportunities, to transform fixed costs into variable advantages, and to achieve market reach that competitors can't replicate. They show up in the power to turn operational complexity into competitive moats, to convert customer data into predictive advantages, and to scale new markets in months rather than years—all while maintaining the organizational agility to pivot faster than smaller rivals and the operational excellence to outmaneuver larger ones.

These drivers might not be visible in the posters or the big statements on the companies' web pages, but they are the ones that govern how these companies prioritize, empower people to lead, obsess over outcomes, and learn and change fast. But these organizations don't just implement a policy or add a new set of procedures; they also live the drivers, breathe them, feel them in their bones. The power of the rhythm lies in how the drumbeat orchestrates the synergistic interplay of all its players, directly shaping culture with every beat—the four drivers working together to create a whole that is greater than the sum of their parts.

This is why your drumbeat isn't merely another business process—it's the living expression, the steady beat of your culture in action. It's the difference between saying, "We are focused," and having a clear, transparent artifact for the entire company to reflect that focus—or the lack of it. It's the difference between saying, "People first," and having consistent, observable, measurable principles and mechanisms that connect people with greater purpose and multiply their opportunities to lead meaningful missions in the organization. It's the difference between saying, "We value results over deliverables," and making the commitment to establish a weekly rhythm that turns that movement into visible progress and lasting impact. It's the difference between saying, "We don't want managers; we want servant leaders," and having regular check-ins where leaders are actively serving their teams to unlock obstacles.

In essence, your drumbeat reveals the gap—or the alignment—between pep talks, grandiose sayings, and what is actually happening within the organization.

The power of shaping a consistent organizational way of working lies not in emulating any one company's approach. Rather, it emerges from applying fundamental drivers within your organization's unique context and challenges. The goal is not to copy but to learn and build—drawing inspiration and insight from the pioneers who have blazed the trail while charting your own course. It's about building and refining the drumbeat of your unique way of working, forging your beat through the maelstrom of FATE.

As the world spins on its axis, ceaselessly hurtling through relentless change and innovation, the organizations that rise above the rest are those armed with a potent sense of rhythm. The most successful

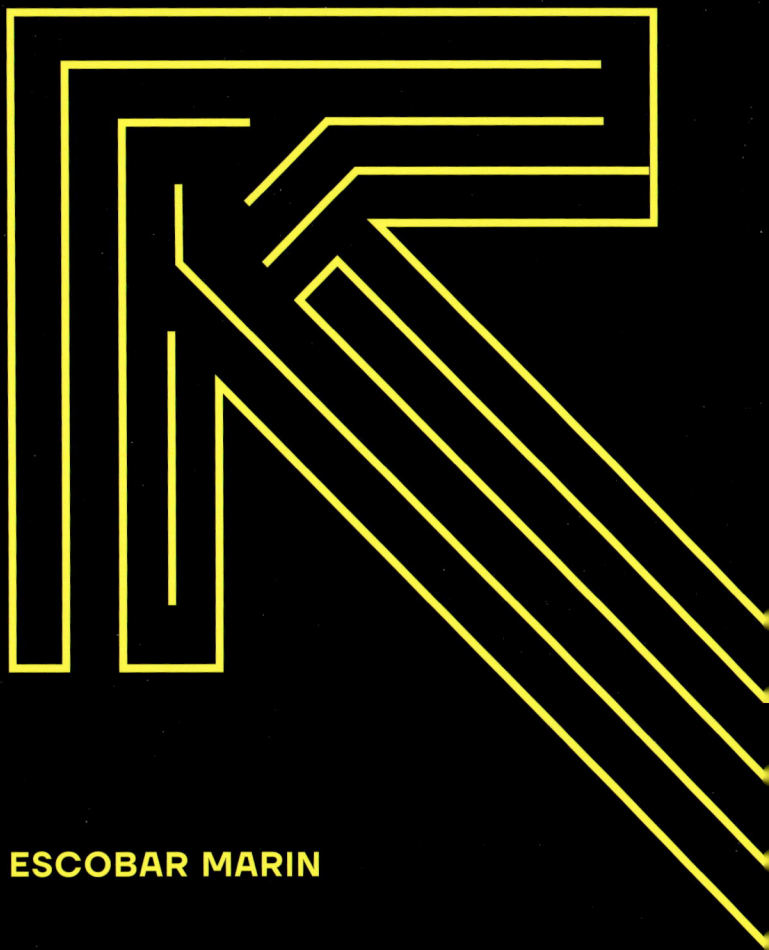

JONATHAN ESCOBAR MARIN

Culture isn't fluffy values or empty hype. It's the beat of behaviors your drumbeat hammers into reality.

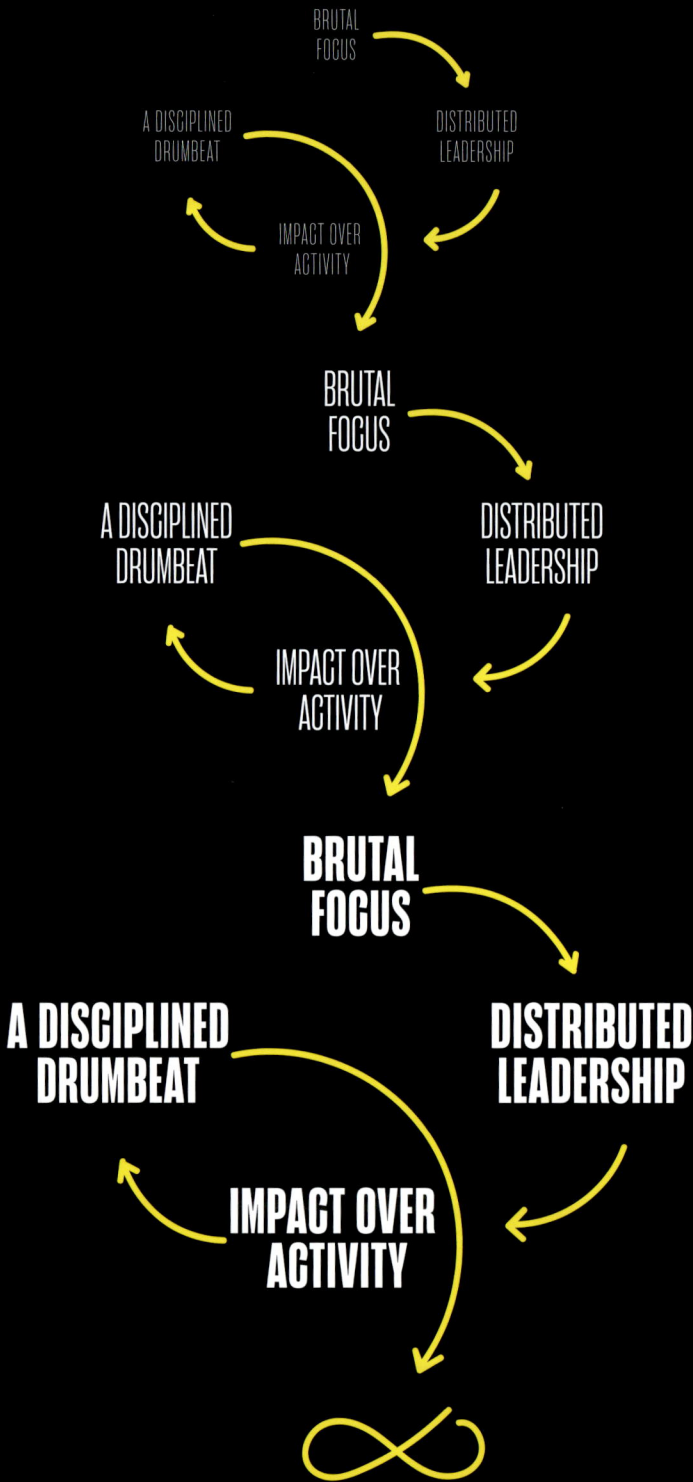

Image 0.2: The four drivers—brutal focus, distributed leadership, impact over activity, and a disciplined drumbeat—shaping the way the world's top firms work

© 2025, Jonathan Escobar Marin

companies forge missions. They break silos. They enable ownership. They unleash execution. They determine their impact or learn. And then they start the cycle over again. At its core, the drumbeat evolves through a complex network of interconnected actions and outcomes, each intricately interwoven to form a powerful, self-reinforcing cycle of success. By disassembling the components of the rhythm, we can see how each element plays a vital role in creating a harmonious symphony of synchronized efforts that drive unparalleled results.

Your drumbeat isn't merely another business process—it's the living expression, the steady beat of your culture in action.

JONATHAN ESCOBAR MARIN

FORGE MISSIONS.
BREAK SILOS.
ENABLE OWNERSHIP.
UNLEASH EXECUTION.
IMPACT OR LEARN.
START OVER AGAIN.

Leading to beat the FATE requires uniting the entire organization around ruthlessly chosen ambitions with clear targets, deadlines, talent, and capital allocation to effectively execute the strategy—in other words, well-defined missions that drive impact. When these missions are embraced across silos and hierarchies by emerging leaders throughout the organization, they catalyze truly distributed leadership. Breaking down the missions into specific bets, initiatives, and milestones creates a comprehensive execution plan. The seamless execution and accelerated decision-making within these missions result in impact, achieving desired outcomes. When we do not achieve the desired outcomes, we learn, iterate, pivot, transform. We start over again as one team, fully synchronized, fully aligned. The drumbeat is common sense with uncommon discipline. This disciplined cadence transforms effort into market-defining impact. The key to achieving that disciplined, collective synchronism lies in ingraining the cycle of rhythmic drivers as a deeply rooted cultural habit. When these drivers are in place and the rhythm kept with exceptional discipline, companies don't just compete; they also set the beat for their entire market. The rhythmic drivers may seem like common sense at first glance, and they are; the uncommon discipline and commitment to consistently applying them are what truly drives success in business. The resulting beat turns chaos into dominance.

The drumbeat is about forging a cultural evolution where your organization's best future becomes inevitable, transforming purpose into a relentless beat of impact to shape tomorrow. Finding the rhythm and keeping your drumbeat consistent—evolving focus, talent, and execution—require courage, experimentation, and the willingness to embrace the discomfort of continuous change. It will demand that you challenge your assumptions, question your orthodoxies, and let go of the practices and mindsets that no longer serve you. But for those who are willing to commit to beat the easy path and set the rhythm, the rewards are immeasurable.

The world of FATE is not for the faint of heart. But for those who are willing to embrace its challenges and seize its opportunities, it offers the chance to make an extraordinary impact—to shape the future rather than be shaped by it. The rhythm of change is growing louder by the day.

The question is, will you lead to beat FATE with your own drumbeat, or will you fall behind, marching to someone else's?

JONATHAN ESCOBAR MARIN

THE DRUMBEAT IS COMMON SENSE WITH UNCOMMON DISCIPLINE.

FOCUS BEATS DISPERSION. CLARIT
DISTRACTION. PRIORITIES BEAT
HESITATION. COMMITMENT BEATS
INDECISION. AUDACITY BEATS FEAR
BEATS OPTIONS. TARGETING BEAT
UNCERTAINTY. RESOLUTION BEATS WA
SIMPLICITY BEATS COMPLEXITY. ESS
DOUBT. DEFINITION BEATS VAGUENES
CONCENTRATION BEATS DIFFUSION. C
COURAGE BEATS CHANCE. IMMERS
BEATS DRIFT. SHARPNESS BEATS BRO
DIFFERENTIATION BEATS SAMENESS

ATS AMBIGUITY. DIRECTION BEATS
SIBILITIES. DECISIVENESS BEATS
ONTEMPLATION. PURPOSE BEATS
ECTION BEATS ABUNDANCE. INTENT
CATTERING. DETERMINATION BEATS
ING. SPECIFICITY BEATS GENERALITY
E BEATS EXCESS. CONVICTION BEATS
ANSPARENCY BEATS MANIPULATION
CE BEATS VARIETY. LESS BEATS MORE
BEATS APPROXIMATION. MISSION
ESS. URGENCY BEATS DELIBERATION
STINCTION BEATS GENERALIZATION

CHAPTER 1

BRUTAL FOCUS

MOST COMPANIES DON'T LACK RESOURCES. THEY LACK FOCUS.

Your strategy is your map to victory; your success depends on how effectively you chart the route and how boldly you travel it. Put simply, your strategy is your blueprint for winning with customers and outmaneuvering the competition; its power lies not in its brilliance alone, but in how ruthlessly you focus on achieving that advantage and how relentlessly and seamlessly you execute what matters most.

Too many companies fall into the trap of investing heavily in grandiose engagement events—off-site extravaganzas meant to rally the troops around a new vision or strategy. Armies of consultants produce flashy PowerPoint tomes articulating lofty ambitions. The executives wax poetic about bold transformations but don't offer any detailed plans for implementation. Far too often, these expensive spectacles amount to little more than theoretical exercises. Once the event is over, that shiny new strategy gets filed away, quickly forgotten amid the whirlwind of daily operations; the whole organization quickly loses focus when it comes to execution.

And please don't get me wrong: Getting strategy right is essential; it's the foundation of every market-making transformation. Yet the masters of value creation know that strategy's power is fully unleashed only when paired with ruthless focus, seamless execution, and the ability to iterate toward victory through market realities. Strategy's true test lies not in management off-sites but in the raw arena where decisions collide with market realities. The greatest strategic minds win not only by envisioning the future, but also by orchestrating their entire organization's energy around the critical moves that translate that vision into market reality. True transformation requires more than just slick presentations and rah-rah rhetoric. Great strategies die in the gap between inspiration and implementation.

This truth emerges from a fundamental principle: Strategy is nothing without execution. It's in the daily decisions, in the market, where strategy truly comes alive. What separates enduring success from fleeting performance is the sustained, intense coordination of every organizational fiber around executing those strategic imperatives. It demands brutal focus on the vital priorities that will achieve breakthrough outcomes.

The difference between good and extraordinary lies in the organization's capacity to maintain this laser-focused execution against strategic imperatives. In an era where fragmentation threatens to pull organizations apart—from splintered consumer segments to fractured supply chains—brutal focus on the vital strategic choices serves as the essential counterforce. Brutal focus is about creating an environment

JONATHAN ESCOBAR MARIN

Your strategy is your map to victory; your success depends on how effectively you chart the route and how boldly you travel it.

Great strategies die in the gap between inspiration and implementation.

JONATHAN ESCOBAR MARIN

where every team member, every decision, and every resource aligns with crystal clear strategic priorities—turning collective insight into market impact. It's about chopping the grandiose plans down to size. It's about being in leadership positions not for the shows but for impact. It's about leading at its maximum expression; focus on what moves the needle, not what looks good on a PowerPoint slide for the next "all-hands." After all, pep talks don't pay salaries. It's about setting ambitions that are grounded in action, not just aspiration. Vision without ruthless execution is just expensive daydreaming.

This is where true market leaders separate themselves: in their ability to combine strategic brilliance with unrelenting execution discipline. They've mastered the art of translating a unified purpose and a compelling vision into concentrated action, operationalizing strategic clarity with a purpose that is worth a lifetime of dedication. In today's market velocity, this combination isn't just advantageous; it's essential for sustained value creation as well. The real challenge—and the real opportunity—lies in forging this relentless collective rhythm around the critical vital priorities that will achieve strategic outcomes and realize the common purpose.

Brutal focus isn't about what to do or not to do; it's about what to achieve or abandon. Outcomes first, actions second. Prioritizing by

GOOD INTENTIONS IN POWERPOINTS, OFF-SITES, AND EVENTS

FANBOYS OF NARRATIVES & PEP TALKS

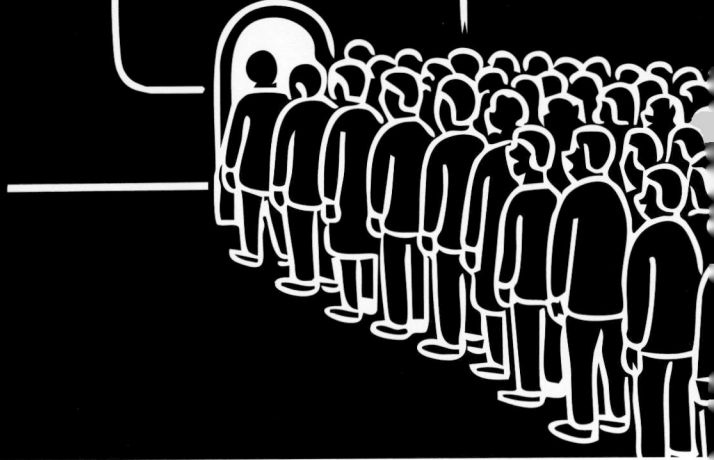

FOCUS THAT CUTS WITH DISCIPLINED EXECUTION THAT WINS

DRIVERS OF FOCUS, GROWTH, WINNING, & CHANGE

Image 1.1: Crowds distracted with PowerPoint karaokes—while the few win with brutal focus. Choose your door. © 2025, Jonathan Escobar Marin

VISION WITHOUT RUTHLESS EXECUTION IS JUST EXPENSIVE DAYDREAMING.

thinking in terms of activity is a relic of outdated playbooks—born in the minds of efficiency cults, where busyness was mistaken for impact and deliverables piled up like trophies. Brutal focus, on the other hand, means deciding and stating unequivocally which goals we pursue and which we do not.

Some leaders resist building brutal focus simply because they lack the ability to decide what is essential to achieve and what is not. They feel comfortable being busy while (usually unaware of it) protecting the indefiniteness of the goals.

Jerome du Chaffaut, CEO of Altadis and general manager of Iberia cluster, Imperial Brands PLC, stands at the forefront of work innovation, visionary leadership, and relentless execution. Jerome said of brutal focus, "This seems to be an approach to strategy execution, but in reality, it's an exercise in elevating leadership to the highest possible level: It moves leaders from the ambiguity of strategy, PowerPoint business reviews, good-intended one-off engagement events to the transparent, unambiguous commitment of choosing and declaring the critical number of pivotal missions . . . and pursuing them with unwavering commitment and military-like synchronization.

"By channeling our collective energy and expertise into these key missions," he continues, "we create a powerful vortex of creativity and meaningful conversations. This strategic alignment becomes contagious throughout the organization, fostering a shared sense of purpose and urgency. It's a commitment to excellence that demands discipline and focus, but the rewards are transformative."[1]

Building brutal focus does not mean each function or department compiling a wish list. That's not focus; to the contrary, this avoids focus. Focus means making bold choices—extremely clear outcomes first, empowered teams determining the how second. Rather than broad philosophies, brutal focus involves North Star metrics that reflect the growth, efficiency, or long-term transformation imperatives of the strategy. These help ensure everyone can see if the organization is moving with the needed urgency and in the right direction. It means missions that define the most significant outcomes—not activities or deliverables—essential to achieving the North Star metrics. Each mission is unambiguously assigned to a specific team, who then defines execution—bets, activities, and deliverables—fostering radical transparency, unquestionable accountability, and extreme ownership. This approach enables powerful collaboration, since every team understands how their work contributes to and impacts the broader strategic goals.

Brutal focus requires conscious talent allocation across silos: Team leaders and members must be responsible for each mission, enabled by dedicated guides (specific members of the executive team). The guides serve as servant leaders who challenge, support, and counsel their teams to achieve beyond what they believe possible, all within an environment of strong trust and psychological safety.

CHALLENGE

How do I empower
talent to unleash their
full potential?

Setting clear and stretching
missions

Expressing and reinforcing
expectations for teams

Breaking self-limiting beliefs
when needed

Giving honest and candid
on-the-spot feedback

SUPPORT

How do I unlock
talent so that they can
be successful?

Creating unconditional
psychological safety

Clearing away the obstacles that
the teams cannot overcome

Facilitating resources that
the teams need but lack

Building belief and resilience
in valleys of disappointment

Image 1.2: Challenge drives the mission, support fuels the rhythm of
execution, guides empower teams to thrive with brutal focus.
© 2025, Jonathan Escobar Marin

Brutal focus is an exercise in elevating leadership to the highest possible level."

—**Jerome du Chaffaut**

The team members will be defined by each team leader who is given the freedom—with some principles aimed at distributing ownership and discovering new talents—to build a dream team. Brutal focus also involves indisputably clear timelines for realizing impact on each mission. The missions' results are defined with specific targets to hit by set periods (e.g., the end of next quarter, the end of the year, in three, five, ten years), creating a timeline that leaves no room for doubt about what must be achieved, by whom, and when. With timelines this well defined, no one can claim the impact to achieve in a given period is not abundantly clear.

THE WALL

Rather than superficially communicating a strategy via some flashy event, brutal focus helps you do the difficult but vital work of operationalizing the organization's purpose and strategy into a powerful Wall that serves as a single source of truth—or, better said, a single source of empowering distributed leadership for impact-obsessed execution.

Since a company's strategy is defined not by its narrative but by what its people actually focus on and deliver, the Wall reveals these true strategic priorities. The Wall serves as a unifying force for effort and execution in an increasingly fragmented business landscape.

With the rise of Agile methodologies—which, at their core, emphasize a focus on customer value, collaboration across boundaries, adaptability, and purposeful iteration—came an unfortunate phenomenon I call *Agile theater*. Instead of embracing Agile foundational principles, it became open offices divided into departments or functional teams (what a funny contradiction) with the walls of the office covered with Agile boards full of sticky notes, arranged in neat columns: "To-Do," "Doing," "Done." At first glance, these walls seem to embody efficiency and transparency. The illusion of progress has only intensified as organizations eagerly embraced digital work management platforms—transforming physical sticky notes into virtual cards, adding layers of complexity with endless

JONATHAN ESCOBAR MARIN

A company's strategy is defined not by its narrative but by what its people actually focus on and deliver. The Wall reveals the true strategic priorities.

subtasks and automated workflows. These tools, much like their physical counterparts, often serve to further fragment work rather than unite it, creating digital silos that mirror our physical ones. But if you look more closely, more often than desired, you'll see a lot of meaningless activity, a lot of work for the sake of work. Two things are missing from these Post-it walls: the connection to the bigger picture—the strategic outcomes behind all the "doing"—and the connection between all the functions where these "Agile boards" exist. Among these functional walls, there is no singular wall that shows the brutally important goals for the organization. The commercialization of pseudo-Agile—marketed under the banner of Agile but missing its essence—which pulled and continues to pull people into workshops and certifications at scale to learn how to manage activity rather than impact, has inadvertently made organizations around the globe lose sight of purpose and context. Functions continue to work in silos, their boards filled with tasks but devoid of the connection to the brutally important outcomes that should give those tasks meaning and purpose.

Beyond simply checking the box by sending employees to certifications or sharing aesthetic photos of Post-it–covered walls on LinkedIn, there is another way to approach work. At least work to make a meaningful impact. By the late 2000s, amid the Agile industry explosion—and after years of experimenting with elevating and connecting activity to impact, outputs to outcomes, execution to results, and talent to the bigger picture—I had the opportunity to learn how Procter & Gamble and Toyota charted a different path. They prioritized purposeful execution, empowered extreme ownership, obsessed over doing only what moved the needle, and pushed themselves to learn faster than everyone else in order to obsessively iterate their approach. What truly set them apart was their ability to seamlessly connect the *why*, the *what*, the *where*, the *how*, and the *learning*—all clearly and visibly integrated on their walls.

They had different kinds of walls from anything I had seen before— ones that perfectly connected the dots of all my previous practice. Their walls always followed a kind of Plan-Do-Check-Act thinking, first with the big blocks of the business—the fundamental priorities that would make or break the company's success in the short, medium, and long term. To achieve these priorities were thirty-, sixty-, and ninety-day action plans with clear ownership defined, detailed plans guiding teams toward their goals. Then, next to these action plans, you had hourly, daily, and weekly tracking metrics offering real-time insights into the teams' progress. When the results fell short, gap analyses and systemic problem-solving appeared, prompting reflection and adjustment. This was pure purpose and execution poetry—not in PowerPoints but in real life, owned by the talent living in the organization.

These walls, although they didn't call them that, were more than just display boards. They were living, breathing entities that connected everyone to the bigger picture. They bridged the gap between grand visions and well-defined outcomes, between corporate strategy and team contribution. In essence, they were platforms of truth, single sources of distributed execution that propelled what truly mattered for the company's success.

This wall—the Wall—was a commitment to transparency, alignment, and shared purpose. Whether it was manifested as a literal wall in an office, a digital dashboard, or a state of mind, the essence remained the same: a single platform of truth where leaders and teams could align, track, and realize their brutally important goals while having honest, sharp conversations to better collaborate without the sticky-note to-do lists, PowerPoints, and pep talks. As Mark Ritson of Gasp! succinctly puts it, "A great [strategy] takes months of thinking but never needs more than a page, usually half a page, to explain to anyone."[2]

The Wall is a beacon of clarity that makes purpose actionable. It connects people's effort, collaboration, and obstacles with the organization's overarching goals. It puts front and center the meaningful impact they seek to achieve. It speaks truths about the company's direction and its execution of this direction. It lives and breathes with the rhythm of the organization, updating as goals are met and new challenges emerge. It explains the "what winning means" behind every

JONATHAN ESCOBAR MARIN

The Wall is a call to bring purpose and context back into our daily work lives, an invitation to tear down the walls that divide us and build a singular Wall that unites us in pursuit of what truly matters.

"where to play." It shows where we are focusing to win and—probably most important—who will achieve those goals: the talent, the most important and scarce asset of any company.

The Wall transforms companies. It breaks down silos, aligns efforts, and ignites a sense of collective purpose. It turns strategy from an abstract concept into a tangible, visible guide. It makes success not only measurable but palpable as well. It's a rallying point, a source of motivation, and a catalyst for collaboration.

The Wall is a fundamental shift in how we visualize, communicate, and pursue what is needed for organizational success. It's about creating a space—physical or virtual—where the brutally important is always in focus, where every action is contextualized, and where every team member can see their role in the bigger picture. It's not merely a management tool; it's a philosophy of organizational clarity and cohesion. The Wall serves as a foundation for building community within the organization, where everyone understands and lives the strategic vision together. What companies *do* matters more than what they *say* about their culture. The Wall is a cultural artifact that shapes how decisions are made and priorities are owned and maintained. The Wall shapes not only results, but also how teams interact, execute, and learn to develop an increasingly sophisticated understanding of value creation that compounds over years. The ability to maintain razor-sharp focus amid complexity becomes a self-reinforcing advantage. It's a call to bring purpose and context back into our daily work lives, an invitation to tear down the walls that divide us and build a singular Wall that unites us in pursuit of what truly matters.

It's a vision for a more aligned, purposeful, and successful way of working. It's a promise that in every organization, there will always be a place where the brutally important is clear, where truth lives, and where every individual can see how their efforts contribute to the greater good.

As we will discover through the concept of the drumbeat, cyclical evaluation and re-creation of the Wall helps establish an intense rhythm of strategy execution and evolution that delivers on the most significant strategic goals. The Wall isn't just an execution tool; it's also the beat of brutal focus that orchestrates your organization's march toward what matters most: what builds lasting strategic advantages. With the drumbeat, each cycle of brutal prioritization strengthens the organization's ability to detect emerging opportunities, allocate talent with dynamism, and create sustainable differentiation. Over time, this disciplined focus compounds into market positions that competitors can't easily replicate. The Wall serves as a guide for building brutal focus for what is important in the short, medium, and long term, and has four fundamental cornerstones: North Star metrics (ideally one, maximum three in complex organizations with multiple categories, customer bases, or P&Ls, based on our experience), specific missions with well-defined targets, unambiguous team staffing (leaders, members, and guides), and indisputably clear timeboxes for realizing impact on each mission. Your North Star metrics translate your organization's purpose into measurable indicators that provide guidance for decision-making and show how well you're delivering on your why. That guiding purpose will help you determine crucial missions to make it happen, and you'll measure your progress with well-defined outcomes, not mere checklists of deliverables. In order to implement those missions, you need a team brutally focused on each one with top executives acting as guides, servant leaders in action. Finally, you'll also need indisputably clear-cut timeboxes for realizing impact on each mission; teams must always know when moving the needle is needed.

The Wall is a living artifact that everyone can access at any time to understand and align with what is needed, building shared awareness, desire, and knowledge about the outcomes essential to achieving strategic goals both in the near term and for sustained market leadership. The Wall brings to life the company why and illuminates the what, the where, the where not, the who, and the when of getting outcomes delivered, empowering everyone with an outward focus on the customer and on economic, societal, and environmental results.

The Wall is designed to eradicate what we call "the Fatal Five"—the strategy killers. The five primary dysfunctions of most strategies are outcome ambiguity, short-term myopia, diffused granular actionability,

JONATHAN ESCOBAR MARIN

THE WALL SPEAKS TRUTHS ABOUT THE COMPANY'S DIRECTION AND ITS EXECUTION OF THIS DIRECTION.

MISSION 1

Reclaim oral care market
leadership by growing volume
share from 38% to >41%

NORTH STAR

Win with those who
matter most to achieve
above 52% market
share in our power
categories by EOY

→

MISSION 2

Cement Petylon market leadership
by extending value share from
73.1% to >75%

MISSION 3

Conquer the premium impulse
category by driving >$300M at
30%+ gross margin

Image 1.3: North Star metric aligns, missions ignite, teams commit, timelines accelerate—
the Wall builds clarity with brutal focus. © 2025 Jonathan Escobar Marín

accountability opacity, and timeline ambivalence. In a landscape where market leadership demands precision, speed, innovation, and growth at scale, these dysfunctions silently erode remarkably promising strategies. The Wall's sharp architecture transforms organizational entropy into focused momentum through five decisive strikes:

1. Where outcome ambiguity dilutes impact, *North Star metrics forge crystalline purpose*. Every decision, every mission aligns to concrete measures of success that make the common victory not only visible but inevitable as well.

2. Where short-term myopia creates false trade-offs between short-term execution and long-term value creation, *the Wall's dual architecture enables organizational ambidexterity*. It simultaneously drives immediate impact through focused execution while nurturing breakthrough innovations and capability building that secure future market leadership.

3. Where diffused granular actionability paralyzes execution, *mission clarity converts strategic vision into right-sized achievable victories* for two-pizza teams, turning grand ambitions into transformative outcomes that teams can own and deliver.

4. Where accountability opacity breeds hesitation, *unambiguous talent allocation across the silos creates unstoppable ownership*. Named leaders, members, and guides form a clear chain of execution, creativity, support, and responsibility from the boardroom to the execution line.

5. Where timeline ambivalence permits endless drift, *crystal clear timeboxing demands specific achievement within defined periods*. Crystal clear outcome cycles forge relentless momentum. Success isn't simply measured; it's delivered through high-velocity iterations and bold pivots, creating the drumbeat of sustained market leadership. There must be no room for interpretation about what must be achieved and when, while teams are empowered to self-organize and iteratively find the best path to delivery. Paranoid clarity about impact and timing unleashes

teams to rapidly design, deliver, measure, learn, and iterate their way to victory.

This isn't merely about alignment; it's about architecting market dominance through ruthless clarity. It forges meaningful discussion around what is critically important to the company and what is actually happening, week by week, to build lasting strategic advantages. It creates a virtuous cycle where execution and evolution discipline feed into creating sustainable value. It makes the theory of aligning everyone with a shared vision and working together as one a reality but in a straightforward, simple, and pragmatic way.

This commitment to ruthless clarity and simplicity resonates with what A. G. Lafley discovered as CEO of Procter & Gamble: that communicating at a *Sesame Street* level of simplicity was crucial. As he explained, "So if I'd stopped at 'We're going to refocus on the company's core businesses,' that wouldn't have been good enough. The core businesses are one, two, three, four. Fabric care, baby care, feminine care, and hair care. And then you get questions: 'Well, I'm in home care. Is that a core business?' 'No.' 'What does it have to do to become a core business?' 'It has to be global leader in its industry. It has to have the best structural economics in its industry. It has to be able to grow consistently at a certain rate. It has to be able to deliver a certain cash flow return on investment.' So then business leaders understand what it takes to become a core business."[3]

It's crucial that the architecture of your Wall is engineered to eliminate vagueness at every level with peak simplicity. This laser focus on clarity is grounded in cognitive science and organizational psychology. John Sweller's cognitive load theory demonstrates that clear, unambiguous information presentation enhances performance.[4] The Wall is designed for this, reducing the mental effort required to understand and act on strategic objectives.

Research by Rizzo and colleagues showed that role ambiguity and unclear goals significantly hamper productivity.[5] The Wall and the later activation of teams with radical clarity about their roles and their unambiguous connection to the goals directly address these issues, fostering a more engaged workforce.

I've observed marked improvements in employee engagement, strategic alignment speed, and execution efficiency in the organizations we work with who have embodied brutal focus. This skill set and the mindset shift required to implement it, rooted in both research and application, enable the creation of environments where vagueness is eliminated, trust is augmented, and minds are activated toward shared goals. By replacing traditional, often nebulous strategic communications with the clarity of the Wall, organizations build the brutal focus necessary for success in today's complex business landscape. This transformation creates a crystal clear understanding of what to achieve, where to play to achieve it, who will achieve it, and when—always powered by a compelling why.

The power of the Wall—and the brutal focus embodied on it—is evident in the transformative experience of Justin Apsey, a leader with over twenty-five years of distinguished service at Unilever, one of the world's leading consumer goods companies. His current role as managing director and executive vice president, Southern Africa, puts him at the forefront of one of the most important markets for Unilever, particularly within the context of emerging markets. His insights on leadership and organizational change are grounded in decades of hands-on experience navigating complex business environments and spearheading strategic shifts across diverse markets.

Justin shares his team's journey in starting with brutal focus, implementing the Wall's conversation and its profound impact. Finding the North Star metrics and the consequent missions to impact them, Justin says, "pushed us to reflect deeply on the legacy we wanted to leave and what would truly make a significant impact on our performance on a global scale. We set ambitious North Star metrics that stretched into the future with missions that were granular and specific enough to deliver measurable outcomes within a financial year. This vision was not static, and over three years evolved into two key items: One, to develop a World

Champion mindset. Two, to build a superior value creating business by improving margin and brand love by absolute numbers every year."[6]

Part of that focus, of finding their guiding light, was a brutal focus on what his business *wouldn't* pursue. "This was intentional because," he says, "before being challenged by the brutal focus and obsession on making clear choices on the outcomes of the Wall, we often found ourselves caught up in a whirlwind of activities, lacking discretion in how we allocated our time and very often built on opinion over data." Busyness buries business, but, Justin says, "Busyness had become our default mode of operation, and we weren't sufficiently focused on the impact of our actions and the allocation of our talent. By crafting the Wall, with crystal clear North Star metrics and key missions, we forced senior leadership to really articulate the priorities, and in doing so, empowered our leaders and teams to say no and be selective about our commitments—a revolutionary shift in how our leaders and teams show up."

Justin and his leadership team developed the missions with clear targets to deliver what was needed for the present and the future. "We approached the missions on the Wall," he says, "through four critical lenses: brand building, market penetration, our business model, and innovations for the future. What truly transformed our organization was the ability to operate ambidextrously—simultaneously optimizing today's business while building tomorrow's opportunities. This was not easy and required us to symbolically define the teams as Perform and Transform. This dual focus prevented the common trap of either being too short-term oriented or too disconnected from current realities that needed us to change into the future. The Wall became our shared cognitive map, providing transparency and aligning everyone around what matters most. Ensuring we beat competition and built the World Champion mindset we knew resonated strongly with the South African psyche." These elements allowed his team to create meaningful shifts toward transformation while ensuring measurability, and they would track their progress on each mission through weekly syncs and review the Wall in quarterly iterations.

BUSYNESS BURIES BUSINESS. A BRUTALLY FOCUSED WALL BUILDS IT.

Justin's experience underscores the transformative power of the Wall to shape brutal focus. His team was able to break free from the trap of busyness and focus on high-impact missions. This shift not only improved their performance in market share, speed to market, and profitability, but also empowered team members to make better decisions about how to allocate their time and resources.

CUT THE CRAP!

The ability to say no to good but noncritical goals and activities is as crucial as identifying what to pursue. This approach allows leaders and teams to channel their energy and resources into outcomes and initiatives that truly move the needle, rather than spreading themselves thin across a multitude of good ideas that aren't the top priority. Selective focus and execution are fundamental exercises in building brutal focus, which we call *cutting the crap*. It means having the ambition to not settle for scattered, to aim to win, and deciding what not to focus on or what to stop doing within the organization. As Steve Jobs famously said, "When you think about focusing . . . you think, 'Well, focusing is saying yes.' No. Focusing is saying no. . . . And the result of that focus is going to be some really great products where the total is much greater than the sum of the parts."[7]

By eliminating good ideas that don't lead the pack, our companies can direct their resources and attention toward what truly matters for achieving strategic outcomes. This requires difficult but necessary decisions; big wins often require brutal choices. To build brutal focus, that segmentation is key.

Behind every company that wins, you can find the Pareto principle, so it's crucial to focus on the 20 percent of strategic bets targeted to deliver 80 percent of impact through the most significant choices while letting go of the rest that aren't the game changers.

Brutal focus isn't just a tactic; it's a mindset as well. It's about cutting through noise and distractions to prioritize the vital areas to win big today and tomorrow. The trade-off is hard but essential: By doing

"When you think about focusing . . . you think, 'Well, focusing is saying yes.' No. Focusing is saying no . . . And the result of that focus is going to be some really great products where the total is much greater than the sum of the parts."

—Steve Jobs

less, you achieve more. Eliminate the 80 percent that dilutes the vital 20 percent.

Cutting the crap involves stopping good efforts that don't hit the top mark and redirecting talent toward what matters most in terms of sustained value and impact. As markets continue to fragment into countless microsegments and opportunities, the ability to decisively choose which fragments to ignore becomes as critical as choosing where to focus. To keep your brutal focus on what is needed, it's fundamental to be fully committed to the things you are going to stop pursuing. These pieces of work go on the back of the Wall—the Stop Wall. The Stop Wall isn't just about efficiency; it's also about maintaining coherence and consistency in an increasingly fragmented world.

Just like the Wall, the Stop Wall must be communicated to the entire company so everyone understands what's not being pursued—which strong options we're dropping. Alongside the Stop Wall, you'll need unambiguous answers to these questions:

- What specific outcomes and activities will we end completely?
- Who needs to be informed of this decision to stop?
- What firm date do we set to ensure this is terminated and off our agenda?
- Who will gain back capacity once these activities cease?
- How do we ensure this stays dead and doesn't creep back onto our agenda?

Think of the Stop Wall like a discarded pile in cards; you know what's there, but those items are out of play. Like defining the wildly important, the brutal focus, deciding which good ideas to ditch isn't a one-time meeting or activity; it's a habit. The Stop Wall doesn't work unless it also becomes a habit. It is sustained by the mindset challenge of ensuring that, a month from now, you haven't filled your agenda with tasks and goals that don't drive the win.

JONATHAN ESCOBAR MARIN

BY DOING LESS, YOU ACHIEVE MORE. ELIMINATE THE 80 PERCENT THAT DILUTE THE VITAL 20 PERCENT.

Radical transparency—communicating clearly and consistently to everyone in the organization what you will not do—enables both brutal focus—the attention on what is really important—and cutting the crap, the ruthless elimination of nonessential work. These elements work in concert to drive meaningful impact. If you lack focus and simply create transparency around numerous initiatives that aren't truly priorities, you'll only generate confusion—what I call "transparent chaos." You've made your activity visible, but without strategic prioritization. However, if you maintain focus but fail to clearly communicate the priorities and nonpriorities throughout your organization, people will continue treating everything as equally important. That's why these concepts must work together: Focus determines what truly matters, cut the crap refers to what is not critical now, while transparency ensures everyone understands both what will be pursued and what will be deliberately set aside.

This is why one of the best practices we have implemented over the last few years is to communicate with equal emphasis both the priorities that are brutally important and what we should no longer spend one minute on.

Image 1.4: If you don't cut the crap, enjoy the busyness trap.
© 2025, Jonathan Escobar Marin

Cutting the crap ties into resource management as well. In the last twenty years of evolving organizations across five continents and multiple industries, I've worked with hundreds of organizations, and there is not a single one where I have not heard the same refrain: "We lack resources." When I hold up the mirror to this statement—not to challenge its validity but to expose its true meaning—top leaders and boards face an unmistakable truth: "We lack resources" really means "We haven't made the bold, strategic decisions about what we cannot neglect to achieve—and what we must stop."

They realize that this phrase reveals a lack of strategic prioritization and decision-making, potentially masking a deeper problem—a shortage of ambition. And they're right, because the most dangerous belief in business is "We don't have enough resources." The right mindset is "How do we win big with what we've got?" Ambition enables proper resource allocation. It's the spark that turns brutal focus into big wins, driving us to say no to good ideas and yes to the vital few. The power of ambition exceeding resources—a principle I first witnessed through Fernando Fernandez, current CEO of Unilever, during our partnership in Latin America and later explored with Nitin Paranjpe, who traced it to C. K. Prahalad's teachings—has shaped into two powerful formulas proven by instilling this mentality in boards across the world: When ambition is

AMBITION GREATER THAN RESOURCES EQUALS RESULTS

Image 1.5: Ambition over resources sparks results—cut the crap; let hunger fuel brutal focus to win big. © 2025, Jonathan Escobar Marin

JONATHAN ESCOBAR MARIN

BUILDING BRUTAL FOCUS IS A HABIT, NOT AN ANNUAL GOAL-SETTING WORKSHOP.

WIN BIG IN A FEW AREAS INSTEAD OF LOSING SLOWLY EVERYWHERE.

R>A=M

RESOURCES GREATER THAN AMBITION EQUALS MEDIOCRITY

Image 1.6: Resources over ambition breeds mediocrity—let scarcity ignite brutal focus instead. © 2025, Jonathan Escobar Marin

greater than resources, results are achieved, leading to annual recurring revenue (ARR). When resources are greater than ambition, mediocrity is generated, resulting in recurring augmented mediocrity (RAM). Ambition isn't a luxury; it's the edge that cuts through the crap.

In the face of resource scarcity, organizations can harness this challenge to build brutal focus. By prioritizing and concentrating on what truly matters, companies can achieve better results. This shift paves the way for ARR, enabling companies to generate consistent, recurring revenue. However, when resources outpace ambition, RAM takes over, leading to stagnation and complacency.

Our responsibility lies not in seeking more resources but in making courageous decisions about what we cannot neglect to achieve—and what we must stop. As leaders, we must own this reality: The scarcity of resources is not an excuse; it's a call to action. Our responsibility is to make courageous decisions, to focus with relentless clarity, and to empower our teams to achieve breakthrough outcomes. Cutting the crap is not just about eliminating inefficiencies; it's also about eliminating the mindset that settles for less and igniting ambition to fuel the fight. It's ambition that turns focus into a weapon and sacrifice into strength.

By adopting an ARR mindset and leaving RAM behind, we build

organizations that deliver not only results, but also transformative, last-ing impact that compounds over years and decades. This is not theory or abstraction; it's a proven pattern I've seen time and again in practice. It starts with ambition. It starts with us. And it's followed by brutal focus and the courage to cut the crap.

As A. G. Lafley explained in an interview back in 2005: "Most human beings and most companies don't like to make choices. And they partic-ularly don't like to make a few choices that they really have to live with. They argue, 'It's much better to have lots of options, right?'"[8]

Lafley also recognized that rejected options often tend to resurface in discussions later. To prevent this from happening, he required teams to create an explicit "not-do list" similar to our Stop Wall: a list of initia-tives they would not pursue as part of their strategic planning process.

"For example, when we chose our corporate innovation programs, we cleared the deck of a lot of other stuff that we were then doing. So we'd have a list of all the things that we're not going to do. And if we caught people doing stuff that we said we were not going to do, we would pull the budget and the people and get them refocused on what we said we were going to do."[9]

Cutting the crap is not only about simplifying—it's also about trans-forming an organization's mindset. It demands correcting lack of ambition, deliberately eliminating distractions, and ruthlessly cutting lower-impact ideas to create space for what truly matters. Courage isn't about starting new things. It's about stopping the non–brutally important ones. This act of subtraction requires bold leadership. When leaders embrace this mind-set and religiously use tools for brutal focus like the Wall and Stop Wall, they don't just improve efficiency; they also fundamentally reshape how their organization thinks and acts. This is the essence of brutal focus: an ongoing act of leadership, courage, ambition, and discipline that separates high-performance, high-impact companies from the merely good ones.

The courage to say no builds organizational muscle memory that transforms short-term discipline into long-term competitive advan-tages. Ambition is the muscle behind that courage—pushing us to reject the good for the great.

JONATHAN ESCOBAR MARIN

THE SCARCITY OF RESOURCES IS NOT AN EXCUSE; IT'S A CALL TO ACTION.

COURAGE ISN'T ABOUT STARTING NEW THINGS. IT'S ABOUT STOPPING THE NON-BRUTALLY IMPORTANT ONES.

AMBIDEXTERITY ENABLED: THRIVING IN DUALITY

Brutal focus is about narrowing down, cutting through distractions, and relentlessly prioritizing the few missions that truly matter. But brutal focus doesn't mean oversimplifying or ignoring the complexity of competing priorities, like balancing short-term performance with long-term growth. It's about making deliberate, unambiguous choices and fully committing to them, without compromise. Nowhere is this more important than in the duality of exploration and exploitation—a concept known as *organizational ambidexterity*. In my experience, mastering this duality has become essential for leaders to navigate the complexities of modern markets and ensure sustained success by winning big today and tomorrow.

The concept of organizational ambidexterity, first introduced by Robert Duncan in 1976 and later expanded by James March in 1991, has gained significant traction in management science.[10] For instance, the Wall enables the capacity to simultaneously pursue both incremental improvements and breakthrough innovations. This duality is the essence of enduring success, allowing companies to simultaneously deliver on their current ambitions while seizing the future's game changers.

The ability to balance exploration and exploitation is no longer a luxury; it's a necessity. In business, we're running a marathon with hurdles—one eye on the path we've paved, the other on the horizon. We need to exploit what works now while building what will win next. This isn't about balance in the traditional sense; it's about dynamic tension—like a bowstring pulled taut—pushing and pulling between today's growth and profits and tomorrow's possibilities. It's about ambidexterity, made real.

This dynamic tension between present performance and future wins is what builds enduring market leaders. Research has consistently demonstrated that organizational ambidexterity is positively associated with firm performance across multiple metrics. The empirical evidence shows clear positive relationships between ambidexterity and sales growth, innovation outcomes, subjective performance ratings, market valuation (measured by Tobin's Q), and firm survival rates. This finding is particularly robust given that studies have used different measures of ambidexterity, various outcome variables, different levels of analysis, and samples from diverse industries. While ambidexterity may sometimes be inefficient and duplicative, the evidence suggests it typically has beneficial effects on firm performance, especially under conditions of market and technological uncertainty. However, the research also indicates that both under- and overuse of ambidexterity can be detrimental, suggesting an optimal balance is needed.[11]

The Wall aligns closely with contextual ambidexterity, which enables individuals to make their own judgments about how to divide their time between conflicting demands for performance-driven delivery and innovation-driven disruption. Cristina Gibson and Julian Birkinshaw demonstrated that this approach leads to superior performance by creating an organizational context that encourages individuals to make their own choices between execution-oriented and transformative-oriented activities in their daily work.[12]

Organizational ambidexterity becomes especially crucial in markets where companies must simultaneously excel in current segments while hunting the next brutal breakthroughs in emerging ones that could represent future growth. Ambidexterity presents a paradox: the simultaneous pursuit of efficiency and flexibility, stability and change, today's growth and tomorrow's disruption. This paradox is not to be resolved but embraced. As noted by Wendy Smith and Marianne Lewis, organizations that can hold these tensions and pursue both poles simultaneously are more likely to achieve long-term success.[13] The Wall embodies this paradoxical thinking, creating a space where exploitation and exploration coexist and reinforce each other to cut the crap on both fronts.

With the Wall, depending on the organization's level of maturity and business context and after several quarters of growing new habits and mindset, we achieve a healthy balance between exploitation and exploration missions. While exploitation naturally initially commands a larger share of our focus, we ensure that exploration gains

JONATHAN ESCOBAR MARIN

WE NEED TO EXPLOIT WHAT WORKS NOW WHILE BUILDING WHAT WILL WIN NEXT.

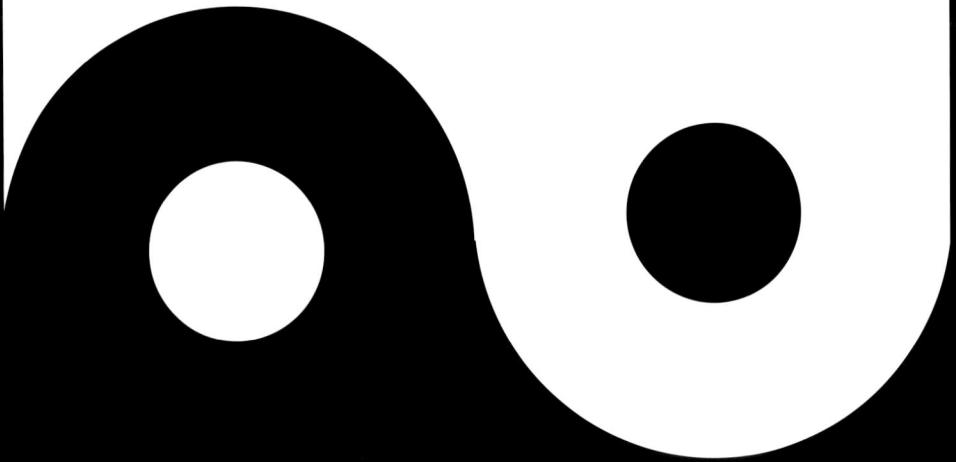

Image 1.7: Yin of today, yang of tomorrow—win with the duality of brutal focus.

substantial dedicated space—typically growing to between one-third and even almost half of our priorities after some time; believe me this is not immediate. This represents quite a good balance, considering that most organizations acknowledge their prior inability to give exploration priorities the right space to simply happen.

This shift highlights a profound change in organizational behavior: Exploration is no longer relegated to the margins of governance or treated as an afterthought, where it exists as a "nice to do but never really do" activity. Instead, it becomes a deliberate, structured effort embedded within the organization's strategic fabric, demonstrating that innovation and exploration for the brutally important can coexist alongside exploitation without being neglected. This balance not only fosters sustained growth, but also ensures the organization remains future-ready in increasingly dynamic and competitive environments.

Exploitation is about execution, effectiveness, and efficiency. It involves leveraging existing capabilities to achieve measurable improvements in performance, growth, cost reduction, and customer satisfaction. These missions are crucial for maintaining a strong market position and generating the resources necessary for future wins.

Exploitation missions on the Wall might include the following:

- Increase market share from X percent to Y percent in markets A, B, and C.

- Improve the customer retention rate from X percent to Y percent through enhanced product use.

- Reduce operational costs from X percent to Y percent through supply chain optimization.

- Boost customer satisfaction scores from X to Y points by eliminating top five pain points.

Conversely, exploration is about experimentation, risk-taking, and discovery in a world where speed and execution reign supreme. It requires a culture that encourages curiosity, embraces failure as part of the learning process, and constantly seeks new horizons—but with empathy as your secret weapon and only for the big wins that redefine markets. Exploration isn't random; it's long-term ambition with a target. Leaders in exploration are visionaries who understand that true innovation stems from decoding the unspoken needs of their clients through deep observation. They drive their organizations toward uncharted territories not merely for novelty's sake but because they've aligned their pursuit of the new with the actual behaviors and desires of their market. These leaders are more than innovators and disruptors; they are catalysts for change who create brutal focus by transforming customer insight into market-making impact. Their potential for transformation comes not just from their courage to experiment, but also from their ability to ground that experimentation in genuine market understanding.

And after some time, we typically dedicate between a third and almost half of our missions to exploration. These missions seek to strike at growth niches, disrupt operations, or seize game-changing impacts of technology for specific, brutal goals. Exploration missions might focus on these goals:

- Generate X percent of revenue from new products or services within two years.

- Establish a foothold in a new market segment, capturing X percent market share within three years.

- Develop the technology that eliminates the top five customer pain points by X percent in not more than eighteen months.

- Create a new business model that doubles margins by X percent in a target market within five years.

- Implement AI use cases that deliver more than $X million in cost savings in the next fifteen months.

- Strike at growth niches in adjacent markets that could become more than X percent EBITDA contributors in five years.

By combining the two types of missions, we avoid the traditional pitfalls where exploration projects are "always on top" initiatives when there is time. The missions delivering on exploitation fuel the resources needed for exploration, and the insights gained from exploration inform and enhance the efficiency of exploitation. This creates a virtuous cycle of continuous disruption through ambition-fueled innovation.

In the last year, we have seen numerous examples across various corporations where exploration teams have discovered pockets of business disruption achievable through new technologies that promise brutal breakthroughs. Meanwhile, exploitation teams have channeled intense focus into winning brands to capitalize on growth areas, delivering substantial returns on new investment bets aimed at discovery and execution. This duality—driven by clarity, ambition, courage, and customer obsession—separates the good from the legendary, the fleeting from the enduring. When focus beats in perfect rhythm, today's performance and tomorrow's innovation dance together.

Case in Point: EV Company

Let's use the example of an electric vehicle (EV) company for understanding organizational ambidexterity in action. The EV company needs to achieve excellence in exploiting electric vehicle manufacturing and commercialization, continually improving brand reputation with desirable, functional, and reliable vehicles while refining production processes and vehicle technology to increase efficiency and reduce costs. Simultaneously, the company must have a relentless pursuit of exploration, from pioneering autonomous driving technology to venturing into energy storage solutions, neural networks for Full Self-Driving software, and humanoid robots. This ambidextrous approach could potentially enable this EV company to not only lead the market in electric vehicles, but also claim the future's biggest wins in transportation, energy, autonomous robotics, and physical AI.

When focus beats in perfect rhythm, today's performance and tomorrow's innovation dance together.

To illustrate the potential impact of such a strategy, let's consider, as an example, how this EV company ambidexterity might translate into measurable outcomes on the Wall:

Examples of Exploitation Missions (Quarter-Year Horizon)

- Electric vehicle market leadership: Increase global market share from X percent to Y percent in electric vehicle sales by [end of year], delivering X million units annually across diverse price points and vehicle categories.

- Manufacturing excellence: Achieve industry-leading profit margins of X percent on electric vehicles by [end of year], by reducing vehicle production costs by X percent through advanced manufacturing techniques.

- Battery range enhancement: Increase vehicle range by X percent across all models by [end of year], solidifying our position as the leader in long-range electric vehicles.

- Battery cost reduction: Reduce battery costs by X percent by [quarter n], enabling more affordable electric vehicles and improved profitability.

- Charging and battery life optimization: Decrease charging time by X percent while simultaneously extending battery life by X percent by [end of year], enhancing the overall user experience and vehicle longevity.

Examples of Exploration Missions (Three to Ten Years Horizon)

- Autonomous driving: Generate $X billion in annual revenue by [year] through widespread adoption of Full Self-Driving technology, including licensing to other automakers and deployment in a robotaxi fleet.

- Robotaxi network: Capture X percent of the global autonomous ride-hailing market by [year], generating $X billion in annual revenue and transforming personal transportation.

- Energy storage: Deploy X gigawatt-hours of stationary energy storage by [year], generating $X billion in annual revenue and accelerating the transition to sustainable energy.

- Robotics: Achieve $X billion in annual revenue by [year] through the development and commercialization of humanoid robots, revolutionizing manufacturing and service industries.

- AI powerhouse: Establish a position as a top-three provider of AI training and inference services by [year], generating $X billion in annual revenue from external customers leveraging advanced computer capabilities.

This ambidextrous strategy, focused on concrete outcomes across both exploitation and exploration, illustrates how a company can position itself to lead in its core market while also redefining multiple industries. By balancing the performance of core competencies with the pursuit of new frontiers, such an approach aims to create diverse revenue streams and help a company maintain a position as an innovation leader across various sectors.

DECISIONS OVER PARALYSIS

As leaders, we must embrace the transformative power of decisive action over analytical paralysis. In today's high-stakes world of business, hesitation can be more costly than making a wrong decision.

This means that, when faced with a decision, we must act with purpose rather than freeze in the pursuit of complete certainty. Too often, companies get bogged down in endless analysis and metrics, losing sight of the bigger picture and the critical decisions that need to be made. Instead, those who master the art of ruthless prioritization—saying no

JONATHAN ESCOBAR MARIN

HESITATION CAN BE MORE COSTLY THAN MAKING A WRONG DECISION.

to the noise—and maintain unwavering focus on market-moving outcomes will dominate their sectors, today and tomorrow.

Making decisions quickly and acting on them with imperfect information is not about being reckless. It's about recognizing that strategic execution must respect the laws of the market, not just the laws of business theory. It's about recognizing that in today's fast-moving markets, the cost of delayed action often exceeds the benefit of perfect analysis. The most successful companies have learned to balance speed and precision; they gather enough data to make informed choices while maintaining the agility to make brutal choices quickly based on real-world insights. This approach turns strategy from an academic exercise into market-dominating reality.

By prioritizing decisive action over analysis paralysis, your company can move quickly and decisively toward your goals. This requires a calculated boldness to take smart risks, to experiment, and to learn from your mistakes. It also requires a high-impact culture that trusts and empowers teams to design, deliver, measure, and learn fast through distributed ownership, open communication, and collaboration—while killing off the distractions that don't matter.

The drivers in this book—the brutal focus of the Wall approach, distributed leadership, the obsession with achieving over doing, and the disciplined drumbeat—serve as a powerful antidote to analysis paralysis by forcing clarity around what matters most, where we need to play to win, who is needed to deliver, and having to forge this clarity when needed, not when our comfort decides. When we visibly decide what is needed to win—the critical priorities and their measures of success—and what we won't pursue, it creates accountability for decisions and their outcomes. Top leaders can't hide behind endless analysis to decide, and neither can teams when their progress (or lack thereof) is transparent to everyone. All this drives a culture of decisive action aligned with strategic imperatives that win big now and seize the future.

Ultimately, breaking free from paralysis means prioritizing what matters most and being willing to make tough choices in order to execute and learn fast, faster than everyone else. It means building brutal focus on what is needed. It's about having the courage to take action—and to say no—and the resilience to learn and iterate when things don't go according to plan. By embracing decisive leadership over paralyzing analysis, companies can build a culture of focus, innovation, speed, and impact that drives long-term success—with ambition as the beat of every move.

CROSS-SILOS COMPASS

Let's be clear: Departments, functions, or regions are not silos by their nature. They become silos when some executives transform them into isolated kingdoms, prioritizing their own agenda over organizational success, building invisible walls, filling out activity for the sake of activity Post-it boards, and operating with hidden interests that undermine collective goals. A silo emerges when a legitimate organizational unit chooses self-interest over organizational impact—and nobody stops it.

And let's continue with straight language: Without the brutal focus that dismantles silos, there is only brutal chaos—the chaos that emerges from masqueraded individuality and self-interest, where hidden agendas drive in different directions while some well-intentioned talent tries to merge impossibly different paths. Beyond its role to dismantle silos, in today's fragmented business environment, the Wall serves as a cross-units compass that becomes essential not only for alignment, but also for maintaining organizational coherence. The Wall prevents the company from fragmenting internally in response to external market fragmentation. By creating a unified vision across units, functions, or departments, the Wall defines what winning means and where we need to play to win. Our missions then serve as our relentless cross-boundary compass, ensuring we collaborate seamlessly to deliver week by week, as one team, with uncompromising clarity and zero hidden agendas. In this way, the cross-functional teams driving these missions don't simply execute; they build relationships, they unleash synergies, they accelerate results, and a clear timeline gives them a window for success or learning fast.

JONATHAN ES

A silo
Leo

The Wall's power lies in its ability to break down silos through shared work to realize common good. The Wall is alive; it captures not only where focus should be, but also how performance, collaboration, and progress are unfolding in real time. Everyone knows what is and what is not prioritized and why, and there's nowhere for territorial games or political maneuvering to hide, creating a unified direction across departments. By offering weekly visibility into progress and obstacles, the Wall enables leaders and teams to rapidly identify where there is no progress, where bottlenecks are forming, and where obstacles are stalling execution—unearthing, in this way, where some might be building moats around their territories that silently erode organizational efficiency and impact.

When everyone can see week by week the progress on the goals, key metrics, responsibilities, and timelines, it's easier to align efforts, bridge departmental gaps, prevent chaos, and work together effectively. This also prevents teams from inadvertently undermining each other's efforts and the quiet construction of new organizational kingdoms.

In many organizations, the most destructive inefficiencies come from fragmented efforts and lack of cross-functional collaboration. These challenges are particularly dangerous because they often masquerade as "business as usual," buried under carefully constructed explanations of why "this department is different" or "our situation is unique." With its dynamic, real-time nature, the Wall exposes these divides, making it impossible for such theatrical performances of (non)collaboration to persist.

With continuous access to the Wall with the status of the brutally important, there are fewer communication gaps, and teams organically align across functions. People don't have to navigate complex reporting structures or wait for cross-departmental meetings to understand status or strategic priorities. This enables more frequent cross-functional collaboration and discussion. When people have context for the bigger picture, they can make better decisions that consider the entire organization, not just their silo.

Brutal focus establishes shared awareness of the strategy and metrics that matter most, eliminating at its root cause the biggest business pandemic: siloed thinking. You can't build brutal focus by explaining a high-level strategy and expecting that everyone translates a high-level strategy into department projects or activities. Furthermore, you can't simply hope that these projects from the different units will all get along together to achieve the desired results that the strategy requires. Brutal focus isn't realized within the walls that isolate silos. It thrives on the Wall that unites them.

It's time to break out of silos. Brutal focus is about strategy execution as simultaneous evolution with synchronization as one team, as one organization: People's evolving understanding of context and meaning doesn't actually stop while waiting for the next communication from management. Instead of a cascade or deployment, or even a translation, it's better to think of strategy leadership—regularly synchronizing a constantly evolving context and meaning simultaneously occurring at all levels of the organization.

This is why the Wall is so much more than a management tool; it is the heart of your organization's execution, learning, and evolution. It keeps strategy alive, updated, and actionable—not buried in last month's PowerPoints or forgotten in folders in the Cloud.

The transformative power of building brutal focus across multiple units is exemplified by leaders who have successfully implemented these principles in their organizations. During her tenure as executive vice president and general manager for beauty and wellbeing at Unilever, Regina Kuzmina demonstrated how to lead and advance a huge unit with full P&L responsibility for the category across the United Kingdom and Ireland, Europe, the Middle East, Turkey, Australia, and New Zealand. She demonstrated how brutal focus can unite diverse regions and functions under a common purpose to win, not just align. Her leadership exemplifies how breaking down geographical and operational silos, while maintaining unwavering focus, drives both team empowerment and business performance, creating sustainable value through truly unified execution.

WITHOUT THE BRUTAL FOCUS THAT DISMANTLES SILOS, THERE IS ONLY BRUTAL CHAOS.

Brutal focus isn't realized within the walls that isolate silos. It thrives on the Wall that unites them.

JONATHAN ESCOBAR MARIN

When Regina launched the way of working to the newly formed organization spanning over twenty countries, I witnessed her demonstrating the essence of building brutal focus. She introduced the Wall to her entire organization like this: "We started with a big ambition, and now I'm just trying also to answer the question on all your brains: 'That is all nice, but what are the top priorities?'" At this point in her speech, the screen revealed the Wall. "These are the top priorities for the leadership team and all of you, all of us. . . . This is where we are going to put brutal focus without distraction. Here is where we are going to put our capital. Here you have what winning means for all of us, and now you are going to own how to win. We, the leadership team, are here to guide and support you when you ask us to do so."

Regina's approach illustrates the shift from abstract strategy to tangible, focused execution. She elaborates on the power of this approach: "Sometimes we perceive strategy as a very big and hairy animal or hundreds of PowerPoint slides or very elaborate Excel sheets. With the Wall, we're able to create a very clear and comprehensive story of what needs to be delivered and how. And how is very clearly linked to what. So it creates transparency, it creates tangibility, and that creates visibility [about the] resources you need to actually deliver on the strategy."[14]

Regina's experience underscores the transformative impact of the

Wall in strategy execution: "The Wall is not creating your strategy, but it's evolving it from day one. It's refining it, making it a winning strategy, because it's reflecting without any piece of ambiguity if your strategy is being executed." More important, Regina continues, "the Wall clearly delineates who owns the outcome and whether the results are being delivered. The entire organization is fully synchronized—through transparency and brutal focus—to deliver results."

Building brutal focus through the Wall transforms strategy from an abstract concept into a living, breathing reality that permeates every level of an organization. When we leaders commit to clarity, transparency, and alignment, we can create an environment where everyone understands not just the why, what, and where of the strategy, but also the where not, together with the how, who, and when of its execution. This real-world example from a leader at one of the world's largest consumer goods companies reinforces the universal applicability and power of building brutal focus. Regardless of the size or complexity of an organization, the principles of clarity, alignment, and focused execution, combined with a commitment to continuous innovation and learning, can drive transformative results.

Rather than relying on ambiguous PowerPoints, forgotten spreadsheets, and disconnected activities, the Wall and the Stop Wall are your compass for ruthless prioritization across silos. With the Wall, you distill your most critical, high-impact missions, each with clear and measurable outcomes. The Stop Wall is equally powerful; it forces you to explicitly decide what you will not pursue and consequently do, ensuring resources and attention remain focused on what matters most. Together, they make the trade-offs of brutal focus visible and nonnegotiable. With them, we operationalize the company's core theory of competitive advantage into a clearly defined set of measurable missions and commitments. With radical transparency around real-time performance toward these missions, every team understands how their work directly impacts and enables strategic success. The Wall provides the living operational system for continuous alignment, fostering shared context and understanding. It forces clarity, accountability, and momentum at every level of the organization. This focus made tangible, married with distributed leadership, impact-obsessed execution, rapid learning, and decisive evolution in the next drivers, is how organizations breathe life into their strategy. It prevents lofty visions from devolving into forgotten rhetoric by translating them into an intense and relentless pursuit of stretch goals at every level of the organization. The leadership team, committed to prioritizing decisions over paralysis, sets the tone for a culture where innovation thrives and challenges are embraced as opportunities for growth. Employees at all levels feel empowered to contribute their ideas and take ownership of their work, creating a harmonious symphony of collaboration and progress throughout the organization.

At the heart of this transformation lies the Wall—a single source of truth that unites the entire company. It's not just a strategy tool; it's also a rallying point that creates crystal clarity about the picture of success.

In essence, building brutal focus is about creating a shared vision so clear and compelling that every team member can see, feel, and taste the victory. It's about turning strategy into a collective journey, where each milestone achieved is a reason to celebrate, and each challenge overcome brings the team closer to that moment when the champagne corks fly. As Jony Ive learned from Steve Jobs, this focus isn't an occasional exercise; it's a constant practice: "Focus is . . . not this thing you aspire to, or you decide on Monday. . . . It is an every minute, 'Why are we talking about this?'"[15] This relentless commitment to focus is how organizations don't just execute strategy; they also live it, breathe it, and, ultimately, toast to its success.

To lead is to make everyone be brutally focused. When you enable everyone to be brutally focused, you beat mediocrity. This is how we shape tomorrow.

WE WILL OPEN

=

IF WE DELIVER THE MISSIONS ON THE WALL

Image 1.8: Deliver on the Wall—pop the champagne of brutal focus

Focus is . . . not this thing you aspire to, or you decide on Monday. . . . It is an every minute, 'Why are we talking about this?'"

—**Jony Ive**

What Is Needed

Answer these questions to beat tomorrow—or watch others lead while you lag. Every honest response separates those who drive the future from those who will chase it.

- ↗ Do you want to keep the strategy as a beautiful PowerPoint, or do you want it to be central to every moment of every day for every member of your team?

- ↗ Have you created total clarity about what success looks like for each strategic priority, or is there still room for interpretation?

- ↗ Do you want to keep spending on off-sites, shows, and events where what is said and promised isn't consistently delivered two months later?

- ↗ Do you want people in the silos to keep fighting with each other about what is most important?

- ↗ Do you want to keep your company running as a factory of projects where everyone is happy completing deliverables?

- ↗ Are you willing to eliminate distractions and focus on the key priorities that will define success?

- ↗ Does every member of your organization know exactly which priorities will make or break your success this year and the next?

- ↗ Have you communicated what you don't want to achieve (cut the crap) so that everyone is as clear about it?

- ↗ Are you willing to go through another year without focusing on the innovation and exploration that will shape the company's success in three to five years?

EMPOWERMENT BEATS CONTROL.
OWNERSHIP BEATS COMPLIANCE. 1
BEATS DIVISION. SEGMENTATION
BEATS HIERARCHY. ALIGNMENT BE
SEGREGATION. AUTHENTICITY BEATS
TRUST BEATS AUTHORITY. OPENNES
RESTRICTION. ALLIANCE BEATS BOUN
COALITION BEATS INDIVIDUALISM.
BEATS DETACHMENT. FLUIDITY BEATS
CAPABILITY BEATS FACADE. COOPERA
BEATS CENTRALIZATION. DISTRIBUTION
BEATS SUPERVISION. PARTICIPATION
FRAGILITY. GENEROSITY BEATS DI

LLABORATION BEATS ISOLATION

BEATS DEPARTMENT. CONNECTION

'S FRAGMENTATION. PARTNERSHIP

SEPARATION. INTEGRATION BEATS

RMALITY. NETWORKS BEAT SILOS.

EATS SECRECY. ENABLEMENT BEATS

IES. SYNERGY BEATS INDEPENDENCE.

WSHIP BEATS SOLITUDE. COHESION

IDITY. LEADERSHIP BEATS HEROISM

BEATS INDIVIDUALITY. MOBILIZATION

TS CONCENTRATION. ACCOUNTABILITY

TS OBSERVATION. ELASTICITY BEATS

N. MERITOCRACY BEATS STATUS.

CHAPTER 2

DISTRIBUTED LEADERSHIP

LEADERSHIP EVERYWHERE.
SILOS NOWHERE.

In an era defined by ambiguity, delivering through brutal focus demands seamless execution that transcends departmental boundaries and hierarchies. Transformative goals cannot be conquered from within the blinders of organizational silos. The number of truly transformative missions a single department can achieve independently is severely limited, often approaching zero.

JONATHAN ESCOBAR MARIN

The number of truly transformative missions a single department can achieve independently is severely limited, often approaching zero.

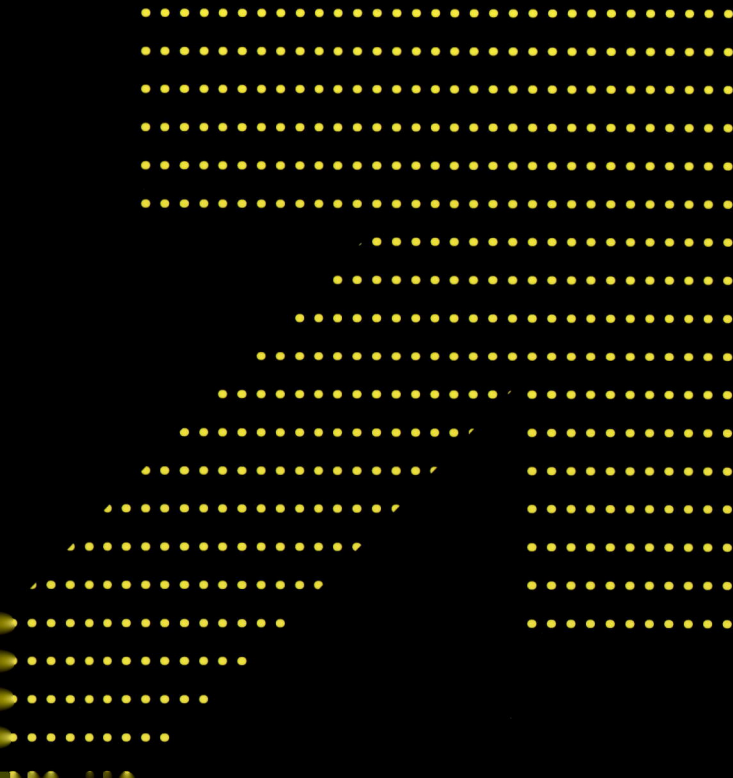

While departments can craft individual strategies and plans, in today's world, customer impact and transformative priorities demand seamless collaboration across boundaries. Imagine trying to complete a puzzle where each department designs its own pieces in isolation. Without a unified vision, the pieces will never perfectly align. You'll waste hours trying to fit them together, only to realize they weren't designed to connect in the first place. Customers don't celebrate departmental plans; they reward the products and services that serve their needs. These emerge through coordinated, cross-functional execution. This is why leadership must flow beyond the boundaries of departments, empowering cross-functional teams to work as an organic ecosystem. It's important to recognize that vertical structures themselves aren't inherently problematic. Do departments or functions need to exist in the future? Yes, more than ever! But not as kingdoms of power and control where talent is caged. The issue arises when verticality exists primarily to maintain status hierarchies rather than to provide clarity and service. When departments transform into centers of excellence and talent pools—where specialists manage functional needs with rigor while flowing to cross-functional teams—verticality becomes a channel for value rather than an obstacle to it. When leadership and ownership transcend silos and hierarchy, organizations can innovate relentlessly and deliver market-defining outcomes that earn customer loyalty while building enduring capabilities that compound over time.

To break free from the puzzle-piece problem of siloed thinking, ideas need to collide and coalesce to build a seamless success picture that will be executed across, not through, silos. No department, function, hierarchy, or category can become an island; an organization's strength is in the synergy of its parts. This is how you create a powerhouse—by connecting everyone around a single unifying wall, the Wall.

Empowering distributed leadership across a fluid network of cross-functional teams is the key. These teams own clear missions, which drive clear execution. Hierarchical constraints dissolve as self-organized teams collectively define the "how" while ruthlessly pursuing their transformative missions. They are always guided by the what, where,

where not, and when—established through brutal focus and made crystal clear on the Wall, all in service of the organization's greater why.

With ownership emanating from those closest to the customer's reality and powered by a winning mentality, these teams accelerate learning cycles, iterating and pivoting when needed. They thrive on first-hand feedback loops, relentlessly evolving while staying locked on their ambitious goals—keeping the beat of progress alive.

Distributed leadership nurtures a culture of accountability and ownership, where team members flow from departments or functions and different levels of the hierarchy to high-impact teams. They are given the power to plan the tactics, make decisions, take action, learn, and correct fast when needed—all to achieve their missions. At P&G, the insights of Arthur W. Jones—echoed in the work of my friend David P. Hanna—instilled in me a principle that my own leadership experience has affirmed time and again: The results you achieve are the ones your organization is designed to deliver; the teams operate as a perfectly designed organism, poised to shatter siloes, embrace the undefined with proximity, and deliver superior outcomes with laser-focused brutal prioritization.

In traditional approaches to leadership, a select few key figures—typically at the top of the hierarchy—drive the majority of strategic but also tactical decisions. This centralized approach becomes problematic when it disregards distributed knowledge throughout the organization and when top leaders confuse hierarchy with privilege, leadership with control, or responsibility with superiority. It stifles execution and innovation and limits the potential for detecting and responding to untagged market shifts across the broader workforce. The issue isn't hierarchy itself—hierarchy can provide clarity, efficiency, and focus when oriented toward serving the organization rather than being served by it. The challenge emerges when those at the top use their power to amass more power for themselves and not to distribute it across the organization to accelerate execution, decision-making, and the capability to win faster. The truth is that when leadership beats in every corner of your organization, silos crumble and collective genius emerges to shape tomorrow.

THE RESULTS YOU ACHIEVE ARE THE ONES YOUR ORGANIZATION IS DESIGNED TO DELIVER.

Just as A. G. Lafley understood that making tough choices and maintaining brutal focus are essential for success, he also recognized that transforming an organization requires more than just top-down decision-making. It demands creating an environment where ambition exceeds resources at every level. This means developing leaders who refuse to settle for mediocrity throughout the organization. In other words, leaders who consciously choose and amplify ARR over RAM. When leadership is distributed, each empowered leader must embody this mindset of ambitious choices and focused execution. In the words of A. G. Lafley, "You can get used to being a player without being a winner. There's a big difference between the two. So I became interested in transforming players into winners."[1] He emphasizes that multiplying leaders who have the hunger to win is a deliberate leadership choice— one that requires intentionality, effort, and conscious action.

In organizations embracing the four drivers of success, the shift from a few to many leaders with the hunger to win encapsulates a transformative approach: creating an environment where real talent can flourish, no matter where it comes from. Leaders everywhere, silos nowhere. And the result can be wild. As Rosa Carabel, CEO of the Spanish cooperative retailer Eroski, puts it, "So far, we've multiplied x15 our strategy owners, and this doesn't stop here. We've amplified the people from Eroski that thrive in the cross-functional teams that lead the brutally important missions of our organization."[2]

Distributed leadership isn't merely about improving current execution; it's about building a powerful competitive advantage that compounds with each quarter. Simple but game-changing design principles of the ecosystem, like one person leading only one mission, fuel the capability of top leaders to go beyond the few usual heroes and open their minds to new talents for today and the future. These new leaders may not be ready to lead from day one as more experienced leaders are, but with the right guidance, coaching, and trust from their guides, they have the growth space to do so in weeks or months, building another leader in the organization.

You can get used to being a player without being a winner. There's a big difference between the two. So I became interested in transforming players into winners."

—A. G. Lafley

Providing uniform growth, learning, and advancement opportunities is crucial for empowering all employees. By facilitating access for your people to lead and be part of important missions, your organization can tap into a broader pool of talent and foster a culture of continuous development.

Radical transparency is the bedrock of distributed leadership. Open communication and accessible information are essential to dismantling silos and fostering a culture of trust and accountability. When employees have access to the same data, strategic insights, and performance metrics as their leaders do, they are better equipped to make informed decisions and take ownership of their contributions.

Regular, transparent synchronizations—or *synchros*—with top executives about mission performance, challenges, and strategic direction ensure that every team member is aligned and informed. This openness encourages dialogue and the sharing of ideas, creating a more dynamic and engaged workforce.

Implementing a digital version of the Wall that provides easy, simple, clean access to the brutal focus in action—the missions, the people owning the missions, their execution progress, and the obstacles they face—allows all employees to see how their work and the work of their peers impacts the organization. This visibility helps to break down barriers and promote a sense of shared purpose.

Distributed leadership transforms our organizations by enabling talent to flourish at all levels. By embracing this driver, our companies can cultivate a dynamic environment where innovation thrives and new leaders emerge. Distributed leadership anchors its design in the principles of radical transparency, unquestionable transversality, accountability, extreme ownership, continuous learning, flow to impact, and autonomy. Guided by these tenets, we leaders, acting more like work architects or servant leaders than traditional managers, do the vital work of enabling cross-functional teams to deliver maximum impact. With key results and timeboxes clearly defined, our teams understand their potential contribution and how it interlinks with others, forming an ever-evolving, high-impact ecosystem.

A singular focus on how to achieve your North Star metrics is driven by three elements: a single specific mission for a single specific team with a single specific execution plan. These three are equal parts of the whole of distributed leadership, creating a formula for achievement that is followed naturally by the most successful organizations. The 1:1:1 formula shapes an ecosystem for impact and seamless execution that cuts through complexity and accelerates results.

The 1:1:1 Formula

- One specific mission
- One specific team
- One specific execution

One specific mission that is crystal clear, measurable, and time bound; one specific team that is cross-functional, cross-hierarchy, and fully empowered; and one specific execution that is unmissable, ruthlessly prioritized, and impact-driven. When these three align, transformation isn't only possible; it's also inevitable. Cognitive psychology tells us that the human brain excels at processing singular, well-defined tasks, while it struggles to handle competing priorities or poorly structured challenges. The 1:1:1 formula leverages this biological advantage by minimizing cognitive overload and allowing teams to focus their mental resources on a single, clear objective. George A. Miller's foundational work on cognitive load theory demonstrated that the brain has a limited capacity for processing multiple pieces of information simultaneously, making it essential to reduce unnecessary demands on attention.[3] Similarly, John Sweller's research on cognitive load highlights that simplifying tasks and removing extraneous complexity enhances problem-solving and accelerates learning.[4]

ONE SPECIFIC MISSION

One specific mission means one mission with razor-sharp goals, definition of success, and timeboxed targets. Clarity is such an underrated superpower in leadership. An unambiguous mission ignites passion and purpose. This isn't about feel-good platitudes; it's about defining a transformative challenge so bright it burns through the fog of corporate inertia and market ambiguity.

Specific missions become especially crucial in the ambiguous waters in which businesses swim today. While markets and competitive landscapes may be unclear, the missions themselves must remain crystal clear, providing a stable foundation for teams navigating uncertainty. Focus on one specific mission to light each market shadow. One at a time.

Top management must enable teams to become high-performing units, first and foremost, with well-defined missions that lock on to the organization's North Star metrics. This alignment enhances motivation and focus, ensuring that every mission drives the overarching common goal and that team members understand their role in achieving it. Goal-setting theory demonstrates that clear, suitably challenging goals enhance performance by providing direction and motivation.[5] Similarly, the balanced scorecard emphasizes aligning individual and team goals with strategic objectives, ensuring everyone works toward a common purpose.[6]

One specific mission is where the 1:1:1 formula begins. A focused mission sparks the formation of a dedicated team, which develops the execution plan required to deliver results. For example, consider a mission to increase market share in a specific region from 5 percent to 25 percent. This mission forces the organization to prioritize and segment its opportunities, moving from broad aspirations to a brutal focus on the most critical levers for success.

Missions do not exist to fill PowerPoints. In fact, they do not require a single one. Instead, they exist to guide the creation of a cross-functional team that empowers distributed leadership and is purpose-built to deliver

FOCUS ON ONE SPECIFIC MISSION TO LIGHT EACH MARKET SHADOW. ONE AT A TIME.

JONATHAN ESCOBAR MARIN

Missions do not exist to fill PowerPoints.
In fact, they do not require a single one.

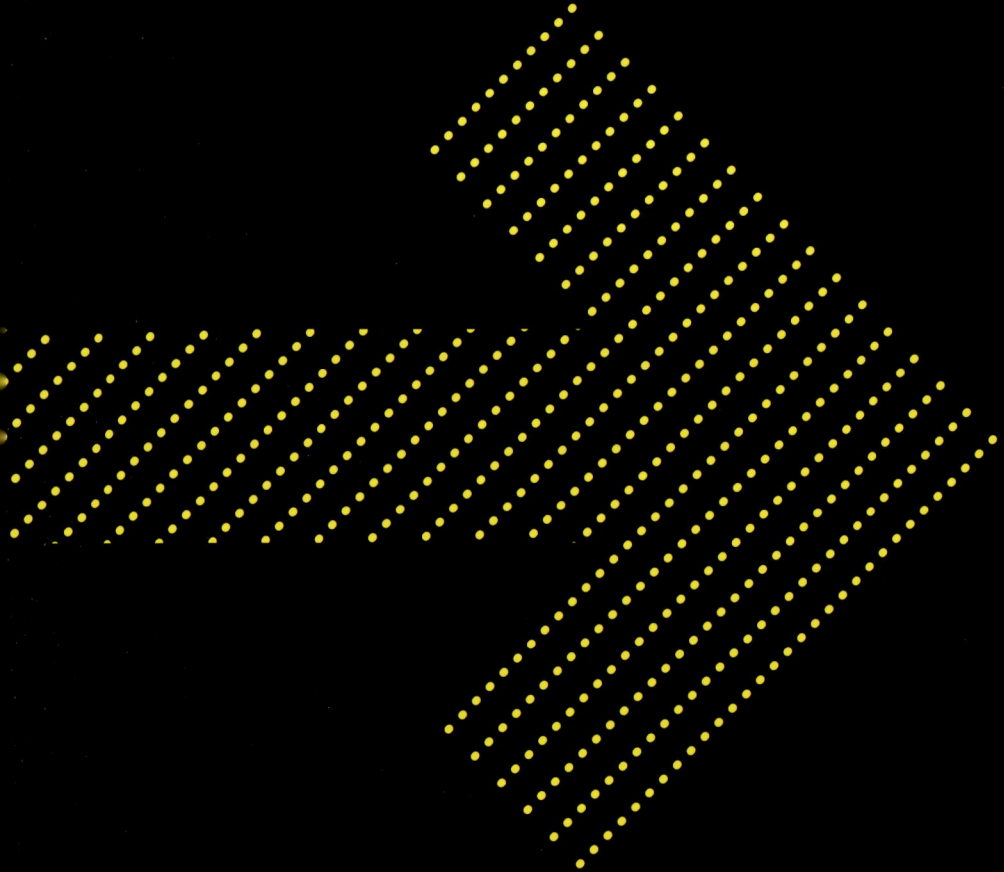

on the challenge. The mission determines the team's composition, ensuring the right mix of expertise, accountability, and diversity of thought. The team, in turn, takes ownership of the mission and transforms it into a clear execution plan. This execution plan is not simply a list of tasks; it is a tactical map that translates the mission into measurable B-I-G choices: bets, initiatives, and glidepath. Ruthless prioritization, driven by a well-done segmentation, ensures that only the most impactful bets are pursued. Every bet, initiative, glidepath milestone, and tactic is directly tied back to the mission's success.

The mission sparks the team, and the team drives the execution plan. This seamless alignment eliminates ambiguity, ensuring that every action contributes to achieving the mission's goal. For example, consider now a mission to improve customer retention rates from 60 percent to 85 percent. The mission immediately requires segmentation to identify the most impactful levers for improvement—whether it's enhancing onboarding experiences, addressing product pain points, or creating loyalty programs. This segmentation informs the selection of a cross-functional team with expertise in customer experience, product design, and data analytics. The team then develops a focused and specific execution plan.

A specific mission transforms ambiguity into clarity, strategy into dream-team staffing and action, creating a direct pathway to execution through the 1:1:1 formula. It ensures the organization's energy is concentrated on what matters most: driving purposeful alignment across all levels. This mission acts as the foundation for assembling a high-impact team and crafting an execution plan that ensures measurable results. Together, these components work in perfect harmony to create the clarity that lights the darkness of ambiguity and drives transformative wins. Remember, without a specific mission, there is only amplified ambiguity. A specific mission gives freedom, not constraint, allowing for creativity and innovation within the unambiguous definition of a strategic choice. The connection among one mission, one team, and one execution is intentional and unbreakable—a leadership beat that echoes forward.

ONE SPECIFIC TEAM

One specific team means one clearly staffed team to focus on the specific mission. This is akin to assembling an elite strike force. It isn't about head count; it's about handpicking a crew of high-caliber individuals whose collective synergy creates a gravitational pull toward success. Break down silos, ignore hierarchies, and empower leadership below the top management to unite diverse talents under a common banner.

Social identity theory, as developed by Henri Tajfel and John Turner, demonstrates that humans perform better when they have a clear sense of belonging and purpose.[7] The 1:1:1 formula creates this environment by staffing one dedicated team per mission. This isn't just feel-good psychology; it's also a performance accelerator. A meta-analysis published in the *Journal of Applied Psychology* showed that team cohesion is positively related to performance.[8]

In organizations who do this well, each team is led by a highly skilled leader, empowered below the level of top management, who is accountable to a specific mission. This leader's sole responsibility is to turn strategy into tangible bets, initiatives, and actions that deliver results, and they are empowered to do so by assembling a team from different departments. This radical approach transforms the traditional function of siloed departments. For example, the CFO's role shifts away from building an army of financial experts and controllers to oversee budgets and toward cultivating a team of financial leaders who can run operations while seamlessly flowing into mission-driven teams, disseminating financial acumen and data-driven decision-making across the organization.

Pol Codina, a seasoned executive with over two decades of experience in the consumer goods and sportswear industries, offers valuable insights into how distributed leadership can revolutionize performance in global organizations. "When I think about FAST," Codina says about PepsiCo's way of working, "I think about distributed ownership. Each one in the FAST ecosystem is accountable for a part of the strategy in full synchronization with the rest. This isn't just about assigning tasks;

JONATHAN ESCOBAR MARIN

The connection among one mission, one team, and one execution is intentional and unbreakable.

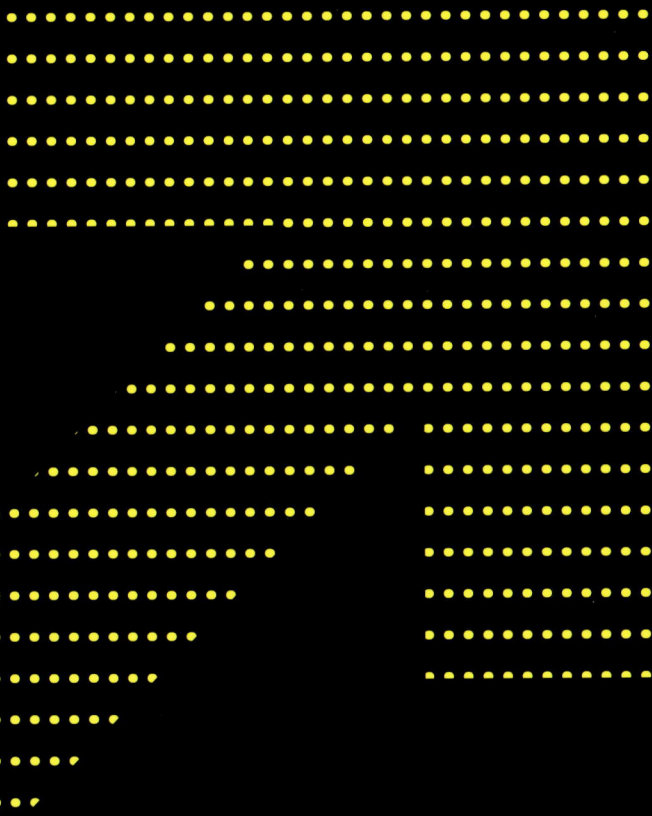

it's about empowering every team to own a clear outcome and the best execution to make it a reality. This distributed accountability has been transformative. We've seen teams break free from silos, collaborating across functions with a shared sense of purpose. The impact on our execution speed and quality has been remarkable. But perhaps the most inspiring aspect is how FAST has unleashed the potential of our people. We're seeing leaders emerge at all levels of the organization, driving change and delivering results."[9] Codina's testimony vividly illustrates the power of distributed leadership in action. It shows how it can be applied in a complex, multinational corporation to dismantle silos, drive accountability, and deliver results.

Moreover, Codina's experience underscores the importance of transparency in this model. For each member to be truly accountable for their part of the strategic missions, they must have a clear understanding of how their work fits into the larger picture. This level of transparency is a cornerstone of the FAST approach and aligns perfectly with the principles of distributed leadership we've discussed.

Distributed leadership evolves the widely recognized T-shaped talent model into what I call an O-shaped talent model, building on its strengths to meet the demands of an AI-integrated workforce. In the T-model, professionals develop deep expertise in a specific domain (the vertical bar of the T) and the ability to collaborate across functions (the horizontal bar). While this model has been instrumental in fostering versatile professionals, current research suggests that traditional organizational structures can limit AI's potential by fragmenting decision spaces.

The O-model empowers organizations to address these limitations by enabling professionals to transform their developed expertise and collaboration skills into leadership across diverse organizational challenges while continuously enhancing their leadership and collaborative capabilities to tackle complex, cross-functional missions, with AI as a force multiplier. It empowers professionals to lead across traditional boundaries, facilitating integrated decision-making through cross-functional teams, aligning with AI's need for holistic optimization. In an era where

AI agents have already joined the workforce and physical AI begins transforming the everyday landscape, this evolution represents both present reality and future imperative.[10]

The O-model reimagines talent as dynamic, adaptable, growth-driven, and capable of leading diverse missions that require cross-boundary execution and decision-making over time, while preserving and enhancing the T-model's emphasis on expertise and collaboration. Physical and agentic AI are transforming the landscape: While AI agents handle knowledge work and decision support, physical AI extends this revolution into the material world, where everything that moves—from cars and trucks to humans operating in factories or laboratories—becomes AI-enabled and robotic. This dual transformation requires individuals who can orchestrate both virtual AI teams and physical autonomous systems.

In this new reality, the O-model builds on the T-model's deep expertise, enabling professionals to apply their specialized knowledge to lead varied challenges sequentially, while their collaborative skills become even more critical for cross-functional, AI-augmented work, to generate organization-wide impact. The ecosystem's collective capabilities expand exponentially, fueled by cross-pollination, shared learnings, and a communal drive to achieve brutally important outcomes through continuous innovation. This expansion accelerates through the two AI waves described previously: first, as AI agents amplify cognitive and decision-making capabilities and, then, as physical AI enables autonomous machines to perceive, understand, and perform complex actions in the real world. The emergence of superintelligence tools catalyzes unprecedented scientific discovery and innovation, requiring a workforce that effectively harnesses and directs these powerful capabilities.

AI acts as a catalyst for this evolution, enabling teams formed by individuals coming from different areas of expertise to augment their decision-making, enhance their productivity, and tackle increasingly complex challenges with confidence. This symbiotic relationship between distinctive human abilities and AI capabilities defines business success in the age of superintelligence. By providing actionable

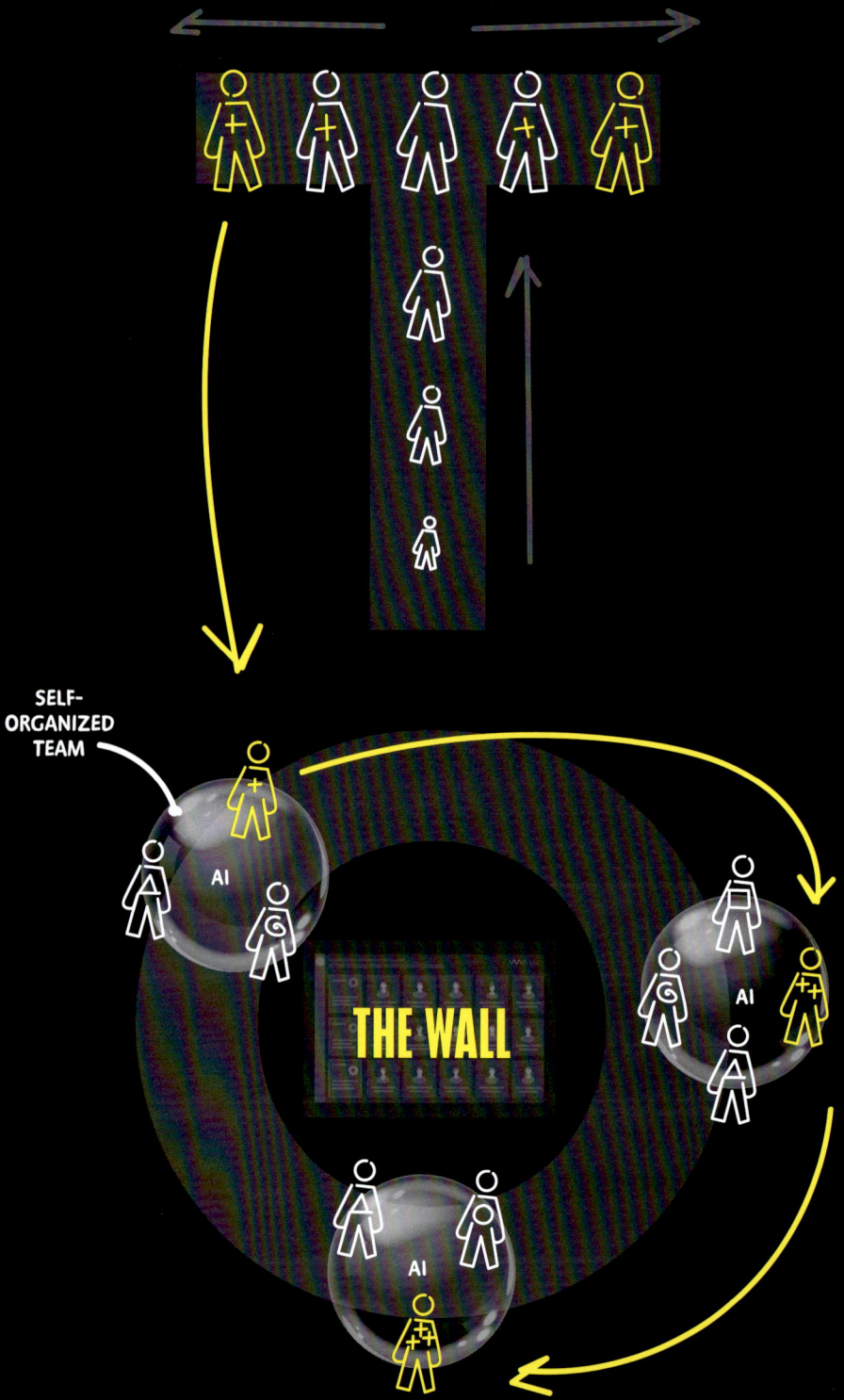

Image 2.1: From T to O—Talent is dynamic, adaptable, and capable of leading diverse missions over time with AI as a force multiplier. © 2025, Jonathan Escobar Marin

insights through advanced analytics, AI helps teams to deliver on high-value, mission-critical work. This dynamic interplay between human skills, sensing, passion, drive, and AI-driven augmentation defines the O-model's strength.

This reimagining requires, also, a profound cultural shift in how companies understand hierarchy, departmental structures, and work responsibility. The challenge extends beyond technology to evolving the organization itself.

This change of paradigm requires that, time and again, individuals from different levels of hierarchy come together into the ecosystem of teams, powered by aim, hunger, and AI, demonstrating the courage to continually challenge assumptions, collaborate synchronously or asynchronously toward shared goals, and discover better ways of working through iterative execution and rapid learning cycles. People formerly confined to siloed departments flow into an ecosystem of cross-functional teams. Both departments and ecosystems are necessary to sustain, evolve, and transform what is needed in an organization. What matters is how they're implemented and how they are synchronized. Departments should evolve from rigid territories into centers of excellence that nurture specialized expertise while enabling talent to flow to brutally important missions. In this model, departments and functions connect people and amplify intelligence rather than enforcing unnecessary separation between organizational layers. The silos evolve to increasingly behave as open talent pools, also supported by AI systems, freely cross-pollinating ideas, sharing learnings from their teams' diverse experiences, and collectively supporting the achievement of critical outcomes.

When these mission-driven teams are given the freedom to self-organize, solutions, AI-powered or not, emerge organically from those closest to the work. Through execution, reflection, iteration, and continuous improvement, these teams profoundly evolve how they operate. And this approach leverages the unique insights and expertise of the team members, driving more impactful and innovative outcomes.

HIERARCHY

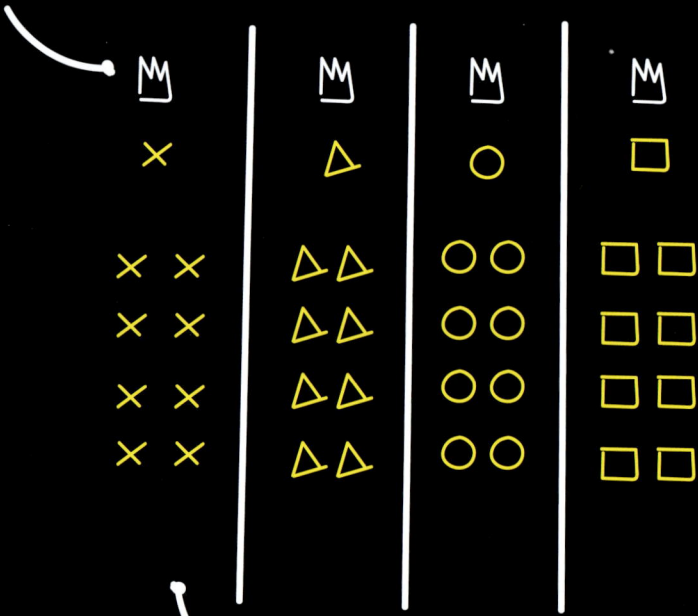

Image 2.2: From silos to teams, departmentalism to unity, hierarchy to ecosystem—distributed leadership with brutal focus. © 2025, Jonathan Escobar Marin

ECOSYSTEM

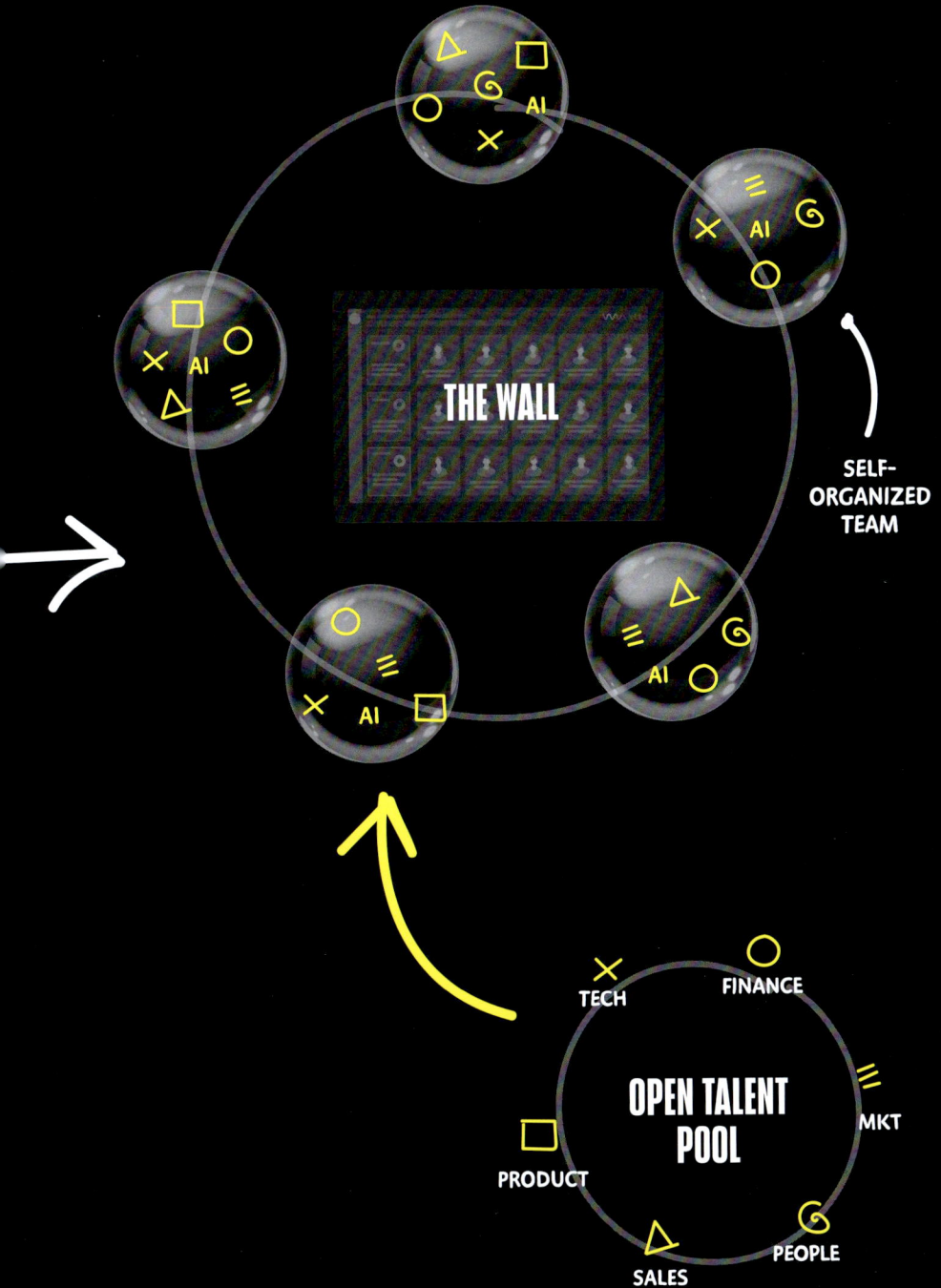

THE WALL

SELF-
ORGANIZED
TEAM

AI

OPEN TALENT
POOL

TECH

FINANCE

MKT

PRODUCT

SALES

PEOPLE

High-impact, high-performing teams consistently exhibit certain characteristics, such as mutual trust and respect, autonomy, effective communication, continuous learning, and functional and hierarchical diversity, which make these teams particularly effective at managing ambiguity because they bring diverse perspectives and expertise to bear on undefined challenges. Their diversity of thought and position helps organizations detect and respond to emerging patterns in unclear situations.

Trust and respect within teams fuel this frictionless exchange of ideas, collaboration, and execution. This observation is supported by research showing that trust among team members correlates with higher levels of cooperation and information sharing, leading to better performance. Amy Edmondson's research on psychological safety highlights that mutual respect helps create an environment where team members feel safe to take risks and share ideas.[11]

We have seen that teams with the freedom to make decisions about their priorities are more innovative and responsive. This autonomy fosters a sense of ownership and accountability, driving team members to excel in their roles. This experience is consistent with J. Richard Hackman and Greg Oldham's job characteristics model and self-determination theory, which highlight that autonomy is crucial for job satisfaction and performance.[12] When team members have control over their work, they are more motivated and engaged.

Maintaining open lines of communication within the team and with their top leaders ensures rapid problem-solving and idea generation. Regular collaboration sessions—such as weekly synchros and quarterly feedback meetups—focus teams on key outcomes to deliver the desired results. These sessions improve overall visibility and foster a safe environment for learning, broadening perspectives and possibilities. Teams share strategies for overcoming obstacles and refine their approaches based on what has proven effective, turning each learning experience into a catalyst for accelerated progress. This approach aligns with principles from Patrick Lencioni's five dysfunctions of a team and various communication models, highlighting the necessity of transparent communication for building trust, resolving conflicts, and driving innovation.[13] Moreover, outcome-focused collaboration transforms the flow of knowledge within the organization, breaking down silos and fostering a collaborative talent pool where specialized knowledge is shared and amplified across the entire organization.

Our high-impact teams embrace continuous learning and regularly review their performance. They learn from their experiences and adjust their strategies, ensuring they remain agile and effective. This practice resonates with Peter Senge's concept of learning organizations, which demonstrates that a culture of continuous learning and evolution is essential for innovation and responsiveness.[14]

When in action, these self-organized teams exemplify the following: the courage to continually invalidate assumptions and conventional wisdom; asynchronous collaboration toward collective goals, transcending temporal and spatial constraints; a relentless focus on discovering and delivering better ways through iterative execution and learning.

These teams also drive individuals' self-transformation—from being process-oriented operatives who are activity-obsessed to mission-driven innovators who are outcome-obsessed, fueled by an insatiable hunger to deliver outsized value for customers.

Open-talent pools are also particularly valuable in today's ambiguous business environment where required capabilities may be unclear or rapidly evolving. The ability to flexibly access diverse talent becomes a key advantage in navigating uncertainty—a distributed leadership beat that cuts through the undefined.

The power of open-talent pools isn't just theoretical; it has also been successfully implemented by forward-thinking companies for years. At Procter & Gamble (P&G), under the leadership of A. G. Lafley, this approach revolutionized how the company innovated and created value. P&G pioneered "connect and develop," an open-sourcing strategy that recognized innovation and expertise could come from anywhere, at any time.[15] This approach led to numerous breakthrough products like Align Probiotic,

Enabling open talent pools

The ecosystem that distributed leadership creates enables an organization where talent flows seamlessly to areas of value creation, transcending the boundaries of silos and also the firm. Much like open innovation, where companies open their doors to external ideas and expertise, distributed leadership allows the organization to dynamically allocate talent—both internal and external—to specific missions where capabilities need acceleration or enrichment. It marks the final leap from the "not invented here" mentality to "invented here, with talent from everywhere, at any time." With AI as a force multiplier, these fluid teams navigate challenges, experiment, and deliver innovative solutions at an unprecedented pace.

Acknowledging the power of these principles is especially important in a world where the new generation of talent no longer clings to static organizations but dynamically flows between opportunities, projects, and challenges where they can maximize their impact. Phil Jackson, the most successful head coach in NBA history, reminds us, "The strength of the team is each individual member. The strength of each member is the team." They are attracted to enriching work environments that allow them to continuously learn, grow, and reinvent themselves. In response, visionary companies have abandoned the notion of closeness with immovable departments and rigid hierarchical structures. Instead, they have given birth to organic, dynamic, fluid, and flexible open-talent pools.

These ecosystems revolutionize how cutting-edge talent is connected, integrated, and enabled. Organizations can't attempt to encapsulate talent within their department cages but, rather, become powerful magnets that fluidly attract talent capital as needed for each mission. These open-talent pools leverage state-of-the-art digital platforms to skillfully identify and incorporate global experts for specific, time-bound projects while building lasting networks of expertise that enrich the organization's capabilities for years to come. AI engineers from Beijing, influencer-marketing strategists from Barcelona, and data scientists from Texas can all be seamlessly onboarded on demand and integrated into self-organized teams.

This open, interconnected talent economy is revolutionizing antiquated notions of the traditional workforce. It's no longer about hiring workers but about dynamically attracting, integrating, and enabling talent on a fluid basis. The end result is an unbeatable organizational model, able to assemble dream teams on the fly for any mission by leveraging global collective intelligence while fostering a mindset of continuous learning and reinvention within a company's own internal workforce. Companies that embrace this open-talent pool, fueled by leaders at every level, will enjoy a competitive advantage impossible to match by organizations anchored to hierarchy, department, and closed structures.

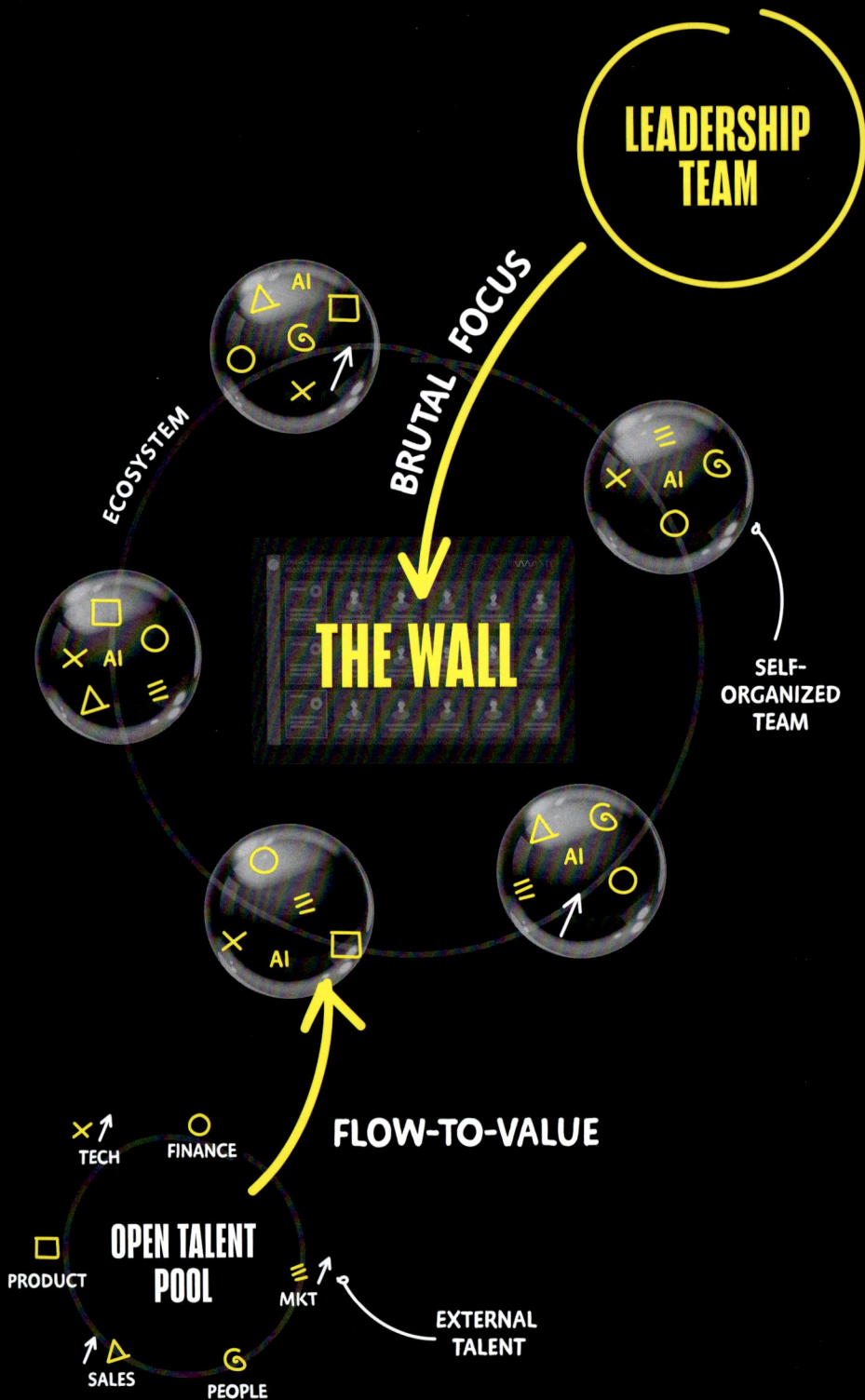

Image 2.3: Dynamic talent allocation, flowing to value—the ecosystem of distributed leadership fueled by open talent pools. © 2025, Jonathan Escobar Marin

Clearblue, and Mr. Clean Magic Eraser.[16] The company understood that while they excelled at understanding consumer needs and commercializing products, they didn't need to own all innovation capabilities internally. Instead, they created fluid partnerships with external talent across multiple domains—from technology development to creative services—paying for expertise when and where they needed it.

Another such leader who has embraced the paradigm shift described in this chapter and with whom I have had the pleasure to partner and learn in different business environments is Alfonso Gómez, CEO of BBVA Switzerland, who says, "When you're surrounded by people who are exceptionally capable, both intellectually and professionally, your role as a leader fundamentally changes. It's no longer about control; it's about creating an environment where their talents can flourish."[17] Even in highly regulated banking environments where reputation is paramount, Gómez has demonstrated how being connected to external talent ecosystems and emerging technologies can drive innovation while managing risk—as evidenced by BBVA Switzerland's pioneering moves into digital assets and blockchain technology.

Since taking the helm of BBVA Switzerland, the group's international private bank, in 2014, Gómez has been instrumental in strengthening BBVA's position as a global player in private banking. Perhaps most notably, his leadership has driven the integration of crypto assets, blockchain technology, and digital innovations, positioning BBVA Switzerland as a trailblazer in bridging the gap between traditional banking and the digital crypto realm. But beyond technological innovation, Gómez's most profound impact lies in his philosophy of distributed leadership and empowerment: "When you give people the power to make decisions, execute them, and be accountable for the results, you're not just delegating tasks; you're cultivating leaders at every level." It's not always easy, though. "Many people struggle with this level of responsibility—not because they are resistant to improvement, but because they haven't been equipped." But when you succeed at transforming into an organization with extreme ownership at every level, "you are rewarded with a

The strength of
the team is each
individual member.
The strength of
each member is
the team."

—Phil Jackson

surge in innovation, a marked improvement in customer satisfaction, and a faster, better, more dynamic, resilient, and responsive organization overall." Your people "become more confident, more capable, and more invested in our collective success."[18]

The rhythm of this kind of change is not always easy to follow and may not be uniform across the organization. Let's return to Justin Apsey, whose account of the gradual shift in team dynamics—from dependency on designated leaders to proactive self-organization—serves as a powerful example of the organic nature of this transformation. He notes, "When we started [this transformation], if a team leader wasn't available for a specific period or session, the team was inclined to slow down execution or even postpone some decision-making. It was a significant breakthrough when teams started to realize week after week, and quarter after quarter that the missions' targets were a real commitment. That no one would come to organize them or impose a specific method to deliver but they were a team that had to find their best way to deliver, that each person had a role, and that top leaders were there to guide and support when they needed it. We called this employee entrepreneurialism and servant leadership, and it was scary to some people. It didn't happen straightway but when they realized that brutal focus and distributed leadership were not intentions but consistent realities, this moment marked a true shift toward self-organization. The teams discovered that their empowerment to deliver missions extended to proactively managing how they had to organize to maximize speed and ensure impact week per week.

"Once we established the rigor and discipline of focusing on key business results with a mindset of removing obstacles and empowering teams," he continues, "our teams began to imagine new ways of working. . . . In essence, we've brought business out of the boardroom. Previously, only a select few were invited into those brutally important priorities. We've moved away from PowerPoint presentations filled with stories about what we might or should do, to an environment where everyone was invited to lead forward, to own key missions, and to

When you give people the power to make decisions, execute them, and be accountable for the results, you're not just delegating tasks; you're cultivating leaders at every level."

—**Alfonso Gómez**

move from players to winners. We have seen leaders growing through action every week, working on the most significant and strategic missions, and we've had incredible surprises about talent we didn't know had this capability to lead. This shift has amplified our talent bandwidth and leadership capabilities in ways we didn't anticipate. If we had stuck to business as usual, we would have remained the few always behind closed doors and our speed of decision-making would have continued to be slow.

"The most profound insight from this journey was recognizing that leadership isn't about position but about contribution. When we distributed leadership across the organization, we unlocked intellectual and creative capital that had been dormant. People who had never been given the opportunity to lead stepped forward with innovative solutions that executives would never have conceived. This created a multiplier effect—where previously we had relied on a handful of leaders to drive change, we now had dozens, even hundreds of individuals taking ownership. The speed and agility this created became our ultimate competitive advantage in a market where sluggish decision-making means death."[19]

Apsey's experience vividly illustrates the organic nature of self-organization. It's not something that can be mandated from the top down; rather, it emerges when teams are given the space and trust to take ownership of their work. The evolution he describes—from hesitation to innovation—is a powerful testament to the potential of distributed leadership.

Perhaps most importantly, Apsey's reflections highlight the multiplying effect of this approach. By bringing business out of the boardroom, organizations can tap into the collective intelligence of their entire workforce, fostering a culture of transparency and shared purpose that drives engagement and innovation.

ONE SPECIFIC EXECUTION

Planning without execution is a hallucination. One specific execution means one unambiguous execution plan seamlessly executed. Teams craft a battle plan so clear, so precise, that it leaves no room for misinterpretation or excuses. It's their iterative glidepath to victory, where every milestone is conquered territory and a learning space on their march to mission achievement.

Ambiguity is the enemy of execution. Simplicity is the ultimate sophistication. In a world of ambiguity and unprecedented complexity, your execution plan should be your sword—sharp, clean, effective. PowerPoint slides dilute your focus. Strip the plan down to the essentials. Define your "where to play" and "how to win" approach through clear outcomes that drive meaningful impact. This is why the 1:1:1 formula demands one unambiguous execution plan.

Through distributed leadership, teams break down missions into one unambiguous plan with discrete outcomes that serve as their directional compasses. Missions don't merely set the strategy; they ensure we make it happen week after week. Fast, dynamic execution powered by clear, unambiguously defined plans allows us to iterate and make consistent progress toward the missions' outcomes—a beat for winning. Brian Tracy tells us that "a clear vision, backed by definite plans, gives you a tremendous feeling of confidence and personal power."[20] That power multiplies through the organization.

To achieve this and effectively break down a mission into superior execution, teams must focus on the B-I-G playing fields: bets, initiatives, and the glidepath. BIG choices are about operationalizing brutal focus, now at teams' execution level, where segmentation is wildly important. Segmentation is about relentlessly and ruthlessly applying the Pareto principle: We must concentrate on the 20 percent of market bets— product innovation, value proposition, promotion strategy, distribution channels, customer experience design, and pricing models—targeted to deliver 80 percent of our strategic mission. It's about creating outsized lasting impact with the minimum possible.

JONATHAN ESCOBAR MARIN

PLANNING WITHOUT EXECUTION IS A HALLUCINATION.

"

A clear vision, backed by definite plans, gives you a tremendous feeling of confidence and personal power."

—Brian Tracy

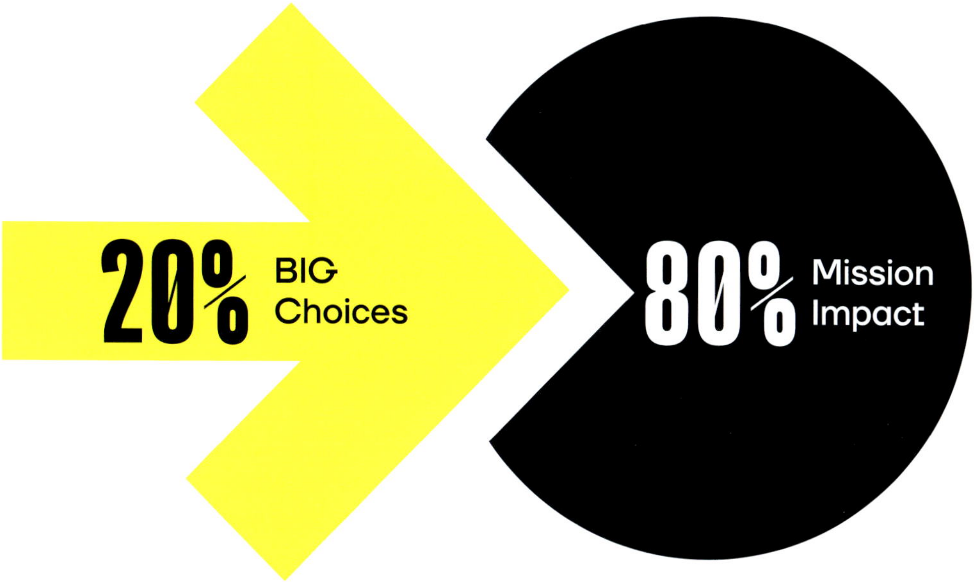

Image 2.4: Target the 20%—unleash 80% impact with clear ownership and brutal focus. © 2025, Jonathan Escobar Marin

Break your mission down: Bet big on what matters. Mark milestones. Execute. Learn. Iterate. Reap results. Bets involve making tactical decisions about the desired outcomes in your chosen playing fields through the right segmentation; this involves setting specific, measurable targets. Initiatives define how you will achieve these outcomes; they are the specific projects or actions that will drive success in the selected areas. The glidepath outlines when you need to deliver to win in each playing field; this involves setting clear milestones and timelines for achieving the outcomes. For example, in a product launch to achieve a targeted market penetration in a specific segment, the glidepath might include milestones for concept prototyping, (in)validation, iteration, and go-to-market execution. Each checkpoint ensures progress, learning, and alignment.

While this structured approach might appear constraining at first glance, the reality is that a specific execution plan with unambiguous BIG choices actually gives teams freedom, not constraint. It creates the space for creativity and innovation within clear strategic imperatives and time frames. In each of the BIG choices, clear ownership is defined. It is crucial to specify who will own the bet, the initiative, and the glidepath milestone each week. This approach ensures commitment, accountability, unstoppable learning, and continuous progress. This way of owning both execution and learning marks a significant behavioral transition: from opinions to data, from failure to learning, and from doing to impact. Teams move from relying on narratives and storytelling to report on traditional business reviews to focusing on forward-looking execution using data. They shift from being content with completing an activity to being focused on making a tangible impact, building deep capabilities that competitors can't easily replicate.

Brutally focused teams never keep their prioritization undone or unled; they make BIG choices with unambiguous targets and owners defined. Teams that commit to nothing will be distracted by everything and armed with endless excuses.

The great paradox I've witnessed time and again in my career is this: When teams publicly commit to their choices and stay paranoidly focused until they learn from their impact (or lack of it), they actually expand their opportunities in the medium and long term. This paradox illustrates how specific execution plans with clear choices enable rather than restrict—providing the foundation for creativity and innovation to flourish within well-defined strategic boundaries. True freedom and transformative choices arise from delivering immense value—a result achievable only through brutal, unwavering, paranoid focus.

JONATHAN ESCOBAR MARIN

Break your mission down:
Bet big on what matters.
Mark milestones.
Execute. Learn. Iterate.
Reap results.

B ETS
Where to Play

I NITIATIVES
How to Win

G LIDEPATH
When to Deliver

Image 2.5: Playing to win is about BIG choices that deliver big wins.
© 2025, Jonathan Escobar Marin

To help their teams ruthlessly prioritize their BIG choices that deliver big wins, successful organizations embrace segmentation. As an example for growth missions in consumer goods, to make segmentation a practical and powerful tool, we usually integrate three frameworks: the first two of which—Advanced Customer Decoding and the Customer Compass—are seamlessly connected to the third, the actionable Six P framework. Together, these frameworks form the ultimate playbook for teams to operationalize segmentation for growth missions, ensuring that every effort is laser-focused on the 20 percent of the levers that deliver 80 percent of results.

It's important to note that while the following examples focus on segmentation as a tool to unlock growth missions of consumer goods organizations, segmentation using other effective frameworks

TEAMS THAT COMMIT TO NOTHING WILL BE DISTRACTED BY EVERYTHING.

Brutally focused teams never keep their prioritization undone or unled; they make BIG choices with unambiguous targets and owners defined.

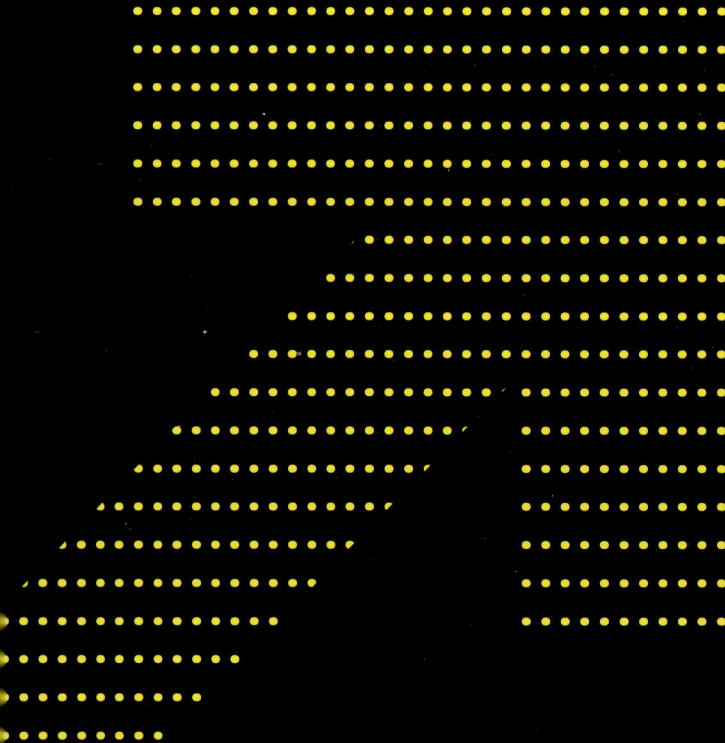

is equally applicable to all kinds of missions and organizations on the Wall. These include not only growth missions, but also bottom-line missions (e.g., driving efficiency or cost reduction) and discovery missions (e.g., exploring new markets or technologies). Different frameworks such as the Ansoff Matrix, the Jobs-to-be-Done framework, portfolio prioritization matrices, value stream mapping, customer journey mapping, and the technology adoption life cycle empower organizations to identify and prioritize opportunities systematically. Complementary metrics like customer satisfaction and Net Promoter Score enhance customer-centric segmentation by delivering actionable insights into loyalty and satisfaction. Additionally, tools like the Business Model Canvas and the Value Proposition Canvas enable the design of value propositions tailored to distinct customer segments, while the human-centered design framework emphasizes empathy-driven approaches through qualitative and behavioral insights, ensuring a nuanced understanding of customer needs and motivations across diverse contexts. All of them can be used in different contexts to prioritize across the unique demands of each type of mission, ensuring that segmentation remains a versatile and impactful tool across various strategic goals.

Let's delve into our examples of segmentation for consumer goods missions.

Advanced Customer Decoding: Deep Understanding of Customers

Effective segmentation begins with deeply understanding consumers. Advanced Customer Decoding is a scientific and data-driven approach to identifying, prioritizing, and acting on the most impactful customer segments. By layering behavioral, psychographic, geographic, demographic, and technographic insights, teams can unlock the true potential of their markets to achieve their missions.

BEHAVIORAL SEGMENTATION:
ACTIONS SPEAK LOUDER THAN WORDS

Decipher patterns in customer actions. For example:

- Purchase behavior: Who are your heavy users, loyalists, and switchers?
- Occasions: What are the key events driving purchase behavior?
- Customer lifetime value: Which customers deliver the highest returns?

RFM (recency, frequency, monetary value) analysis allows teams to identify high-value customers and tailor strategies to retain and grow these segments.

PSYCHOGRAPHIC SEGMENTATION:
UNDERSTANDING THE WHY

Align with deeper customer motivations, such as values, aspirations, or lifestyles. This approach helps craft emotionally resonant communication and product positioning. For example:

- Values and beliefs: Eco-conscious consumers may prioritize sustainability.
- Lifestyle alignment: Fitness enthusiasts may seek performance-driven products.

GEOGRAPHIC SEGMENTATION:
WINNING WHERE IT MATTERS

Tailor strategies to the distinct needs of regions, climates, and urban versus rural preferences. For example:

- Macro level: Identify trends by continent, country.

- Micro level: Use hyperlocal marketing based on region, state, or city.

DEMOGRAPHIC SEGMENTATION:
THE BASICS, EVOLVED

Segment customers using quantifiable data like age, income, and life cycle stage. For example:

- Younger audiences may demand innovation and eco-friendly solutions.
- Older segments may seek simplicity and reliability.

TECHNOGRAPHIC SEGMENTATION:
THE DIGITAL DIFFERENTIATOR

Understand customers' technology adoption and usage to optimize digital experiences. For example:

- Early adopters drive trends; mainstream users scale adoption.
- Device preferences (e.g., mobile-first consumers) dictate engagement strategies.

The Customer Compass: Focusing on Key Moments of Truth

The power of Advanced Customer Decoding amplifies when paired with the Customer Compass, which identifies the five critical stages that define the customer experience:

1. Discovery: ensuring customers find your brand in the right channels
2. Preference: becoming your customers' first choice
3. Onboarding/unboxing: delivering a seamless first impression

4. Usage: enhancing the product experience to drive satisfaction

5. Retention: building loyalty and repeat purchases

By mapping these moments of truth against segmented customer insights, organizations create a strategic blueprint for understanding how to deliver superior value at every touchpoint.

The Six P Framework

To transform segmentation insights into actionable choices in the form of bets, initiatives, and milestones, we leverage the Six P framework, a time-tested approach to achieving superiority. By aligning customer insights with the Six P's—product, packaging, proposition, promotion, place, and price—teams test, learn, and evolve their BIG choices to build unshakable execution. Each iteration sharpens their understanding and refines their choices, turning hypotheses into market-validated solutions. Here's how the Six P's come to life using different segments and journey insights.

PRODUCT: INNOVATE FOR THE RIGHT SEGMENT

- Use behavioral segmentation to prioritize features for heavy users or loyalists. For example, focus on innovation or premium features for high-value users while simplifying functionality for casual users.

- Employ technographics to ensure products meet the needs of early adopters or mainstream users, tailoring features to align with their technology preferences.

PACKAGING: TAILOR TO SEGMENT NEEDS

- Transform packaging aesthetics for psychographic or geographic preferences. For example, concentrate on sustainable materials for eco-conscious segments or culturally resonant designs for specific markets.

- Consider packaging functionality and size based on behavioral insights—offering trial sizes for acquisition-driven segments and larger formats for high-frequency users.

PROPOSITION: SHARPEN THE BRAND PROMISE

- Use psychographic insights to craft propositions that resonate with values and lifestyles. For example, emphasize luxury and exclusivity for premium, high-income segments, or affordability and practicality for cost-conscious consumers.

- Align your proposition with the emotional drivers of each segment, such as sustainability, innovation, or convenience.

PROMOTION: CREATE PRECISION MARKETING

- Target promotions using behavioral data (e.g., personalized loyalty programs for high-value customers or targeted acquisition campaigns for light users).

- Leverage technographics to optimize digital campaigns for the most-used devices and platforms, ensuring seamless engagement across channels.

- Consider psychographic messaging that resonates with customer values—such as sustainability-focused campaigns for eco-conscious segments or aspirational messaging for premium segments.

PLACE: OPTIMIZE ACCESSIBILITY

- Use geographic segmentation to ensure availability in high-potential regions. For example, focus distribution on urban areas where demand is highest or tailor rural strategies for specific consumption patterns.

- Incorporate technographics to optimize e-commerce platforms for mobile-first segments, ensuring convenience and accessibility across devices.

- Use hyperlocal insights to align distribution strategies with micro-geographic preferences.

PRICE: DELIVER PERCEIVED VALUE

- Demographic segmentation informs more than price points—it drives decisions on product portfolio, packaging, and quantity to match income levels and consumption habits. For example, develop functional, affordable products with smaller pack sizes for low-income segments while introducing premium packaging and high-value features for affluent customers.

- Behavioral segmentation helps identify price elasticity and value perception—offering tiered pricing models or bundling strategies to maximize appeal across segments.

- Use psychographics to guide premium pricing strategies for value-driven customers, where exclusivity and exceptional quality justify higher price points.

Segmentation Unleashing Bets

To operationalize segmentation frameworks, teams define their bets— clear, measurable choices targeted to deliver on mission goals by leveraging the depth of segmentation insights. For example:

BET 1

Increase revenue from X to Y in Market A by targeting high-value customers and heavy users.

BET 2

Drive X percent growth in Market B by winning with tech enthusiasts, with key sales uplift from early adopters.

BET 3

Boost penetration from X to Y in Market C with full focus on eco-lovers and premium segments.

Each bet connects segmentation insights to actionable objectives, ensuring every initiative will be grounded in reality while delivering measurable results.

From Bets to Initiatives

Once our strategic bets are established, we create initiatives that clearly define how to deliver these objectives. Each bet demands initiatives are fully aligned with the depth of segmentation insights and the precision of the Six P's. Initiatives are not vague ideas but specific, measurable moves connected to each market's distinct characteristics and needs.

Let's start with Market A; for this market, we begin by conducting RFM (recency, frequency, monetary value) analysis to identify high-value customers, identifying the top 20 percent of customers who contribute 80 percent of the revenue. Then, we might develop and launch a loyalty program tailored to heavy users, increasing the repeat purchase rate by 25 percent within six months. Finally, we personalize communication and offers based on user behavior data, achieving a 15 percent increase in conversion rates on personalized offers.

For Market A, technographics can also reveal the digital platforms most favored by loyal customers. Initiatives might include designing precise campaigns on those platforms, increasing engagement rates by 30 percent, and leveraging customer testimonials and reviews to build trust, increasing the retention rate by 25 percent. By integrating behavioral and technographic insights, Market A initiatives create a comprehensive plan to drive both immediate and sustained growth.

Let's continue with Market B to focus on tech enthusiasts and early adopters. Their technographic segmentation might include researching and listing the top tech blogs, forums, and social media channels. Our initiative would be to establish partnerships with ten key tech platforms, creating compelling content showcasing new product features, and achieving a reach of 500,000 impressions within three months. Then, we might collaborate with influencers and opinion leaders in the tech community, driving 50,000 new visits to the product page through influencer campaigns. Notice that each initiative has a concrete, crystal clear measure of success.

Behavioral segmentation for Market B might focus on early adoption patterns, allowing us to develop an early access program for new product launches. This program could enroll 50,000 early adopters within the first month, offering exclusive deals and previews to these customers, achieving a 15 percent sales lift. Crucially, we would gather feedback from early adopters to refine product features, implementing at least three feature improvements based on their input, ensuring alignment with their expectations.

Finally, Market C. Here we need to win with our eco-lovers and premium segments. We might segment them psychographically by highlighting sustainability features and eco-friendly practices in marketing materials. Our initiative would be to increase brand affinity scores by 20 percent among eco-conscious consumers. If we partner with environmental organizations for cobranded campaigns, we'd aim to achieve a 10 percent increase in market penetration in eco-conscious segments. We could also host events and webinars focused on sustainability issues, generating 100,000 new leads from sustainability events.

Segmenting Market C by demographics might mean going beyond premium pricing. Instead, we would focus on premium positioning in both product and packaging: developing bundles with exclusive features for high-income segments and using culturally resonant packaging to drive emotional connection with premium buyers. Initiatives might include achieving a 20 percent increase in average order value from premium bundles. Another initiative could be increasing lead acquisition among high-income segments by 200 percent through targeted presence on the top five luxury platforms. This approach ensures that demographic insights are leveraged to create holistic strategies that feel distinct and relevant to the segment.

From Initiatives to Glidepath

Finally, for execution to thrive, we need a clear timeline of success—one that evolves through continuous learning; this is our glidepath. We can measure that in milestones rather than in specific time periods, but those milestones should be attached to target periods, such as the next week or in two weeks—and let's demolish a common misconception right here: This isn't about short-term thinking any more than a pilot's constant course corrections reflect a lack of destination. Weekly tension points are the radar pings that keep us locked on long-term value creation. Those who confuse high-frequency execution rhythm with short-term thinking probably also mistake a heart monitor's beeps for the patient's life purpose.

These precise, time-bound markers drive sustained market leadership through unstoppable momentum, not through sporadic bursts of quarterly heroics. Each milestone compounds into lasting competitive advantages, forming the steel thread that transforms strategic vision into market dominance. This isn't about myopic quick wins; it's the disciplined cadence that separates market leaders from market followers.

Great missions demand bold bets. Bold bets demand precise action. Precise action demands clear deadlines. Clear deadlines fuel relentless learning. This is how superior results are delivered. This cycle turns ambition into measurable outcomes.

Let's say our first milestone is to conduct market research and set up analytics. We'd start with detailed market research to identify the key segments in Markets A, B, and C, completing segmentation analysis and identifying the target segments. We'd then implement tools to track customer behavior and campaign performance, establishing baseline metrics for customer engagement and sales.

With this foundational understanding, our second milestone would focus on launching initiatives specific to each market. For Market A, we could launch the loyalty program targeting heavy users, achieving a minimum of 10,000 enrollments after the first week, while initiating digital campaigns on favored platforms to increase engagement by 20 percent after the first four weeks. For Market B, we promote new product features on key tech blogs, achieving the first 100,000

Great missions demand bold bets. Bold bets demand precise action. Precise action demands clear deadlines. Clear deadlines fuel relentless learning. This is how superior results are delivered.

JONATHAN ESCOBAR MARIN

impressions after three weeks, and launch the early access program, targeting to enroll over 10,000 users in the first week. For Market C, we begin sustainability campaigns to increase brand affinity scores by 10 percent after the first month and launch premium-positioned advertising to drive a 20 percent lift in purchase intent among high-income segments already in the first two weeks.

Weekly cadences and milestones are the atomic units of long-term transformation and ensure steady progress. By wielding the principles of BIG—focusing on critical bets, executing targeted initiatives, and following a well-defined glidepath—missions can maintain momentum, and the teams driving them can shift rapidly to any changes. This disciplined approach guarantees measurable progress and learning every week, ensuring each initiative directly contributes to our strategic goals and amplifies our market endgame.

Ultimately, segmentation serves as a foundational tool for prioritization and focus across all mission types. While this chapter emphasizes growth missions in consumer goods as examples, similar frameworks and principles apply to bottom-line, digital, and discovery missions. By tailoring segmentation insights to the specific goals of each mission, organizations can achieve clarity, precision, and measurable impact—regardless of whether their focus is on scaling growth, reducing costs, or pioneering new frontiers.

LEADERS BUILDING NEW LEADERS

In today's ambiguous environment, developing new leaders becomes even more critical as organizations need multiple sensors and decision-makers to detect and respond to unclear market signals. Spread ownership: Ignite leadership everywhere. Distributed leadership ushers in an environment ripe for swift execution through unimpeded collaboration across diverse departments and hierarchies. In this revitalized ecosystem built on the O-model foundation, talent isn't shackled but flows purposefully within the organization—and even among organizations. It assembles into high-impact teams united by common transformative goals. Moreover, it cultivates a culture where leaders build new leaders throughout the mission-focused teams. Noel M. Tichy wrote in *The Leadership Engine*, "The scarcest resource in the world today is leadership."[21] Distributed leadership fills your coffers with that scarce resource. This is why your greatest legacy won't be the new leaders you unleash, but the culture where leaders always create new leaders, as an unstoppable cultural rhythm.

A culture of radical transparency empowers these teams composed of emerging and future leaders to swiftly learn, accelerate progress, and deliver results at an impressive pace. Driven by collective accountability and absolute ownership, leadership becomes a shared responsibility rather than remaining centralized.

This comprehensive overhaul lays the groundwork for an organizational model characterized by unmatched agility. The paralyzing impacts of bureaucracy and siloed thinking are replaced with a fluid network designed for continuous advancement. Rooted in customer-centric realities through on-the-ground leaders, these vibrant ecosystems of teams consistently realign themselves around crucial objectives.

The result is an organization primed for rapid innovation, smooth idea exchange, and steadfast delivery of results that turn ambitious goals into measurable achievements. This transformation prepares the stage for sustained competitive advantage through the regular attainment of strategic objectives while fostering a culture that continually develops new leaders ready to face future challenges—a rhythm that shapes tomorrow.

In the landscape of organizational evolution toward an ecosystem fully staffed by mission-committed leaders, the voice of Rosa Carabel, CEO of Eroski, resonates with the authority of a leader who has not just led change, but actively engineered it as well. Recognizing the untapped potential within Eroski, Rosa embarked on a mission to exponentially expand the company's leadership ecosystem. Under her guidance, what began as a core group of thirty key individuals, then a hundred,

FROM FEW

TO MANY

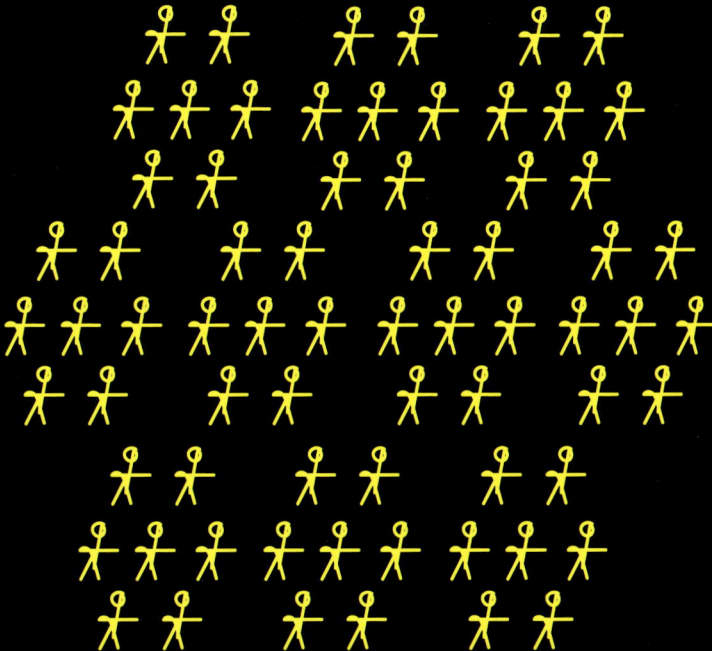

Image 2.6: From few to many—unleashing distributed leadership for multiplied capability and collective intelligence. © 2025, Jonathan Escobar Marin

has blossomed into a dynamic ecosystem that will soon have more than five hundred people, with the ambition to expand in the next few years—creating the granularity that the business requires. The result is a perfectly synchronized ecosystem where each team drives Eroski's accelerated growth and transformation.

As the largest cooperative of the Mondragón Corporation group—the world's largest industrial cooperative—Eroski operates as a worker-consumer hybrid cooperative with more than 1,500 outlets across Spain. The scale of this operation is impressive: Eroski counts more than 27,400 cooperative members and workers, of whom nearly 9,000 [in proximity to several other numerals] are owner-members. This workforce count doesn't include the employees from more than 620 franchised stores.

Rosa's partnership with my team, initiated three years ago, was born out of a keen interest in the tangible results achieved by other CEOs. This collaboration has since become a catalyst for Eroski's organizational metamorphosis, demonstrating Rosa's commitment to pioneering new approaches to work that create lasting competitive advantage.

Her insights offer a rare glimpse into the mind of a leader who has successfully scaled leadership across a large organization fostering a culture of shared accountability. Rosa's experience showcases how distributed leadership can transform not only business outcomes, but also the very fabric of an organization's culture.

"When I took on the responsibility of being CEO of Eroski," Rosa says, "we faced significant challenges: managing unprecedented inflation in food prices, combined with supply chain tensions due to the geopolitical and global tensions we all know."[22] They also had to reorganize their financial and debt structure while determining a new strategy to chart their goals and identify strategic lines that would set priorities for the next five years.

She continues, "I knew that there were thirty executives who would be key in accelerating results and evolving the organization at the corporate level, because they were and continue to be people with enormous

JONATHAN ESCOBAR MARIN

Your greatest legacy won't be the new leaders you unleash, but the culture where leaders always create new leaders.

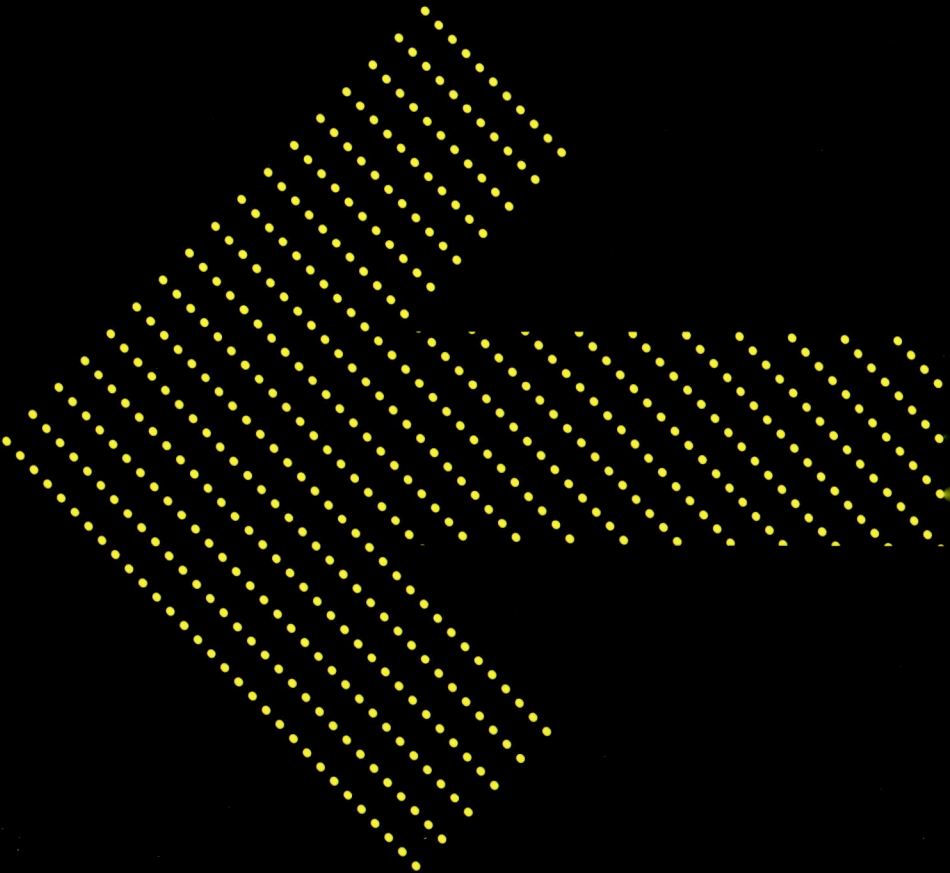

capabilities and qualities, but those thirty people alone can become bottlenecks. I was convinced that, beyond those thirty great professionals, there were many more people who could become leaders, protagonists of driving our organization to the next level. From those thirty we will soon be more than five hundred. Today, every week we know in real time if we're going to take the organization to where we want it to be in terms of results but also transformation. With all that we learn, we make every quarter the right choices to refocus, reenergize, and renew where needed. We all have our finger on the pulse of the organization. Now leadership is not about control; it's about multiplication. Thanks to this multiplication, we are more agile, more flexible, have greater adaptability, and therefore we are better and more prepared for the future. My intention is to continue multiplying leaders. In a couple of years, I am convinced we will be many more than five hundred, leading to build the tomorrow of this great organization that is Eroski."[23]

The success of this transformation illustrates how the principles of brutal focus, distributed leadership, impact-obsessed execution, and continuous evolution are deeply interconnected.

The transformative power of distributed leadership is not confined to any single industry or organizational structure. Its principles resonate across sectors, from retail giants to tech innovators. Christine Doig-Cardet is a visionary leader who has been at the forefront of personalization and product innovation at some of the world's most influential tech companies. As the current director of product, personalization at Spotify, she brings a wealth of experience from her similar roles at Netflix and Google. Her career exemplifies the cross-functional expertise and leadership that flourishes in environments embracing distributed leadership.

"What sets a dream team, a high-performing team, apart from others [is] ownership," she says. "People on the team need to feel responsible and accountable for the results of the entire team. It's like a team sport, not an individual sport. People who have embraced being team players feel that they matter and have a contribution to make, understanding that the outcome is the result of their collective work."[24]

Her perspective underscores the vital role of collective ownership and accountability across all organizational levels. This insight speaks to the heart of creating an organic ecosystem optimized for impact. It highlights the necessity of dissolving silos and nurturing an environment where diverse skill sets and perspectives can thrive. "The most impact an organization can have," Christine says, "is when cross-functional teams are working together, realizing that to really drive missions that are impactful to the business, you need people with different skill sets and functionalities. You need to allow them to work autonomously, trust them to make decisions to drive those initiatives forward."[25] These insights guide us toward a future where leadership permeates throughout the organization, enabling rapid innovation, seamless execution, and sustained competitive advantage.

True distributed leadership isn't about giving up the conductor's baton; it's about creating an orchestra where every section can lead the beat. Distributed leadership transforms organizations into ecosystems of leaders, where every individual is empowered to contribute, innovate, and own outcomes. By breaking down silos, embracing radical transparency, and fostering cross-functional collaboration, we create a dynamic environment where talent flows seamlessly to the missions that matter most. This is not just about achieving results today; it's also about building a culture where leaders create leaders, driving sustained innovation and long-term competitive advantage. The strength of tomorrow's organization lies in its ability to evolve—seamlessly aligning purpose, priorities, people, and performance. When leadership becomes a shared responsibility, and every team self-organizes with brutal focus and unstoppable execution, we're no longer managing an organization; we're igniting a movement. A movement that doesn't just deliver results, but also redefines what's possible in what is needed.

What Is Needed

Answer these questions to beat tomorrow—or watch others lead while you lag. Every honest response separates those who drive the future from those who will chase it.

- ↗ What percentage of your organization's talent is currently leading strategic missions?
- ↗ How many potential leaders remain untapped in your current organizational design?
- ↗ What's the real cost of keeping transformative missions trapped in silos?
- ↗ Are you willing to let go of traditional hierarchies to enable leadership to emerge organically?
- ↗ Is your leadership model built for control or value creation?
- ↗ How quickly can your talent mobilize to seize market opportunities?
- ↗ Are you measuring leadership by titles or by mission impact?
- ↗ Are your teams' execution plans driven by ruthless prioritization?
- ↗ How are you leveraging AI to amplify leadership impact across your organization?
- ↗ Does your organization enable or inhibit the flow of talent to critical challenges?

What sets a dream team, a high-performing team, apart from others [is] ownership."

—**Christine Doig-Cardet**

RESULTS BEAT EFFORT. PRACTICE BEATS
ACHIEVEMENT BEATS MOTION. OUTCOME
BUSYNESS. DELIVERY BEATS PROMISES.
PROCESS. REALITY BEATS THEORY. IMPLE
PERFECTION. REALIZATION BEATS PREPAI
BEATS DISCUSSION. MEASUREMENT BE/
ATTEMPTS. PRODUCTION BEATS PROJECT
BEATS CONSIDERATION. ADVANCEMENT I
POTENTIAL. LEARNING BEATS KNOWING.
BEATS OPINION. VALUE BEATS VOLUME. (
PRESERVATION. MOMENTUM BEATS INEF
BEATS SIZE. INITIATIVE BEATS DELAY. BRA
BEATS RELUCTANCE. COMMITMENT BEAT

RATIVES. EXECUTION BEATS PLANNING.
EAT INTENTIONS. PERFORMANCE BEATS
ION BEATS ANALYSIS. PROGRESS BEATS
TATION BEATS IDEAS. REFINEMENT BEATS
ON. SPEED BEATS REPORTING. CREATION
ESTIMATION. ACCOMPLISHMENT BEATS
BUILDING BEATS WAITING. GENERATION
S VICTIMISM. TRANSFORMATION BEATS
NAMISM BEATS IMMOBILISM. EVIDENCE
TING BEATS TALKING. ITERATION BEATS
BOLDNESS BEATS CAUTION. VELOCITY
Y BEATS BUREAUCRACY. DETERMINATION
ONVENIENCE. IMPACT BEATS ACTIVITY

CHAPTER 3

IMPACT OVER ACTIVITY

WINNING ISN'T JUST AN OPTION, IT'S A LONG-TERM COMMITMENT.

To win in the big leagues, and in a world of relentless turbulence, anything that doesn't make an impact is pointless. If you tell a joke and no one laughs, has it made an impact? Of course not. It has only served to please yourself. It's the same in business: When people plan a lot, do a lot, and don't move the needle, they are just telling jokes to themselves. Business is about playing to win. But true winning isn't about short-term victories at the expense of long-term health.

That's a recipe for bankruptcy. The real game is building for decades by winning in weeks. To play to win is to play to make a lasting impact, and for this you need to execute, embrace turbulence, make decisions, learn fast, and iterate even faster. This iterative process inherently involves taking smart risks and temporary setbacks—not because we embrace failure itself, but because we embrace the pursuit of victory, in an unpredictable world, and this necessarily involves failing forward.

Or as I learned almost two decades ago, first from A. G. Lafley, playing just to participate leads nowhere. It's a guaranteed path to mediocrity. Winning isn't just an option; it's everything. It's the ultimate measure of whether your BIG choices succeed or teach you the next winning move. Winning is about victories that create lasting competitive advantages. True market leaders understand that today's rapid execution and learning compounds into tomorrow's sustainable differentiation.

This winning mindset isn't about avoiding failure; it's about having the courage to fail bigger, learn faster, and rebuild stronger than those who play it safe. Research in cognitive psychology and performance science provides robust evidence for the interconnection between winning mindsets and productive failure. The work of Anders Ericsson and others on deliberate practice demonstrates that experts achieve mastery specifically by targeting their weaknesses and embracing temporary failures in pursuit of higher performance.[1] Carol Dweck's research on growth mindset shows that individuals who view challenges as opportunities to win, rather than threats of failure, consistently outperform their peers.[2] These findings directly support what we observe in business: The pursuit of winning creates the optimal psychological conditions for learning from failure.

What does winning look like? It's about creating something special, something uniquely transformative with enduring greatness. It's about pushing boundaries beyond what's comfortable or proven—a journey that inherently involves temporary setbacks and revolutionary breakthroughs. It's about positioning your business, your brand, your product in a way that distinctly solves an unsolved problem. You must deliver

JONATHAN ESCOBAR MARIN

WHEN PEOPLE PLAN A LOT, DO A LOT, AND DON'T MOVE THE NEEDLE, THEY ARE JUST TELLING JOKES TO THEMSELVES.

an experience and value so compelling that your chosen consumers, customers, or users can't help but notice the difference. This level of differentiation doesn't come from playing it safe; it comes from numerous iterations, failed experiments, and continuous refinement guided by an unwavering vision of victory. That's how you build real competitive advantage. And to be absolutely clear, as we learned earlier, you don't need to win with everyone—just the people who truly matter to you: your core consumers who drive your BIG choices and against the absolute best in your field. When you truly win with customers and outperform your competition, something magical happens: You create superior value for everyone involved—your customers first, but also your partners, your shareholders, your employees, society, and every stakeholder in between.

Walking into companies around the world, I see too many leaders and teams settling for average results simply because they're afraid—afraid to take risks, fail, or stand out. They're content just to maintain the status quo and keep their jobs. But the irony is glaring: In their desperate attempt to avoid failure, they fail at the one thing that matters most—winning. This fear of failure paradoxically leads to the biggest failure of all: the failure to truly compete.

The winning mindset liberates us from this fear; it gives us permission to fail intelligently in pursuit of extraordinary success, learning systematically from each setback to move closer to breakthrough innovation. Winning isn't just a goal; it's also the most powerful driver of meaningful learning.

It's a myth that you learn just by working. Activity for the sake of activity doesn't create learning; it simply creates sameness, continuity, and comfort. And that's okay, but comfort is not the same as growth. If you're working without a deliberate aspiration to achieve something greater, you're not learning. You're rehearsing sameness.

When your ambition is to win, every failure becomes a critical feedback loop that sharpens your strategy and your BIG choices, strengthens your execution, and propels you forward.

JONATHAN ESCOBAR MARIN

Playing just to participate leads nowhere. It's a guaranteed path to mediocrity. Winning isn't just an option; it's everything.
It's the ultimate measure of whether your BIG choices succeed or teach you the next winning move.

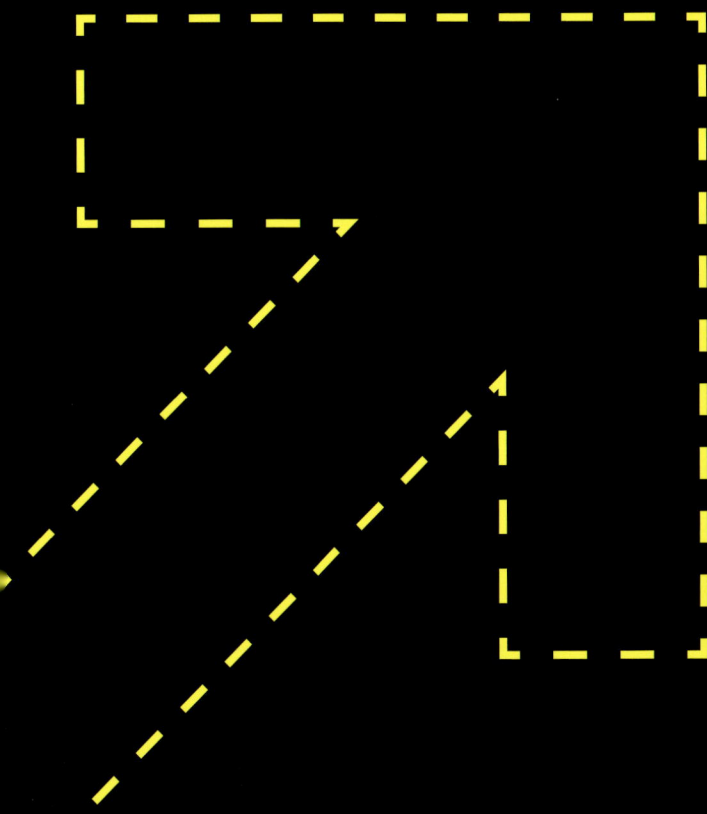

True learning happens in the tension between your aspiration to win and your current results. Without that aspiration, there's no gap, no tension, and ultimately no learning.

When this gap is intentionally created across the entire ecosystem of teams—fueled by distributed leadership and a paranoid obsession with impact over activity—you're no longer just creating progress; you're building an ecosystem of learning. When you compress these learning cycles into weeks while keeping your eyes on decades, something magical happens: You create an accelerated path to long-term superiority.

And if you are aspiring to win in today's world (I do hope you are), speed in decision-making is the price of entry, the right to compete, and the foundation of strategic advantage. This speed usually means that your decisions must be made with a certain level of uncertainty, which entails risk. Talking about strategy, decisions, and failure at an event from Y Combinator's Startup School at Stanford University, Mark Zuckerberg was absolutely clear: "The biggest risk is not taking any risk."[3] Without taking risks, you will be late in making a decision. Sure, it is important that risks are contained in business, but not by avoiding moving fast and making BIG choices, as we already learned how to make them. In today's rapidly evolving marketplace, one truth stands above all others: The true risk isn't in moving too fast; it's in moving too slowly to build something lasting. Victory belongs to those who dare to learn faster than the rest do. Your speed of learning determines your speed of winning. This is why we must put our BIG choices into action through weekly cycles, enabling rapid learning and reinvention to serve customer needs, while keeping our focus fixed on decades-long impact.

This velocity isn't about short-term acceleration at the expense of sustainable growth. Rather, it's about building an organizational metabolism that turns rapid learning into lasting competitive advantages. When teams excel at quick execution and iteration, they don't just win today's battles; they also develop the muscle memory and collective knowledge that shapes tomorrow's victories. For this reason, once you have built brutal focus and empowered distributed leadership, the next

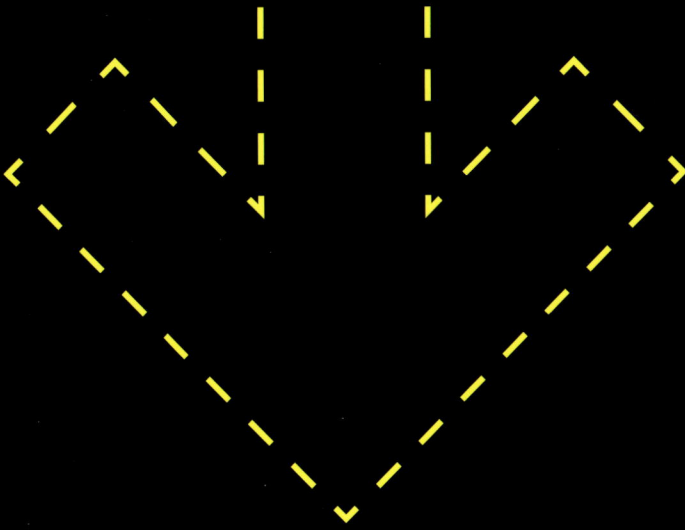

JONATHAN ESCOBAR MARIN

True learning happens in the tension between your aspiration to win and your current results. Without that aspiration, there's no gap, no tension, and ultimately no learning.

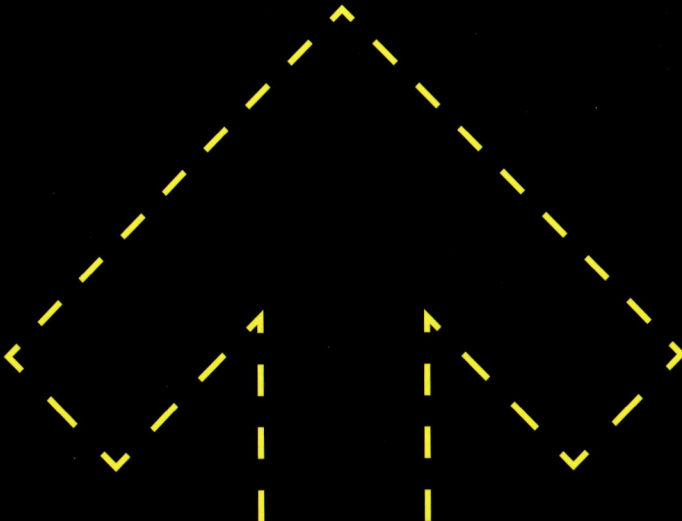

"

The biggest risk is not taking any risk."

—Mark Zuckerberg

YOUR SPEED OF LEARNING DETERMINES YOUR SPEED OF WINNING.

step is to accelerate execution, decision-making, and learning to impact your strategic missions in a timely and efficient manner. Here's the essential truth: Speed follows focus and precedes impact. Each week becomes a building block in your journey of enduring impact. Once we have decided what we need to achieve, we all focus on it: We move fast to meet a goal, achieve it with quality and impact, and move on to the next goal.

This principle comes to life through creating a fast-paced ritual of connection between your teams and top leaders—the synchros—that is transparent and accessible for all so that it also enables the connection between the teams working in each iterative cycle and the executives, the top leaders, guiding them. These weekly rhythms create the foundation for long-term transformation. The discipline of this ritual in a fixed cadence unlocks a steady pace of execution, fuels distributed leadership, and enables frequent conversations to unearth obstacles and accelerate the current speed of decision-making in the organization. That decision-making velocity accelerates the impact of execution. It's not so much about asking everyone to go faster; it is more about creating the stability that releases agility so that, when decisions need to be made or obstacles surface, they are tackled efficiently in the shortest possible period of time. This is how you turn weekly victories into decades-spanning advantages.

By placing impact over activity, speed over comfort, and learning over fear in these synchros, you will inevitably uncover numerous obstacles—decisions and actions stalled by bureaucracy. Bureaucracy is the silent killer of speed, impact, and—ultimately—winning.

I've seen the tremendous power of making these synchros a weekly rhythm, as it's key to cutting through these barriers decisively. You cannot let bureaucracy and obstacles linger in your organization for more than one week if you want to deliver lasting impact. Your solutions must be as close to the problem as possible, eliminating unnecessary steps and approvals. Remember, this isn't about managing layers; it's about dissolving those layers into swift, effective action that drives

JONATHAN ESCOBAR MARIN

Speed follows focus and precedes impact. Once we have decided what we need to achieve, we all focus on it: We move fast to meet a goal, achieve it with quality and impact, and move on to the next goal.

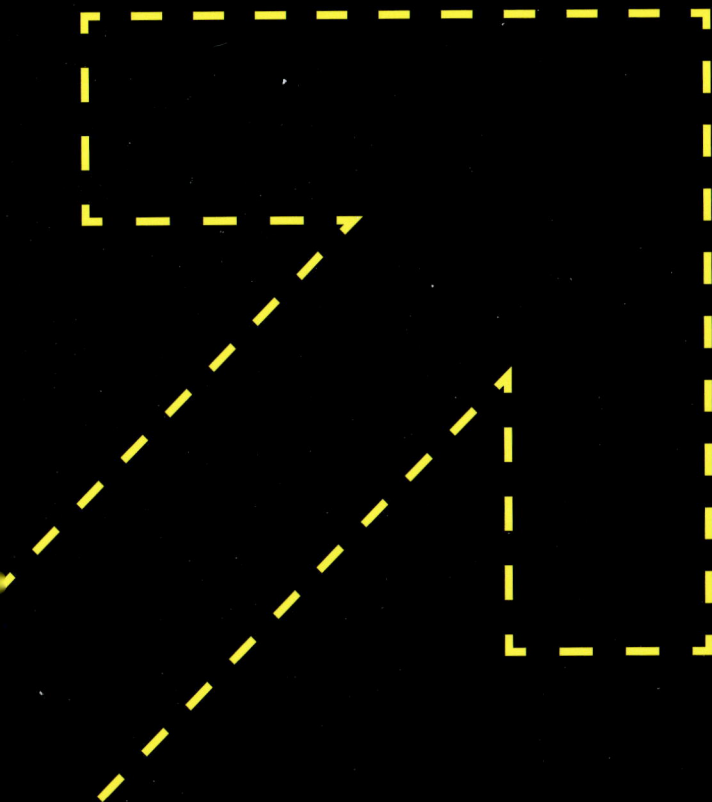

real impact. When you combine your ritual of connection with this bias toward immediate action, you create an environment where decisions flow naturally, impact becomes inevitable, and seamless execution is the norm.

Here's an example that illuminates the transformative power of impact over activity as a part of an integrated way of working. In the dynamic landscape of the food industry, few stories are as compelling as that of Frit Ravich, a family-owned enterprise that has become a beacon of innovation and growth. At the helm of this remarkable journey is Judith Viader, a visionary leader who embodies the spirit of entrepreneurial courage and transformative leadership. Under Judith's stewardship, Frit Ravich has not only flourished as a manufacturer of its own brand of potato chips, snacks, and nuts, but has also become a key distributor for global giants like Mars, Nestlé, and Ferrero. This unique dual model of operation has allowed the company to leverage the best of both worlds, serving an impressive 50,000 points of sale each week across various channels.

Frit Ravich's work philosophy, the FRIT WAY, is encapsulated in Judith's powerful words: "The FRIT WAY ensures that every action we take moves the needle on our most critical objectives, and especially more important for us, that we provide opportunities for talent to grow by leading multidisciplinary teams to achieve these objectives.

"What makes this way of working truly transformative is how it balances long-term strategy, execution speed, and human development—focusing on growing people to become protagonists in the impact of business missions that are vital for today and tomorrow. We progress week by week, deliver results quarter by quarter, and build capabilities for many years.

"And when I speak of capabilities, I'm not just talking about technical or business skills, but also that we've gained in generosity, cohesion, synchronization, and transparency. The FRIT WAY turns cross-collaboration at different hierarchical levels and between different departments into a tangible reality. Always to achieve our strategic priorities, which

BUREAUCRACY IS THE SILENT KILLER OF SPEED, IMPACT, AND —ULTIMATELY— WINNING.

we've defined together, all as one team—something we hadn't achieved with any other work practice before.

"I still remember when, a few months after beginning to work this way, a brand manager explained in the weekly synchro (after having been in the field that week with the different teams involved) why they had modified the packaging of a new product to facilitate startup and stability in the supply chain while simultaneously improving the consumer experience, without affecting the launch timeline. This is the FRIT WAY."[4]

DECISIONS OVER PARALYSIS

As we strive for impact, the crucial knowledge we need to win comes from data, facts, and insights. However, as we emphasized earlier in the driver of brutal focus, we must avoid getting trapped in endless analysis, particularly when facing frequent upheavals. Speed today builds strength tomorrow. When it comes to providing solutions to your customers, it's important to prioritize execution and making BIG choices over being overly precise on every single decimal. By moving quickly, even when there's a degree of uncertainty, you can create real value and deliver results that bring a smile to your customers' faces. Or as Mark Twain is said to have put it, "The secret of getting ahead is getting started." This mindset is crucial in order to avoid delays in decision-making that can hold back progress and prevent an organization from achieving its strategic objectives.

To combat analysis paralysis, install this question in the organization: What if the company's future hinged on making this choice within a week? Excuses are the enemy of progress. In a world where every second counts, there's no time for "we can't." Your mantra should be "how do we?" This is the mindset of those who play to win—with determination, not justification. Remember, winning is about having more ambition than resources.

At its core, impact over activity is our commitment to positively

The secret of getting ahead is getting started."

—Mark Twain

WINNING IS ABOUT HAVING MORE AMBITION THAN RESOURCES.

impact customer needs and ensure the future of the organization. For this, speed in decision-making is crucial to deliver what is needed, when it is needed, and to whom needs it—those who drive our BIG choices. Weekly synchros become invaluable here—not only in uncovering obstacles, but also in creating the beat for decisions to flow at the pace of the business. By maintaining this rhythm, teams stay aligned, focused, and equipped to act decisively without unnecessary delays. Weekly discipline transforms. In a recent interview with Lex Fridman, Jeff Bezos delved into the intricacies of decision-making. He highlighted the pitfalls of common resolution mechanisms such as compromise and attrition, advocating for more effective strategies that prioritize truth and efficiency. Bezos emphasized the importance of decisive—and speedy—action in maintaining high velocity within an organization: "Moving forward quickly on decisions, as quickly as you responsibly can, is how you increase velocity. Most of what slows things down is taking too long to make decisions."[5]

But speed isn't the only metric—you have to make *good* decisions at speed. To do that, you need trustworthy data combined with direct observation and a deep understanding of the facts from those closest to the execution and its impact. Building on the O-model, AI is no longer just a tool; it's a new team member. In the same way that finance or HR business partners have been integrated across teams in the past, today, AI agents and humanoid partners augment our capabilities and amplify our impact.

AI AS AN IMPACT PARTNER

As AI has evolved from perception-based models that understand images, words, and sounds, to generative AI that creates content, and now to agentic AI—where systems can reason, plan, and act autonomously—it has become increasingly evident that while data and computational models are foundational for progress, they are insufficient for capturing the full spectrum of human context and nuance

Moving forward quickly on decisions, as quickly as you responsibly can, is how you increase velocity. Most of what slows things down is taking too long to make decisions."

—**Jeff Bezos**

in the near term. To make the best decisions, we need not only data and insights, but also direct engagement with the facts and realities of the work itself. As Taiichi Ohno emphasized, "going to the *gemba*"—observing what is actually happening in the place where value is created—remains essential.[6] Pairing data, scenario analysis, and AI-driven insights (or even AI-generated decisions) with firsthand observation and contextual understanding ensures decisions are both analytically sound and grounded in human reality.

As AI drives rapid execution, organizations must also implement appropriate governance to manage issues of bias, transparency, and ethical use that could otherwise undermine long-term trust and effectiveness. Its true power lies not in short-term gains but in building organizational intelligence that compounds over time. Each learning cycle strengthens your competitive position for years to come.

By leveraging AI to augment human intelligence, we can enhance human creativity, understanding through firsthand observation, and decision-making with the precision and speed of AI, unlocking new levels of efficiency and innovation. Building on its agentic leap, AI introduces reasoning, planning, and autonomous action but remains fundamentally constrained by its reliance on structured data, predefined objectives, and programmed heuristics. These constraints, while narrowing, continue to hinder its ability to fully grasp complex, unquantifiable human factors such as tacit knowledge, emotional intelligence, and cultural nuance. Beyond this, physical AI represents another level of evolution, integrating virtual intelligence with real-world interaction and enabling robots to engage with physical spaces through reasoning and action.

Yet, even with physical AI, a fundamental question arises: Can humanoid robots truly replicate the depth of contextual understanding and human sensing required to navigate the intricacies of human reality? While advancements in robotics and machine learning have made significant strides, the current evidence suggests that physical AI excels in repetitive, structured, or hazardous tasks—where precision, endurance, and strength are paramount—but it encounters significant limitations when addressing the fluidity and ambiguity inherent in human social, emotional, and cultural environments. For instance, while a humanoid robot might interpret facial expressions or tone of voice using advanced machine learning models, it lacks the lived experience and implicit understanding that humans rely on when interpreting subtle emotional cues or unspoken societal norms.

In the long term, as AI systems continue to evolve, some of these limitations may narrow or disappear. However, in the present and in the next few years, we can accelerate impact through the augmented intelligence of humans collaborating with artificial intelligence; this is what we call AI[3].

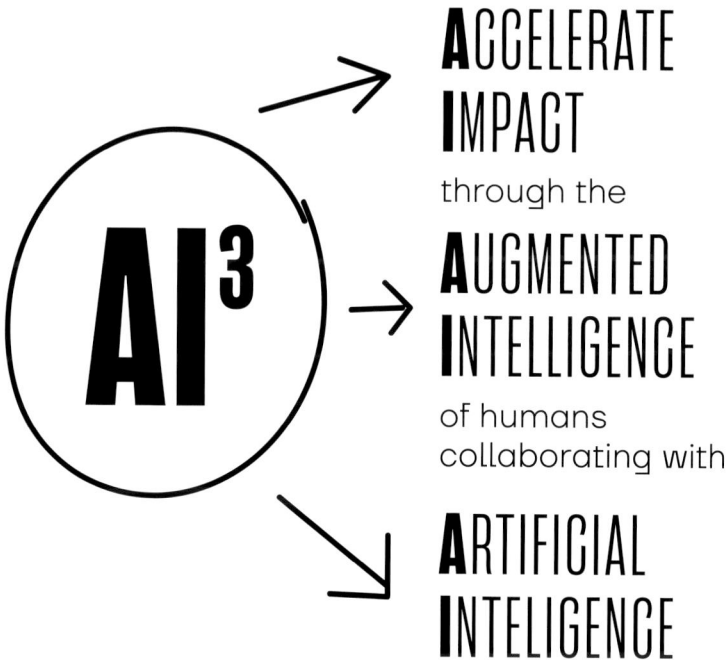

Image 3.0: The AI-human synergistic formula of success
© 2025, Jonathan Escobar Marin

The future of this collaboration depends not only on advancing AI's capabilities, but also on recognizing the unique strengths that humans bring to the table: the ability to synthesize meaning from diverse, dynamic contexts, the capacity for ethical reasoning, and the irreplaceable depth of human creativity and emotional intelligence.

In today's turbulent markets, AI becomes a critical tool for sensing and responding to rapid changes. However, human judgment remains essential for navigating unprecedented disruptions and making sense of chaotic market signals. By transforming traditional silo structures and embedding AI into our ecosystem of teams, we can transform decision-making and execution, enabling rapid iteration and continuous learning. This approach ensures that every decision is informed by data and facts, every action is optimized, and every team member is empowered to contribute to their fullest potential.

A PARANOID OBSESSION ON OUTCOMES

To avoid getting overwhelmed by the mountain of data and insights we might have to climb even without our new AI agents or team members, we'll need a laser focus on taking that data and moving forward with it quickly. However, moving forward doesn't just mean *doing something*; it also means *doing something that matters to win*. It means truly making an impact. We need to transform doers into impact makers. This transformation is essential for creating a culture where execution is intrinsically tied to meaningful outcomes.

Today, in an era where overwork, well-being, and work-life balance dominate corporate conversations no matter what company I step into, I stumble upon a fascinating irony. Walking into business reviews across the planet, I witness team after team fixated on activities, deliverables, and vanity metrics—all spinning furiously, yet without any clear link to impactful outcomes. Quite a contradiction, isn't it? This approach breeds nothing but busywork that fails to move the needle on wildly important missions, leaving people exhausted from doing much while seeing little. Ironically, it's this very disconnect that becomes the perfect fuel for burnout—both mental and physical—and the ultimate enemy of the well-being we claim to cherish.

To break free from this paradox, we leaders and our teams must pivot from mere doing to making tangible impact. The cornerstone of this transformation lies in putting our BIG choices to win into action—and as we execute, learn fast, and understand what works and what doesn't, these choices become our guiding compass. In this learning journey, sacrificing activities, deliverables, and good but not great ideas—cutting the crap—is not weakness but, rather, our greatest strength—a profound testament to strategic resilience and our unwavering paranoid obsession with honoring the sacred trust of our clients, users, consumers, shareholders, employees, and the society we serve. When refinement is needed over weeks of execution, the Pareto principle guiding proper segmentation remains our sharpest tool to refine these bets, initiatives, and glidepaths to focus on only what truly matters. By anchoring ourselves to BIG outcomes, our teams naturally gravitate toward high-impact work, leaving the allure of busy, useless work behind.

The glidepath serves as our flexible impact compass—not a rigid, deterministic plan, but rather the best plan ahead with the best knowledge we have today (though maybe not tomorrow) to create substantial impact and to eliminate any distraction that simply doesn't make the cut. This dynamic approach ensures that every action taken is a deliberate step toward a meaningful bet and initiative, not just motion for the sake of motion.

This focus on impact over motion is especially crucial as we continue to witness what I earlier described as *Agile theater*. Instead of embracing pragmatic, business, impact-first, customer-obsessed approaches, organizations have fallen into a proliferation of sophisticated activity-for-the-sake-of-activity methodologies under the inadequately used banner of Agile, often losing sight of Agile's core values and principles. Some of these approaches—favoring process over outcomes, bureaucracy over responsiveness, and reporting over impact-driven conversations—have often been implemented as ends in themselves rather than means to an end. Organizations have invested heavily in workshops and training sessions focused on these methods, without adequately integrating them into a cohesive management or operating system. This misguided, method-centric approach has several drawbacks, including a loss of context, fragmentation, and artifacts, or theatrical adherence to a script. Consequently, when executives push isolated methods without connecting them to organizational impact, teams risk becoming method-focused kingdoms, leading to silos and communication barriers within the organization. Most concerningly, workshop activities like design and ideation sessions are conducted, but they rarely translate into meaningful innovation that drives business results.

The path forward is clear: The solution lies in integrating some of these methods—the valuable ones—into a comprehensive impact-driven system. This integration ensures that methods serve as tools to achieve impact rather than being pursued for their own sake.

This comes back to impact over activity: We start with an outcome-oriented execution plan, where we visualize the key bets and their expected impact—not just activities. We use these methods when needed to move the needle in a specific outcome-defined bet, but the method is never the point. Next, we need communication, alignment, and synchrony: regular check-ins—the synchros—that prioritize alignment about outcomes, BIG choices, and actual or potential obstacles, not just status updates on activities. We then use Agile and Lean values and principles to self-organize, collaborate, learn, and rapidly iterate on our plans based on real-world impact, not simply to follow a prescribed process. Finally, we use the impact over activity mindset to define the best ties to our intended business outcomes and customer value, not just internal or vanity metrics. By shifting from doing something to making an impact, our teams can harness the power of various methodologies while maintaining a laser focus on outcomes. This approach creates a virtuous cycle where brutal focus leads to execution, execution leads to impact, impact informs future actions, and the organization as a whole moves forward with greater velocity and purpose. In this paradigm, team members at all levels become pilots in their own right, each steering their part of the organization toward meaningful results. This collective piloting, guided by a shared understanding of desired outcomes, is what truly accelerates organizational impact and decision-making.

Placid Jover, executive vice president and chief human resources officer at Teva Pharmaceuticals, brings a wealth of experience and a track record of driving innovative people strategies across global organizations. Placid says of the importance of moving beyond isolated methods to create truly integrated, impact-driven organizations, "It's easy to talk about Agile or OKR or any other fancy method. The real challenge—and the real opportunity—lies in transforming the entire operating system of a company to truly embody the principles of uncompromising focus, empowered distributed leadership, swift decision-making, and ceaseless transformation. . . . It's about more than just adopting new methods or getting certifications. It's about fundamentally changing how we organize work, unleash talent, allocate capacity, prioritize impact, and make decisions . . . moving beyond the theater of workshops and training sessions to create a truly integrated, impact-driven system."[7]

As Placid recognized, the true value of methods lies not in their isolated application but in their integration into a cohesive, impact-driven organizational system. As we continue to evolve from doers to impact makers, it's this holistic approach that will drive meaningful transformation and sustainable success.

FROM REPORTERS TO PILOTS

In the journey toward accelerating impact and decision-making over the illusion of movement and activity, organizations must transform their workforce from mere reporters of past events and lagging metrics into proactive pilots steering toward future success through leading metrics and outcome-oriented bets, initiatives, and glidepath milestones. This transformation is crucial for creating a culture of accountability, foresight, and agility.

In many organizations, employees spend a significant portion of their time, up to 40 percent, in the two layers below the leadership team according to our measurements during the last few years—reporting past activities, actions, and hollow metrics. Business reviews frequently focus on what was done with lots of vanity and lagging metrics presented as misleading averages, without addressing future execution plans with clear outcome-oriented BIG choices. This backward-looking approach, while informative, fails to drive the organization forward. It's funny how obsessing over past glories means your customers only get to see your back.

To shift this dysfunction, companies cultivate forward-thinking individuals and teams who take ownership of future outcomes, what I call *pilots*.

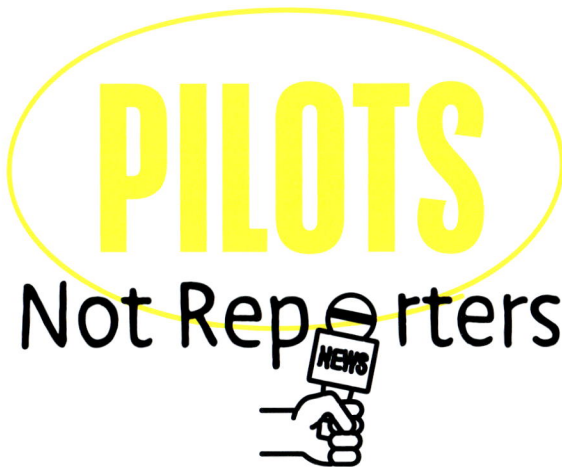

Image 3.1: Pilots, not reporters—driving the future, not reporting the past
© 2025, Jonathan Escobar Marin

This transformation hinges on four key habits: First, pilots continuously monitor their progress toward mission targets, maintaining a clear

As pilots, we...

Monitor our confidence to land on time

Own our landing coordinates

Maintain a clear execution plan

Never ignore gremlins on the wing

Image 3.2: Pilots drive—own, lead, deliver, and tackle gremlins with a winning mindset.

understanding of their current position relative to their goals. Next, pilots possess the ability to anticipate where they will land relative to their targets—whether above or below and by how much—taking full responsibility for the outcome. Pilots maintain a clear set of bets and initiatives with a clear glidepath (their set of critical milestones) for the upcoming weeks to ensure their mission's success. Finally, pilots never ignore gremlins on the wing—those sneaky elements that might seem minor, imaginary, or too early to worry about at first glance but, in reality, demand immediate action to prevent cascading disruptions. I have always believed anticipation is one of the most underrated behaviors in business. A responsible pilot immediately sees the risks, investigates thoroughly, and tackles these gremlins head-on before they can jeopardize the mission's success.

It's funny how obsessing over past glories means your customers only get to see your back.

JONATHAN ESCOBAR MARIN

By shifting the mindset from reporting to proactive piloting, organizations can enhance accountability as pilots take ownership of future outcomes. They become outcome-oriented, challenging their teams to refine their approach based on real-time data and feedback. They establish clear execution plans through glidepath clarity; this ensures that their teams have a clear focus for the upcoming weeks and can effectively make an impact through their plans. And they foster proactive synchrony by never ignoring the gremlins on the wing, creating a culture where problems are celebrated, not hidden, and addressed immediately through servant leadership and swift obstacle removal. In winning organizations, where talent, time, and leadership are appreciated and acknowledged as the scarcest assets, teams must be maniacally focused on the impact and the future; there is little value in reporting on the past when it doesn't serve a better future.

By cultivating these pilot qualities in our teams, organizations create a more agile, forward-thinking environment that accelerates impact and decision-making. This evolution from reporting to piloting represents more than an operational shift; it's a strategic transformation in how organizations create enduring value. Pilots don't just navigate today's challenges; they also build the capabilities and market insights that compound over years. The ability to anticipate, learn, and act becomes a self-reinforcing advantage that grows stronger with each cycle.

To truly understand the power of this transformation, let's turn back to Placid Jover, a leader who has lived, led, and breathed this change. Placid held various leadership positions at Unilever, ultimately rising to become Unilever's Chief Talent, Learning, and Reward Officer. He first partnered with my team to reshape the company's ways of working when he was VP of HR for Unilever LatAm—an $8 billion business spanning twenty-three countries with 30,000 employees. The results were so impactful that, since then, he's been on a mission to spread these practices globally in all roles he has had.

"We didn't just change how we worked," Placid says. "We fundamentally shifted our entire mindset from reporters to pilots. Value and impact became our new language, permeating every conversation, every decision. It was exhilarating to see how this focus on transparency and outcomes cuts through the noise of internal issues and busywork." It was especially effective when it came to those potential problems often hidden behind a locked cockpit door: Those problems "signaled where

JONATHAN ESCOBAR MARIN

Teams must be maniacally focused on the impact and the future; there is little value in reporting on the past when it doesn't serve a better future.

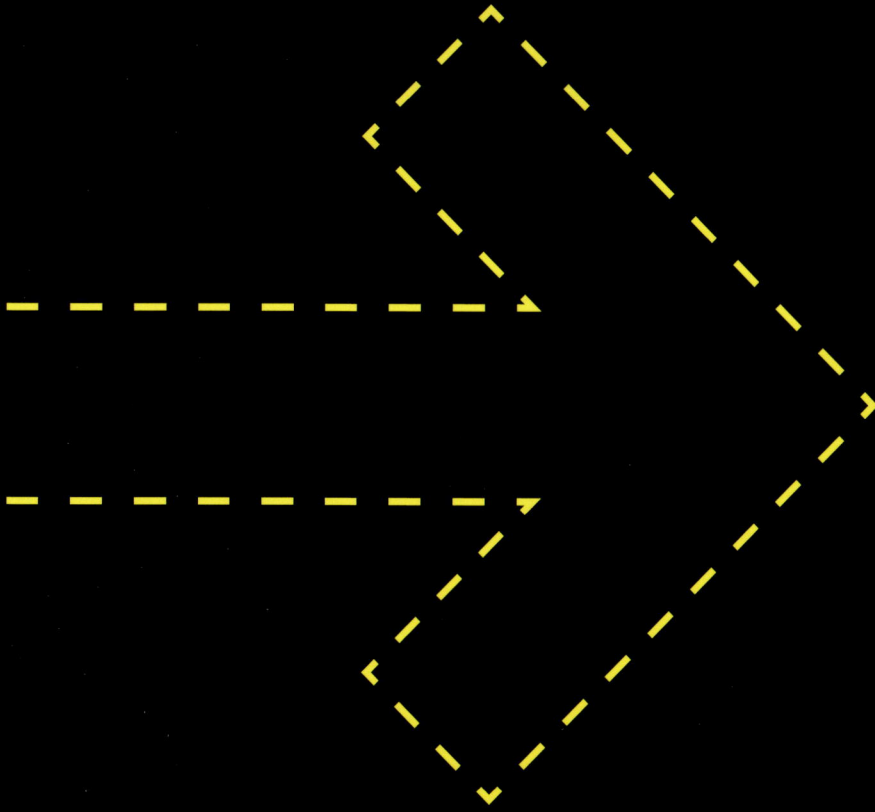

we needed to rally, where we could make a real difference. It's not about failure; it's about stretching, growing, and tackling challenges head-on. That's the true spirit of becoming pilots, not passive passengers, and it's absolutely transformative."[8]

Just as pilots must navigate through turbulent conditions, our talent must become leaders who guide their teams through constant market disruptions. The ability to anticipate, adjust, and maintain course despite turbulence becomes critical for success.

SYNCHRONY OVER CHAOS

The hardest thing after prioritizing BIG choices is the synchronized teamwork required to achieve them. Impact emerges from the thousands of small decisions, iterative learning loops, and aligned execution across leaders and team members.

Just as a flight crew operates in perfect coordination with the air traffic coordination tower, ground teams, and each other, business teams need regular, structured check-ins to stay aligned and effective. The pilot's way of working represents a master class in synchronized teamwork—from preflight briefings to constant tower communications, from cabin crew updates to real-time weather monitoring. Every person knows their role, communication channels, and check-in schedules.

In today's turbulent business environments, synchronized execution becomes even more crucial. Like pilots coordinating during storm conditions, teams need clear communication channels and decision protocols to maintain stability amid market volatility. This aviation-grade synchronization prevents the chaos of uncoordinated decision-making, eliminates dangerous information gaps, and avoids the risks of fragmented communication where critical stakeholders might be left out of the loop. In addition to operational efficiency, this level of synchronization fosters mental clarity and reduces stress by providing predictability and structure—key factors in building psychological safety within teams. To mirror this world-class synchrony in business, we've demonstrated how a simple, pragmatic weekly check-in, the concept of synchros—already referenced earlier in this chapter—prevents the chaos of coordinating on short notice for ad hoc meeting times, eliminates piecemeal communication, and ensures all necessary stakeholders are involved. When everyone knows there's a set time to connect, discuss progress, and address issues transparently, the entire organization moves forward in unison, like a well-coordinated flight operation.

In many organizations, the synchro takes the form of a ten-minute weekly (or biweekly, for longer-term missions) ritual—much like a pilot's position check-in. Having validated this practice across a wide range of cultures, contexts, and business sectors, I can confidently assure you that a ten-minute weekly synchro can save more than ten hours of individual misinterpretations, frustrations, and wasted work—both among team members and top leaders. But beyond time saved, these synchros create a sense of reliability and mental stability, as team members know exactly when and where they can align, voice concerns, and clarify priorities. This rhythm reduces the cognitive load of juggling competing demands and eliminates the uncertainty that often comes with fragmented communication.

Like the structured communication between the cockpit, crew, and traffic coordination tower, this consistent, transparent ritual of connection between teams and leaders serves not as backward-looking report sessions but as forward-focused discussions. Teams express their confidence levels, share supporting data and facts, outline their brutal focus for the coming weeks, and request leadership support in eliminating obstacles—similar to pilots updating their expected landing, flight conditions, fuel status, and the glidepath with potential weather challenges or (hopefully not) gremlins on the wings. It also serves as a transparent invitation for team members and other stakeholders to stay informed and aligned. Several of our synchros, across different organizations, attract communities of fifty to one hundred people who connect voluntarily, drawn together by openness and shared responsibility. This allows those who need to collaborate, whose work may influence or be influenced by the team's efforts, or who simply want to learn from the team's approach, to get information firsthand.

This disciplined cadence creates a mental stability that paradoxically unleashes agility, ensuring that when decisions need to be made or obstacles arise, they are addressed swiftly and efficiently, with everyone who needs to be involved fully synchronized, both in knowledge and timing. Crucially, this stability also contributes to well-being by fostering trust and a shared sense of purpose. Team members add value, get value, and feel valued and supported, which strengthens morale and builds resilience, particularly in fast, high-pressure environments.

Having a predictable way of working with a language that is shared across the organization fosters an environment of reliability and excellence. Teams can concentrate on their tasks with the assurance that their efforts will seamlessly integrate with the broader organizational goals. We've measured in different organizations that without a stable ritual of connection and consistent pace, teams collectively spend sixty to ninety times the duration of a typical synchro in fragmented, one-off conversations—repeating the same information, correcting misunderstandings, and resolving communication gaps. For a ten-minute session, this equates to ten to fifteen hours of inefficiency, which could have been avoided through structured, transparent, and forward-focused discussions—a cultural beat that cuts chaos. Ten minutes of synchronous synchros outweigh days of asynchronous chaos.

The fundamental misconception plaguing modern productivity discourse isn't that meetings exist. It's that we've failed to distinguish between hollow reporting and PowerPoint karaoke time-drains, and precision synchronization instruments to align execution and decision-making to surface what no one wants to talk about but is needed. It is not about eliminating meetings; it's about eliminating all the waste in them and making sure that they become high-leverage synchronization points that accelerate decision velocity and eliminate costly misalignments.

When there is no common ritual of connection, people waste time in one-on-one or siloed forums, increasing the risk of broken-telephone scenarios with multiple lines of communication. This lack of coordination

TEN MINUTES OF SYNCHRONOUS SYNCHROS OUTWEIGH DAYS OF ASYNCHRONOUS CHAOS.

not only slows decision-making, but also increases frustration, erodes trust, and contributes to a sense of chaos in the workplace. By instituting a regular cadence of weekly synchronizations, organizations create a culture of continuous improvement and accountability, while also promoting the mental and emotional well-being of their teams. People thrive when they feel part of a well-coordinated and reliable system, reducing burnout and frustration while enabling them to contribute at their best.

By committing to these regular synchronization points, we create the same high-reliability environment that makes commercial aviation one of the safest industries in the world. When everyone operates on a shared frequency—whether in the air or in business—teams can focus on delivering excellence while maintaining perfect coordination with the broader mission. Teams operating on shared frequencies—why, what, when, and how—don't just perform; they transform. They shape tomorrow. The result is an organization that moves with the precision of a well-orchestrated flight operation, where every team member knows exactly what, when, how, and why to contribute to the mission's success.

Each of these synchros isn't just a meeting; it's also a cultural beat that reinforces how the talent in organizations thinks, performs, and acts. The weekly synchro serves as a continuous culture and talent observatory, where leaders can spot emerging potential and address both cultural and performance gaps in real time. Unlike traditional talent reviews that happen once or twice a year, these weekly touchpoints provide around forty-five opportunities annually to observe how individuals handle pressure, collaborate across functions, and drive outcomes. This frequent exposure helps leaders make more informed decisions not only about business choices, but also about culture health and talent development.

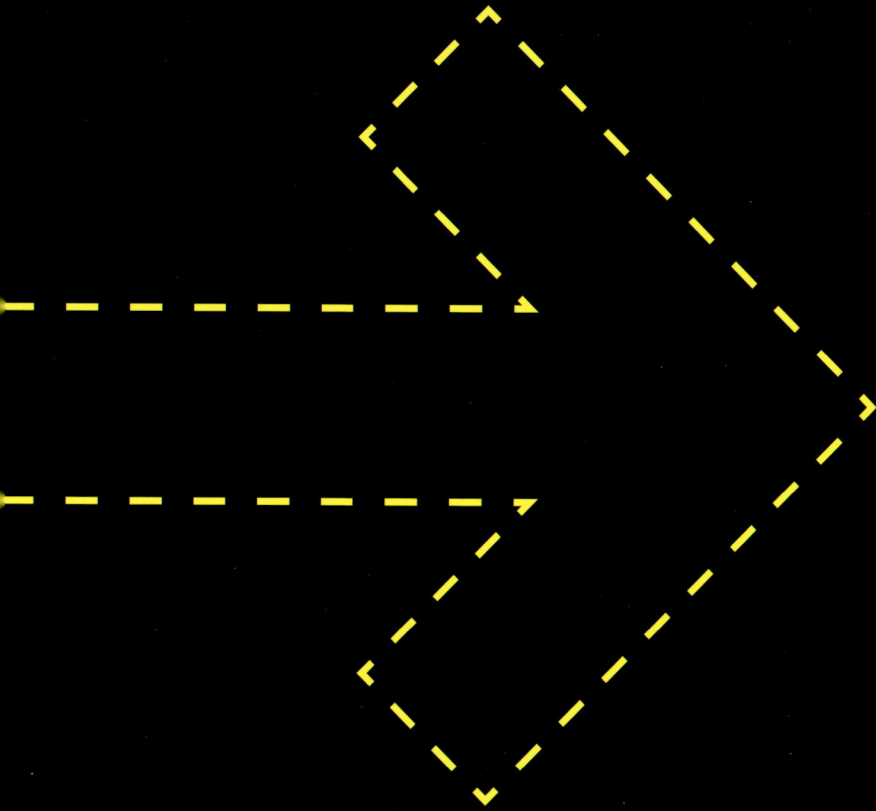

JONATHAN ESCOBAR MARIN

Teams operating on shared frequencies—why, what, when, and how—don't just perform; they transform. They shape tomorrow.

EXECUTION IN THE SHADOWS, IMPACT IN THE LIGHT

Teams' confidence in synchros comes from unseen execution in private. This confidence about their capability to achieve the expected impact on their mission is earned in the work done between them. What teams bring to the table during a synchro is the result of disciplined, focused, and unseen execution that happens away from the public forum.

Be aware that not everyone will like the synchros, especially when they happen on a weekly rhythm. You will get pushback from the same people consistently. This resistance often stems from a discomfort with the transparency and accountability that synchros demand. When teams know that private execution feeds directly into a public rhythm, there's no room for ambiguity, excuses, or unproductive activity—and this can feel threatening to those who have been living for years on the shoulders of narratives, reporting, and vague delivery.

Synchros ruthlessly expose inefficiencies and demand substance. Narratives don't have a single second of space in synchros. Neither do excuses. Reporting is forbidden. Synchros are not about storytelling or justifying past actions—they are about impact, future, alignment, and decisions. They force teams to focus on what truly matters: outcomes over effort, clarity over ambiguity, and execution over talk.

For those accustomed to using narratives to explain away underperformance, synchros can feel like a hostile environment. But for those who embrace the discipline of execution, synchros become a powerful tool for driving focus, enabling speed, and eliminating waste. They create a rhythm that rewards focus, accountability, execution, and results—leaving no room for anything else.

FAST ENOUGH TO SEE WHERE WASTE IS

Speed isn't about rushing—it's about finding the perfect rhythm where execution meets impact or loses it, and where its presence or absence fuels collective learning for the next iteration. Don't forget that speed follows focus and, in turn, highlights the waste that hinders impact.

✓	Monday	✗
✓	Tuesday	✗
✓	Wednesday	✗
✓	Thursday	✗
✓	Friday	✗

Weekly
RESULTS

Weekly
EXCUSES

Image 3.3: Synchros drive results—no excuses, just daily execution for weekly progress and learning. © 2025, Jonathan Escobar Marin

You can't move quickly when you're burdened by the fat of bureaucracy. Speed eliminates organizational dead weight.

Speed is uncomfortable but vital. Speed exposes inefficiencies, unclear priorities, and unproductive habits that were previously hidden in slower, more forgiving workflows. As Shigeo Shingo is said to have noted, "The most dangerous kind of waste is the waste we don't recognize." Speed demands transparency, and transparency can feel threatening to reporters, bureaucrats, and the mediocre who are accustomed to hiding poor results. When the pace quickens, there's no room to mask anything.

This resistance often highlights where progress toward impact is lacking—because speed demands clarity, and clarity exposes waste. When we set out to move fast, we bring to light all the inefficiencies caused by the seven capital sins of business impact: ego, fear, overdoing, bureaucracy, redundancy, mediocrity, and lack of alignment. These hidden inefficiencies are particularly dangerous because they often go unnoticed, buried under layers of busyness and complexity. Those of us who grew up obsessed with driving *impact over activity*, and who know that focus and speed precede impact, grasp this truth well: Speed doesn't just accelerate outcomes; it also reveals the cracks in our systems that slow us down.

Speed eliminates organizational dead weight.

JONATHAN ESCOBAR MARIN

Synchros are a powerful antidote to these sins because they enable the speed that exposes the five most common wastes in organizations:

1. **Overload:** Time wasted by people working on things that do not serve any purpose, such as PowerPoints, to report on what can no longer be changed.

2. **Inventory (of trophies):** Time lost in a surplus of projects that have served a few heroes to win a "trophy" for activities, awards, and vanity metrics with zero impact on those who matter the most.

3. **Mediocrity:** Time wasted trying to convince mediocre people that they should strive and improve every day even though they are not (yet) robots, but human beings with the ability to think critically, feel, learn, and improve.

4. **Rework:** Time lost due to rework caused by the tolerance of mediocre processes and deliverables accepted as good enough, creating problems and rework for others.

5. **Reporting:** Time wasted explaining to ourselves what we did to get a pat on the back. This is the fuel for adults raised with incentives of external recognition rather than effort, readily practiced in hour-long sessions where everyone agrees on the poetry of the past but knows nothing about the verses of the future.

Leaders who embrace synchros as a disciplined rhythm of execution and alignment not only accelerate outcomes, but also systematically surface and eliminate these wastes. Synchros, when implemented with focus and consistency, do more than coordinate teams—they transform them. By forcing decisions to be made and obstacles to be addressed in real time, synchros ensure that organizations don't just move faster; they also move smarter—shaping tomorrow's wins.

The result? Organizations and teams that run leaner, waste less time, and focus only on what truly matters. Leaders who adopt this approach shape the beat of their organizations—driving innovation, collaboration, and impact at the speed the present demands. As Rupert Murdoch may once have said, "Big will not beat small anymore. It will be the fast beating the slow."

This reflection encapsulates the essence of synchros: Speed is no longer a luxury—it's a necessity. Synchros create the structure needed to sustain that speed, enabling teams to leave behind inefficiency and mediocrity and operate with brutal focus, learning agility, and impact.

This truth echoes Shingo's wisdom about hidden waste. Just as the most dangerous waste is the one we don't recognize, the most powerful advantage comes from the speed that makes waste impossible to ignore. As synchros quicken the pace, we uncover the root causes of waste: overloaded teams working on low-impact activities, redundant projects pursued for vanity metrics, mediocrity tolerated in the name of comfort, rework caused by poor deliverables, and endless reporting designed to celebrate effort over outcomes. These inefficiencies aren't just inconvenient; they're also the silent killers of impact and innovation. When the pace quickens, every inefficiency screams for attention. But speed, when paired with focus and impact, eliminates waste by forcing clarity, discipline, alignment, and accountability.

Speed doesn't just help us work faster; it also makes us work smarter by cutting the waste and focusing only on what drives impact.

TRANSPARENCY OVER SECRECY

Another key aspect of accelerating execution and decision-making to drive real impact is the transparency that fosters cross-connection and alignment. Synchros—when they are open to all who can benefit from the dialogue—become powerful enablers of collective intelligence and collaboration. We've consistently seen that when companies make their stable cadence of execution and decision-making ritual transparent and inclusive across all teams, they foster a powerful culture of empathy, generosity, and knowledge sharing. This approach has enabled teams across continents and sectors to work together effectively, align their efforts precisely, and make informed decisions that serve both the needs of customers and the organization as a whole.

NVIDIA's CEO Jensen Huang exemplifies this with his unique leadership style. Rather than relying on one-on-one meetings, he holds rituals that prioritize direct, transparent communication with sixty colleagues at once. Huang ensures that all communication and decision-making processes are transparent and inclusive. Everyone in the room hears the same information simultaneously, fostering a unified understanding and enabling the entire team to contribute to problem-solving. This open approach, which perfectly aligns with our experience and practice, dissolves hierarchical barriers, accelerates decision-making, and ensures that feedback is shared broadly, empowering all team members.

In an interview with Patrick Collison on his understanding of leadership in the era of AI, Huang said, "Almost everything that I say, I say to everybody all at the same time. . . . These are the challenges of the company, or this is the problem I'm trying to solve, or this is the direction we're trying to go into. . . . This isn't working, that's working well. And so all of this type of information, everybody should be able to hear. . . . [At NVIDIA] There is no privileged access to information, [and] we're able to all contribute to solving a problem."[9]

Huang's approach aligns perfectly with our principle of transparency over secrecy. He believes that almost everything he says should be heard by everyone at the same time, emphasizing that there is no information that only one or two people should have access to. This transparency ensures that the entire team understands the challenges, problems, solutions, and directions of the company. Team members are empowered to contribute effectively, knowing that they have equal access to all pertinent information.

Moreover, Huang's method of giving feedback in front of everyone underscores the value of collective learning. Instead of depriving others of valuable lessons learned from individual mistakes, he reasons through issues publicly, allowing the entire team to benefit from the

"[At NVIDIA] There is no privileged access to information."

—Jensen Huang

discussion. This approach not only accelerates learning, but also fosters a culture where mistakes are openly addressed and used as learning opportunities. By doing so, NVIDIA minimizes the layers of communication, reduces the time spent on redundant conversations, and enhances overall organizational efficiency. This transparency and openness drive a more collaborative and informed decision-making process, aligning with the goal of fostering a culture of collaboration and knowledge sharing throughout the company. He rejects the notion of compartmentalizing feedback to one-on-one conversations, instead advocating for leveraging each individual's missteps as teaching moments that can enlighten the entire team.

Ultimately, Huang paints a vision where mistakes are not shameful deficits to be hidden but precious seeds for cross-pollinating insights that elevate everyone's capabilities in the journey to win. This culture of radical transparency transforms errors into opportunities for growth and continuous improvement, fueled by the collective's lived experiences—failures included.

ITERATION OVER ROMANTICIZATION

Have you ever seen a customer rewarding a good idea? Of course not. Customers only ever value the execution that deserves their smiles; they don't romanticize any idea that doesn't satisfy their needs. It's easy to talk about the next billion-dollar idea, but the real challenge lies in turning that idea into a billion-dollar positive business impact. Great visionary ideas are necessary, but they are just the beginning; the true magic lies in the craft of execution. Execution driving impact requires craftsmanship, attention to detail, and a commitment to iterative refinement. By embracing impact-driven loops of rapid prototyping, fast feedback, informed learning, and decision-making, our teams can navigate the journey from concept to successful outcome.

Steve Jobs said, "After I left [Apple] John Sculley got a very serious disease. I've seen other people get it too. It's the disease of thinking that a really great idea is 90% of the work. And that if you just tell all these other people, 'Here's this great idea,' then, of course, they can go off and make it happen. And the problem with that is that there's just a tremendous amount of craftsmanship in between a great idea and a great product."[10]

This craftsmanship is not just about doing the work; it's also about operationalizing the mindset and way of working necessary to ensure the disease of idea supremacy has no opportunity to appear again.

The consistent pace of regular synchros creates a rhythm of momentum—where teams move beyond ideas and into action through iterative loops. These disciplined check-ins provide the clarity to iterate, the focus to sharpen priorities, and the urgency to execute. They aren't just meetings; they're also catalysts for progress, turning ambition into outcomes and obstacles into opportunities.

Arantxa García, global culture and talent acquisition director at Danone, echoes this sentiment, emphasizing the transformative power of impact through ownership and iteration within teams. With years of experience driving cultural and organizational change, she has seen firsthand how empowering teams to become pilots—not only of their ideas, but especially of the execution, learning, and iteration of their plans—leads to extraordinary and creative outcomes.

"When you empower teams to decide their own execution plan and support them," she says, "their level of responsibility and creativity skyrockets. They become far more accountable because it's their ideas, their plan, their execution; they own it, live it, and feel it. Moreover, teams become significantly more ambitious, creative, more grounded in action, and less prone to victimhood about resources. When plan A doesn't work, they innovate plans B, C, D, and as many as necessary to deliver on their mission because they also know that their guides, the top leaders, will be there for whatever is needed in the next synchro. This way of understanding that ideas are only the first step in the chain of impact—and we can't fall in love with them if they do not work—automatically unleashes talent, creativity, collaboration, ownership, and, of course, achievement, impact, real outcomes."[11]

IDEAS GET IT STARTED. ITERATION GETS IT DONE. IMPACT GETS IT REMEMBERED.

ONE WEEK OF FOCUSED LEARNING THROUGH EXECUTION ECLIPSES MONTHS OF PLANNING.

With each cycle, synchros sharpen alignment and compress the time between insight and impact. They ensure that every challenge is confronted, every decision is made swiftly, and every action drives tangible results. This rhythm of iteration fuels continuous improvement, where learning becomes faster, execution grows sharper, and progress becomes unstoppable. Ideas get it started. Iteration gets it done. Impact gets it remembered. This sequence turns potential into lasting value.

Success in today's fast-paced and turbulent world belongs to those who can iterate faster, smarter, and with greater purpose. Short-term discipline creates long-term advantage. Synchros are the cornerstone of this advantage by fostering a culture of achievement, seamless execution, collective learning, and continuous, uncomfortable improvement.

Winning is about more than just achieving goals; it's about creating a way of working where impact becomes inevitable, learning becomes instinctive, and progress becomes unstoppable. It's about transforming organizations into ecosystems of teams with brutal focus, extreme ownership, fearless execution, and continuous iteration. Teams that embrace this mindset don't just adapt to change—they shape it as well. Weekly wins compound into market dominance. They don't wait for perfect conditions—they create impact with the tools and knowledge they have today, knowing that each step forward sharpens their edge for tomorrow.

In a world that rewards speed, clarity, and courage, the ultimate victory belongs to those who dare to move fast, learn faster, and act with purpose. One week of focused learning through execution eclipses months of planning.

The difference between doing something and making an impact is everything. Playing is not the goal; winning is. Working is never the goal; impact is. Teams that win don't just aim to participate—they also commit to win. Because when you focus on impact over activity, iteration over perfection, and outcomes over excuses, you're not merely playing the game. You're defining it—and winning it.

The brilliance of this truth is deeply moving and transformative: Success isn't achieved by simply outthinking the competition; it belongs to those who consistently outexecute them with an unrelenting hunger to win.

The pursuit of impact over activity fundamentally reshapes how organizations build lasting value. While BIG choices drive immediate focus, the real transformation happens as teams master the art of balancing urgent execution and continuous iteration with strategic foresight. Each cycle of learning and adaptation strengthens the organization's capacity to detect emerging opportunities, navigate complexity, and build sustainable competitive moats.

Playing is not the goal; winning is. Working is never the goal; impact is.

JONATHAN ESCOBAR MARIN

JONATHAN ESCOBAR MARIN

SHORT-TERM DISCIPLINE CREATES LONG-TERM ADVANTAGE.

Success isn't achieved by simply outthinking the competition; it belongs to those who consistently outexecute them with an unrelenting hunger to win.

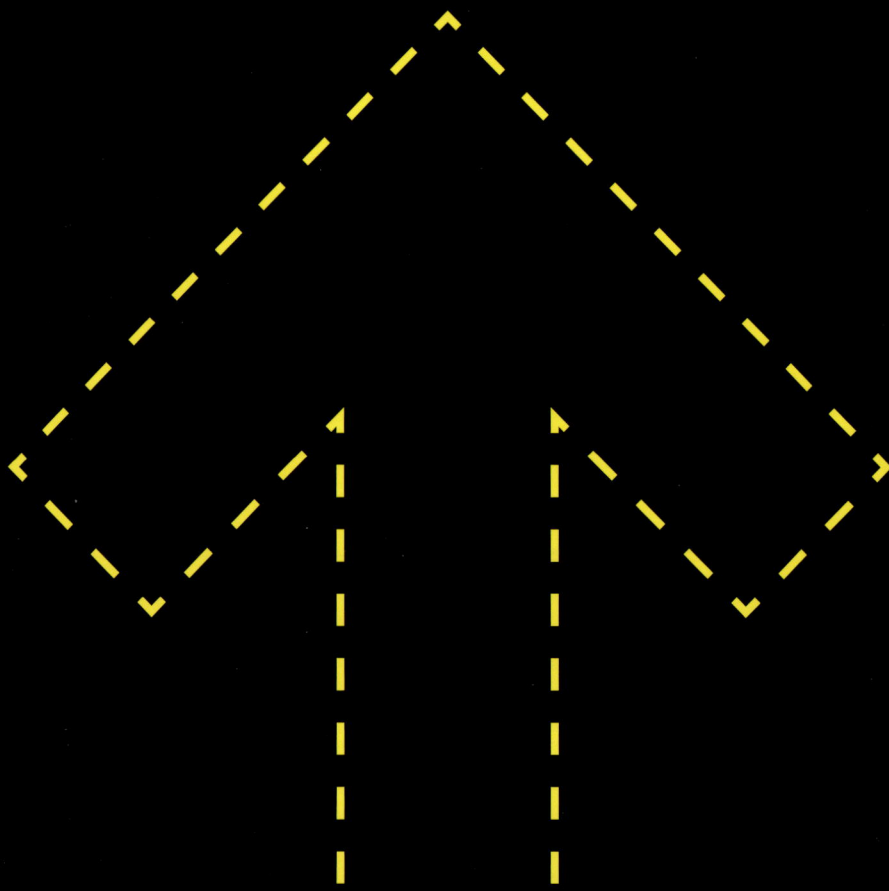

What Is Needed

Answer these questions to beat tomorrow—or watch others lead while you lag. Every honest response separates those who drive the future from those who will chase it.

- ↗ What percentage of your leaders' time is spent reporting on the past versus piloting the future?
- ↗ How much of your organization's activity directly drives market impact?
- ↗ What's the real cost of your bureaucracy in lost market opportunities?
- ↗ Is your organization prepared to make swift decisions with calculated risks rather than seeking perfect information and excuses?
- ↗ How many critical decisions are stalled in your organization right now?
- ↗ Are problems surfaced and solved in hours, or hidden until they become crises?
- ↗ What percentage of your meetings drive measurable outcomes versus sharing updates?
- ↗ Are you ready to stop celebrating narratives and PowerPoint's promises and start rewarding tangible, measurable outcomes?
- ↗ How quickly does your organization translate customer insights into market action?
- ↗ Can your leadership embrace radical transparency to accelerate decision-making and execution?

EVOLUTION BEATS STAGNATION. F

BEATS IRREGULARITY. DISCIPLINE B

PERMANENCE. CADENCE BEATS RAND

HARMONY BEATS DISCORD. PATTE

CONFUSION. PROACTIVITY BEATS REAC

SIMULTANEITY BEATS LINEARITY.

CONTINUITY BEATS INTERRUPTION.

STRATEGY. SYSTEMIC BEATS SPOR

ARRANGEMENT BEATS HAPHAZARD. EC

POLITICS. ORCHESTRATION BEATS D

COORDINATION BEATS DISSONANCE.

CONSTANCY BEATS VOLATILITY.

STRUCTURE BEATS ARBITRARINES

HM BEATS CHAOS. CONSISTENCY

S IMPULSE. METAMORPHOSIS BEATS

ESS. STABILITY BEATS FLUCTUATION

BEATS DISORDER. ORDER BEATS

TY. SEQUENCE BEATS IMPROVISATION

NTICIPATION BEATS ADAPTATION

W BEATS BATCHING. CULTURE BEATS

C. FORMATION BEATS SCATTERED

Y BEATS PRIVILEGE. FAIRNESS BEATS

RRAY. SYMMETRY BEATS IMBALANCE

NCHRONIZATION BEATS DEPLOYMENT

RSISTENCE BEATS INTERMITTENCE

EXCELLENCE BEATS MEDIOCRITY

CHAPTER 4

A DISCIPLINED DRUMBEAT

THE DRUMBEAT IN BUSINESS IS AS VITAL AS BREATHING IN LIFE.

The drumbeat keeps all other drivers in sync, shaping the company beat—its rhythm of focus, leadership, impact, and evolution. It bridges your long-term aspirations, ambitions, and purpose with the discipline to evolve, learning from seamless execution and the FATE (fragmentation, ambiguity, turbulence, and entropy) of the world we lead to beat. When that company rhythm beats with the greater rhythm of change—or, better yet, drives it forward—it will sing your success.

Culture isn't what you say; it's the beat created by what you repeatedly do through the drumbeat. The drumbeat is not simply one of the drivers; it systematically shapes culture by powering, harmonizing, and propelling all other drivers: the brutal focus, the leadership multiplication, the obsession with impact, and the force to learn and evolve as a habit. It connects your organizational purpose to the discipline of empowering more and more people to lead and grow. It's the mechanism that turns business and cultural aspirations into collective realities. And yet, it requires something far more fundamental than intelligence or innovation; it demands discipline. As a quote attributed to Warren Buffett reminds us, "We don't have to be smarter than the rest. We have to be more disciplined than the rest."

The drumbeat is the vital force driving your business and culture—when it beats strong and steady, transformation becomes inevitable and impact becomes unstoppable. The drumbeat is not simply a governance for cross-company collaboration and execution. In an environment where entropy constantly erodes competitive advantages and organizational capabilities, it is the operating rhythm that serves as your defense against decay—a predictable, consistent cycle that ensures everyone and everything evolves and transforms in sync. The drumbeat serves as the foundation for prioritizing, communicating, staffing, executing, aligning, and evolving as we learn. The wisdom here is profound: Discipline turns intention into impact.

While driving renewal through its own disciplined cadence, the drumbeat interacts with the other three drivers like the instruments of an orchestra, propelling them forward on rhythm, connecting the conversations between top leaders, team leaders, and team members, creating a symphony of impact. A drumbeat that is disciplined creates life-giving consistency. This stability creates the agility needed to unleash creativity and deliver results in between cycles, as teams are freed from uncertainty about when things will happen, who will

JONATHAN ESCOBAR MARIN

The drumbeat serves as the foundation for prioritizing, communicating, staffing, executing, aligning, and evolving as we learn.

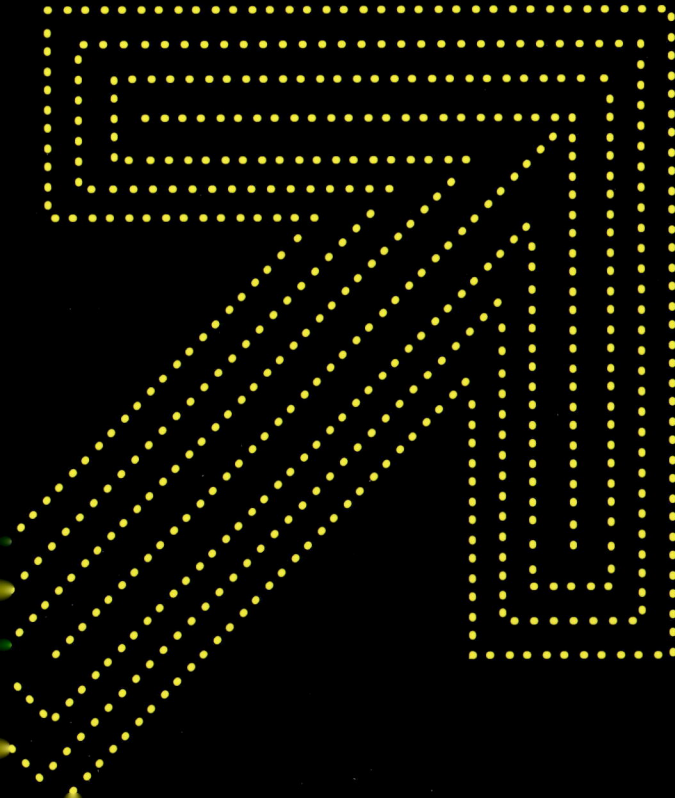

be there, and what is expected. It must be steady enough to anchor your organizational habits, but flexible enough to shift tempo when the rhythm of change demands it. Conducted by your leadership, the drumbeat is an unwavering pattern driving execution and evolution—a persistent rhythm that propels your talent, business, and cultural systems forward, to shape tomorrow.

Again, discipline is the defining factor here. As the saying goes, "Discipline is choosing between what you want now and what you want most." The drumbeat must not change on a whim but only when the speed of evolution demands it and when there is commitment across your organization to change it, all in, without individual agendas, as one team. This ensures that the entire company moves as one, avoiding fragmented rhythms that lead to misalignment. It is this discipline that transforms the drumbeat from mere repetition into a force that inspires, aligns, and drives progress.

Leadership is the conductor of this rhythm. The drumbeat depends on leaders who can set a cadence of accountability and focus, ensuring the organization moves forward in concert. Don't confuse the drumbeat with old-school command and control. It's not about micromanagement. It's about creating the cultural rhythm that enables autonomy within alignment. The drumbeat provides the framework within which teams can operate with freedom and creativity. The drumbeat clarifies not only when things happen, but also the standards by which they happen: what inputs to bring, what outputs to expect, who will be there, and their roles. It is not imposed from the top; it is felt across every level, from teams to executives. Without discipline, the drumbeat becomes erratic, and without rhythm, even the most talented teams fall out of sync.

CONSTANTLY EVOLVING THROUGH THE DRUMBEAT

Any song can last only so long before you have to start another or at least change up the key. But evolution isn't about abandoning your drumbeat; it's about making it stronger, clearer, and more compelling

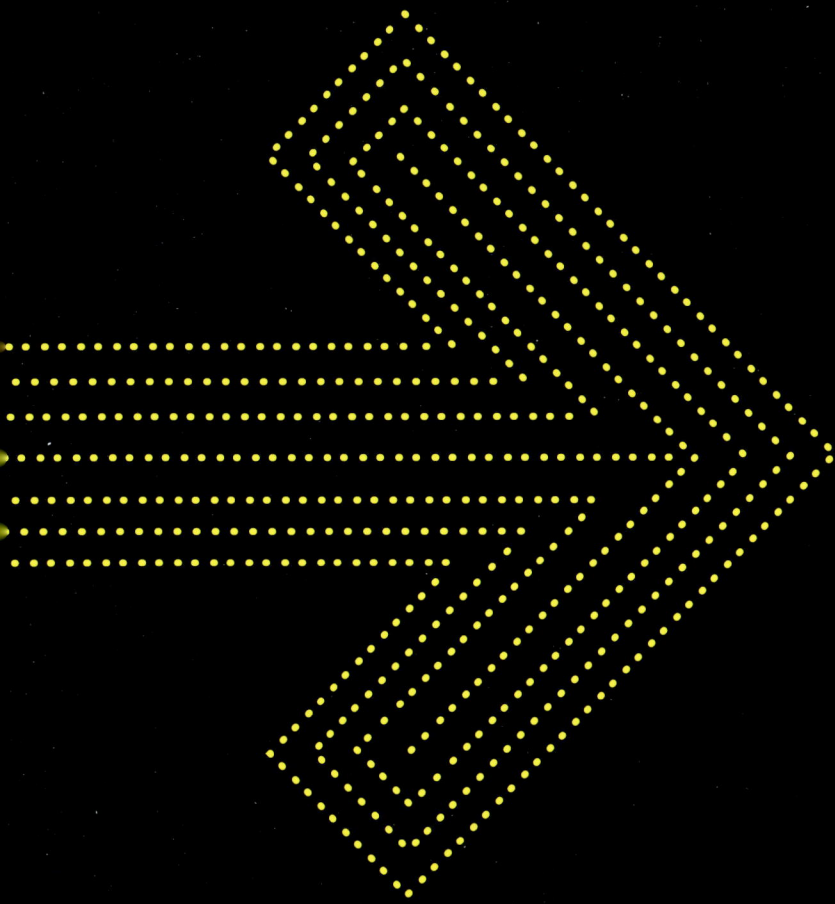

JONATHAN ESCOBAR MARIN

The stability of a disciplined drumbeat creates the agility needed to unleash creativity and deliver results in between cycles, as teams are freed from uncertainty about when things will happen, who will be there, and what is expected.

EVOLUTION ISN'T OPTIONAL; IT'S EITHER YOUR CHOICE OR YOUR FATE.

with each cycle. In organizational terms, this means periodically challenging and refining the missions on the Wall, the sacrifices that must be made on the Stop Wall, the talent required to deliver them, the mechanisms empowering distributed leadership, and the way we lead by service to enable the seamless execution that drives real impact—not just movement.

The drumbeat is the bridge between the courage to dream big and the discipline to learn, evolve, and deliver. Evolution isn't optional; it's either your choice or your fate. In the most demanding business environments—and especially in today's world defined by the fate of FATE—organizations must embrace both the constancy of their drumbeat and the adaptability to shift keys when the moment demands it. You cannot thrive with your customers or outpace your competitors without an operating rhythm that ensures consistent execution and continuous evolution, through collective intelligence and learning.

When you sync long-term aspirations with disciplined evolution, the drumbeat powers the organization's beat, ensuring it doesn't just adapt but continuously evolves as well—amplifying impact and empowering its people to lead and grow. The need for consistency must be paired with the humility to throw away your plans and challenge them all again. Seasoned leaders I've worked with have been caught off guard by unexpected market changes, making it even more critical to maintain a brutal focus on the essential.

Each cycle of iteration and evaluation, with the insights gained from this periodic reflection, drives the company to become more focused, faster, stronger, leaner, and better. This isn't just a slogan or catchphrase; it's also an ethos that defines leadership and strategy execution. At least every quarter, throw away your plans and challenge them all again.

The drumbeat isn't about playing catch-up; it drives the company's beat forward and leads the charge. It prompts organizations to continually evolve their strategies and missions to maintain competitiveness amid rapid change by being present in the places where work is done and decisions are made.

JONATHAN ESCOBAR MARIN

You cannot thrive with your customers or outpace your competitors without an operating rhythm that ensures consistent execution and continuous evolution.

For this reason, the drumbeat transcends being just a mechanism; it embodies an ethos enabling your company to learn fast through consistent feedback loops and stay one step ahead in the permanently unpredictable business landscape. The discipline to maintain this rhythm becomes a strategic advantage that grows stronger with each cycle over the years.

The *Gemba*

The necessary evolutions through the organizational rhythm can only be determined through firsthand observation and engagement at the *gemba*—the place where real work happens, where value is created or delivered, and where customers' expectations are either met or missed. The *gemba* is not just a location; it is also a way of thinking and leading, rooted in direct observation and engagement with the facts of the work itself.

As discussed earlier, Taiichi Ohno emphasized the power of the *gemba*. After decades of working with organizations across diverse cultures and continents—from tech giants to traditional brick-and-mortar businesses, from American to European, African or Asian cultures, from entrepreneurial cultures to highly bureaucratic ones—I've seen this truth reinforced time and again: The deepest wisdom lies not in remote analysis, but in the rich tapestry of daily work life, where real people tackle real challenges and create real value. True understanding and transformative insights emerge when we immerse ourselves in the heart of where work happens and where value is appreciated or not by customers, engaging directly with them, witnessing their challenges, triumphs, and disappointments, and learning from their lived experiences.

In other words, to truly learn, you need data, facts, eyes, hearts, and brains—not in mass, but only what is needed of each. Too much data detached from facts creates noise; facts without data can create blind spots or misperception. The eyes are needed to observe what is real and undeniable. The heart is essential to empathize with the people, teams, and customers involved. The brain is critical to analyze, reflect, and synthesize the insights.

When data and facts are augmented through this human lens of observation, empathy, context, and reflection, they transform into actionable insights that drive meaningful change.

This is why the drumbeat thrives on leaders who go and see (not to be seen; please don't confuse it with management by walking around) the execution in front of their customers, who reward them with observations and feedback but also with the subtle insights revealed through customers' interactions with the product or service. These interactions often illuminate unmet needs, including those desires that remain unspoken or unexpressed.

At the *gemba*, you experience the true beat of your customers and your organization—not through presentations, but by witnessing it firsthand. The knowledge, insights, conversations, and collective understanding built through visits to the *gemba* and during weekly synchros fuel the exercise of refining the Wall and the Stop Wall.

Keep, Improve, Start, and Stop

As leaders delve into the refinement of the Wall and the Stop Wall, their mindset is "faster, stronger, leaner, better." This resonates perfectly with the cultural beat of the best companies in the world, which are driven by leaders who go and see and learn from the actual work being done, ensuring the organization is obsessed with the brutally important and cutting out the crap when and where necessary.

The leadership team must determine what to keep doing as they are doing it; what is worth doubling down on? For those items that might not be kept as they are, can they be improved so that the team can keep doing it but in a better way? What bets did they discover in the previous cycle that are necessary to begin now? What must they stop doing because they have learned that the investment doesn't pay off in the short, medium, or long term?

JONATHAN ESCOBAR MARIN

AT LEAST EVERY QUARTER, THROW AWAY YOUR PLANS AND CHALLENGE THEM ALL AGAIN.

JONATHAN ESCOBAR MARIN

To truly learn, you need data, facts, eyes, hearts, and brains—not in mass, but only what is needed of each.

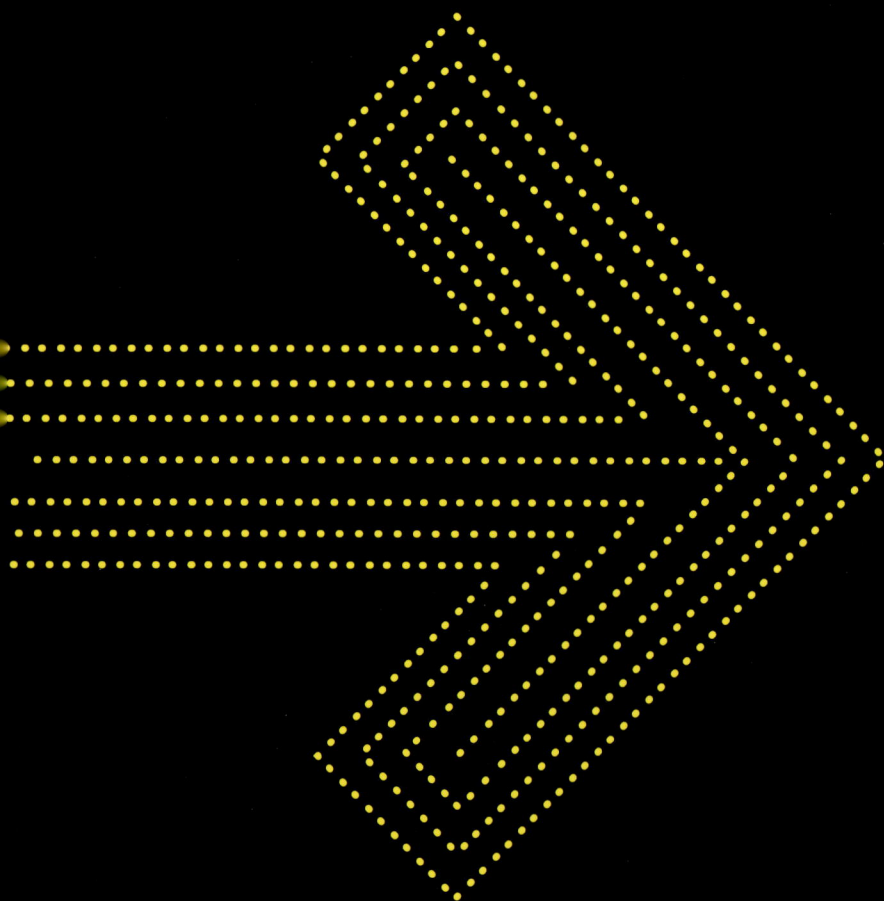

In my experience, this self-reflection is equally important when you are in trouble and need a turnaround as when you are winning and must fight against complacency. This fight against complacency is a challenge that even the best-performing organizations face. As Satya Nadella, the CEO of Microsoft, once said, "It is natural that, when you're doing so well, the culture feels like, 'Yeah, [we] know it all.'"[1] This statement captures a critical truth: No matter how successful you are, ongoing growth and learning are essential to avoid the dangerous trap of believing you've figured it all out.

Even the most successful organizations must ensure they never settle into the mindset of "knowing it all." The drumbeat enables this by creating a mindset that promotes humility, learning, and action. The drumbeat is collective coherence, consistency, and honesty in motion.

Refining the Wall

The heart of our strategy execution, the Wall, now becomes the center of our attention once again. A peacetime Wall doesn't serve its purpose in wartime. When market conditions change dramatically, impact metrics and priorities must shift accordingly. This is why, in regular cycles, top leaders gather as one team to review each element on the Wall, applying the principles of Keep, Improve, Start, and Stop to ensure alignment with our evolving reality:

- North Star metrics: Are these still the right indicators of our strategic direction? Have we discovered more precise or relevant metrics to guide us?

- Missions: Which goals have we achieved? Which need adjustment? What new objectives have emerged from our learnings? And which should we stop because they no longer deliver value?

- Team leaders, members, and guides: Has our experience revealed the need for changes in leadership, membership, or guidance for specific missions?

- Timeboxes: Do we need to adjust our timelines based on our progress and new insights?

This isn't a mere check-in; it's a rigorous examination of the strategy in action. We celebrate our successes, learn from our challenges, and refine our focus based on real-world outcomes. Wall refinement becomes even more critical as entropy accelerates the decay of strategies and capabilities. What worked last quarter may already be obsolete, making continuous evaluation and adjustment essential.

The drumbeat ensures that the Wall is more than a unique source of truth; it is a living connection between long-term strategic ambitions, immediate priorities, and the discipline to evolve through the learning from every step.

Renewing the Stop Wall

Equally important is our review of the sacrifices on the other side of the Wall, the Stop Wall, with the things you have chosen not to do. We ask ourselves three killer questions:

1. Which items have we successfully stopped pursuing? Can they be removed from the Stop Wall?

2. Are there initiatives we decided to stop but that have crept back in? Why, and how do we address this?

3. What new items we have decided not to pursue should be added to the Stop Wall?

Start less. Impact more. Remember, the Stop Wall is not just a list; it's also a commitment to maintaining our brutal focus to push impact by continuously cutting the crap.

As we complete the cycle, we return to where we began—now equipped with new insights, achievements, and a sharper focus gained through a strong iteration process, active presence at the *gemba*, and continuous proximity to our teams through the weekly synchros.

JONATHAN ESCOBAR MARIN

THE DRUMBEAT IS COLLECTIVE COHERENCE, CONSISTENCY, AND HONESTY IN MOTION.

Start Less.
Impact More.

JONATHAN ESCOBAR MARIN

Simultaneity + Transparency = Synchronized Evolution

As we renew the Wall and the Stop Wall, we ensure that these changes are owned deeply across the entire organization simultaneously. This isn't about cascading information down through levels of management; it's about having a profound and solid comprehension of our strategy as one unified team.

Business-wise, this ends up in an increased accountability for the brutal focus needed in the next cycle or cycles, never spending time defending the past, regardless if it worked or not. Successful organizations are continuously looking into the future; they do not defend the past. The most powerful organizations aren't built on past trophies, but on the courage to throw them away to start over again as if it were day one. This is how they constantly shape tomorrow.

To operationalize this forward-looking mindset and this seamless construction of the future, we build on the powerful synergy of simultaneity and transparency.

Starting with simultaneity, this requires aligning brands, categories, functions, markets, and talent in a cohesive manner. In other words, bringing the right people from each area together in the same place, at the same time builds the right symphony of innovation. This underscores the importance of moving in unison to cultivate dissent, seek diverse perspectives, and listen attentively to make well-informed decisions. It operationalizes during Wall refinement sessions where the top leaders from diverse business areas leading a P&L come together to

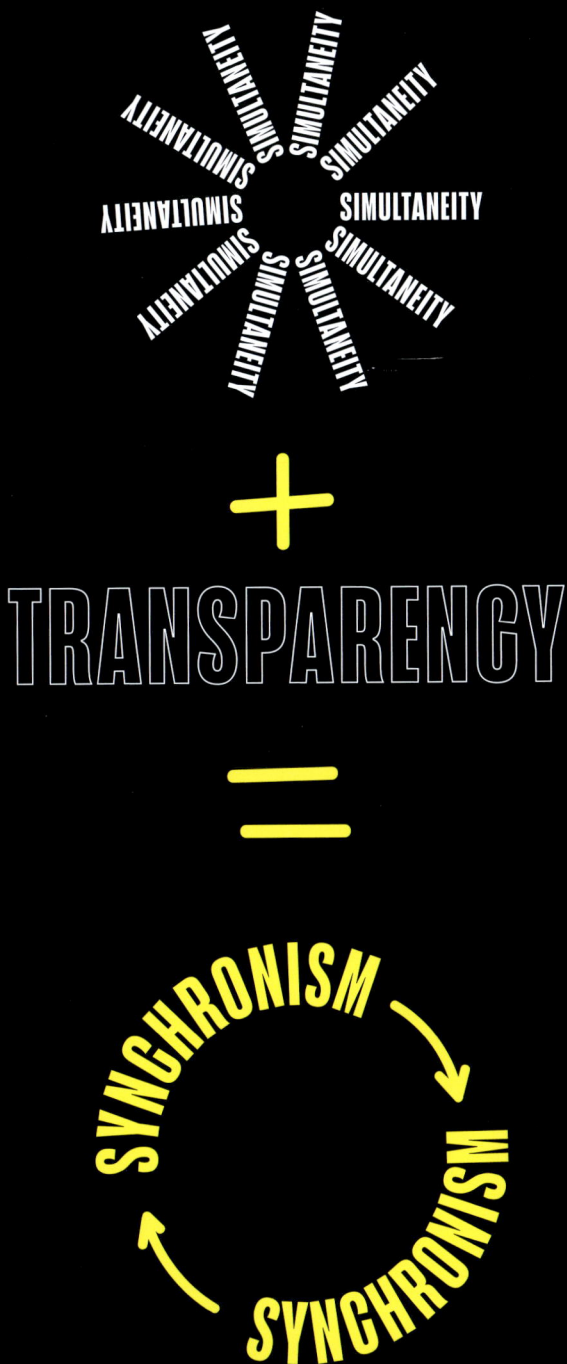

Image 4.1: Simultaneity plus transparency equals synchronism, enabling learning, alignment, and focus. © 2025, Jonathan Escobar Marin

build the common Wall for the next quarter, actively farming for dissent. This rigorous process ensures that everyone works diligently to reflect, evaluate, and rethink shared goals and objectives, aka missions on the Wall, thereby eliminating silos and fostering a culture of collaboration. When knowledge is synchronized across the organization, a robust collective vision emerges, one that is comprehended and embraced by all.

Furthermore, once a decision is made about any change on the Wall for the next quarter, everyone, including those who advocated for different approaches, adheres to the principle of "disagree and commit." This ensures that the outcome is as successful as possible, as dissent has happened, a decision has been made, and with it everyone feels the commitment of the leadership team from the outset to the conclusion.

Once the simultaneous alignment produces a brutally focused Wall, every member of a musical ensemble must be able to hear the rhythm and play within it.

Transparency, like simultaneity, lies at the heart of the drumbeat; it prevents redundancy, ambiguity, and uninformed decision-making. The Wall becomes the single source of truth for the entire organization, integrating brands, categories, functions, markets, and talent to follow the same song sheet.

This clarity in decisions and focus for the upcoming quarter leaves no room for ambiguity or miscommunication. Transparency goes beyond merely sharing information; it encompasses the commitments made by the organization without gray areas, without duplications, without hidden agendas. Everyone knows precisely what the goals are, what is expected of them, and why these goals are crucial. This lucidity eliminates political strife and misunderstandings, ensuring that all parties are aligned toward a common objective.

By making everything transparent—from strategic missions to team contributions—organizations create an environment where everyone is aware of their role in the bigger picture. Transparency isn't just about sharing information; it's also the active empowerment of distributed leadership, ensuring that every person understands their contribution to

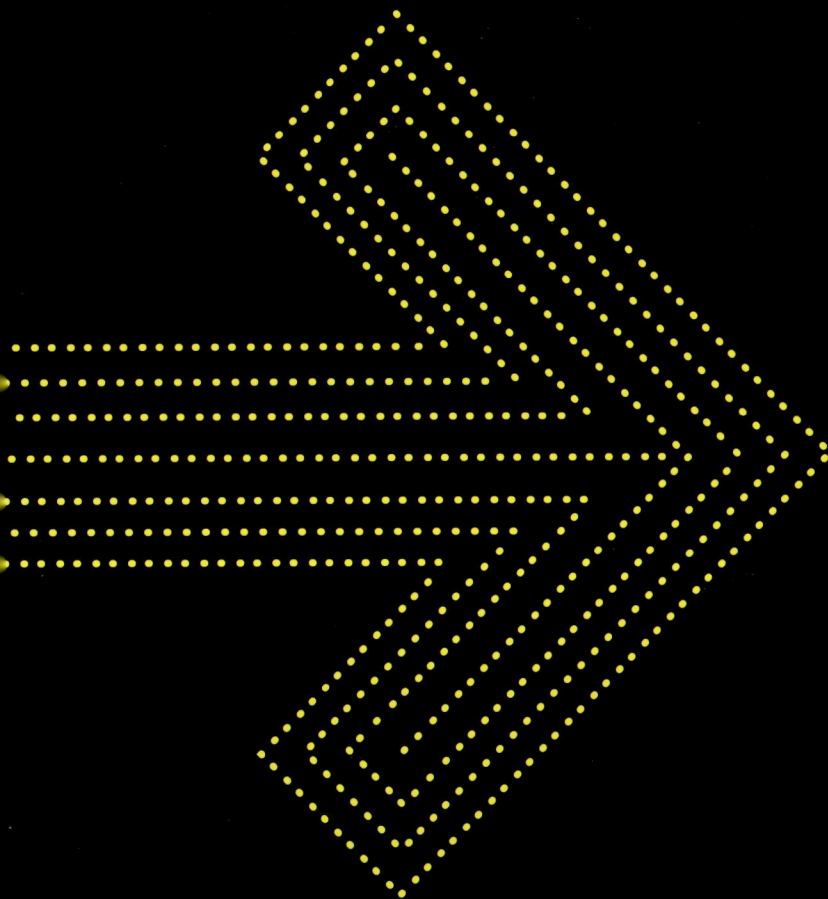

JONATHAN ESCOBAR MARIN

The most powerful organizations aren't built on past trophies, but on the courage to throw them away to start over again as if it were day one. This is how they constantly shape tomorrow.

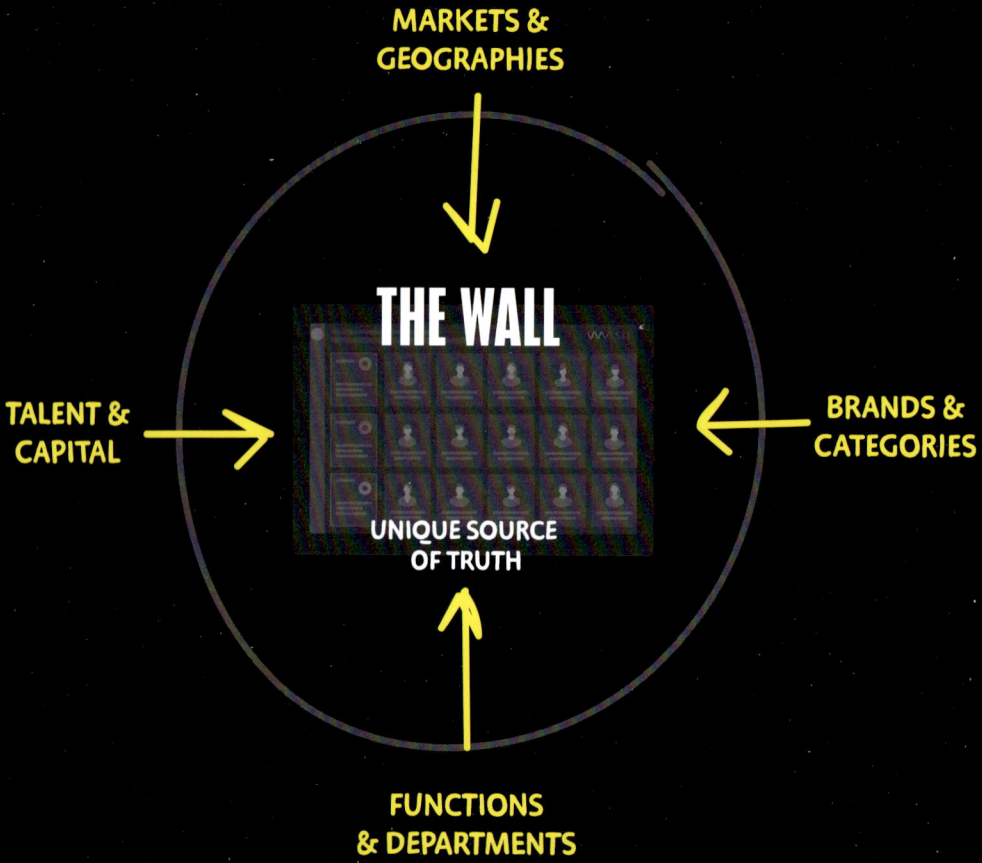

Image 4.2: The Wall unites all—right people, same place and time, all-in without privileges. © 2025, Jonathan Escobar Marin

the overall purpose. This shared understanding promotes accountability and drives collective progress. No one can claim ignorance of the goals because everything is laid bare for all to see, fostering a culture of trust and mutual respect.

Transparency also plays a vital role in empowering distributed leadership in avoiding duplications and gray areas. When all information is openly accessible, it becomes easier to identify and eliminate redundant efforts, ensuring that resources are utilized efficiently and the right people are at the right place at the right time. Gray areas, which often lead to confusion and inefficiency, are illuminated, allowing everyone to operate with a clear understanding of their responsibilities and the organization's direction. This level of transparency ensures that no effort is wasted and that everyone is working toward the same clearly defined objectives, minimizing the risk of overlapping initiatives and uninformed decision-making. This alignment and clarity empower our organizations to turn uncertainty into their greatest advantage, achieving bold goals and driving transformative growth.

Transparency and simultaneity ensure organizations operate without gray areas, duplications, redundancies, overlaps, individual agendas, unknown bottlenecks, hidden problems, wasted time, misinterpretations, confusion, or political games. In other words, transparency kills confusion, and simultaneity kills politics. The truth is that when the brutally important is built simultaneously by all, there's no space to hide, distort, or delay.

THE DRUMBEAT SHAPES CULTURE WITH EVERY BEAT

Culture isn't just about values and sloganized statements; it's also actual behaviors demonstrated through real business practices and rituals, ones that the drumbeat establishes with blunt pragmatism where no one can hide. This is why the drumbeat is not merely a business evolution cadence; it is the power that actively counters organizational inconsistency and entropy. It enables actual behaviors to be demonstrated, not just shown in flashy presentations. The drumbeat is the force that propels the culture's beat, ensuring every system, capability, and individual aligns with the company's North Star metrics and key missions. It creates a feedback-driven culture where continuous improvement is embedded into the fabric of the organizational culture, not as an aspiration but as a way of operating. This rhythm drives a seamless connection between strategy, execution, talent, and culture, ensuring every quarter builds on the learnings of the last while creating the vision of the future.

As market positions decay and capabilities become outdated, cultural evolution is not a luxury but a necessity. Culture becomes either your greatest defense against entropy or its greatest enabler. At its core, the drumbeat fuels a cross-company, cross-silo, cross-hierarchy learning loop to make culture the most powerful organizational force.

High-performing, high-impact cultures emerge from authentic values, consistently demonstrated in how you prioritize (or fail to), how you empower distributed leadership (or restrict it), how you accelerate impact (or impede it), and how you enable learning and evolving as habits (or resist them). The only way to create such a strong culture is to empower everyone to live and demonstrate it daily. The drumbeat strengthens the cultural beat by embedding it into every practice, ritual, and system.

This cultural reinforcement isn't wishful thinking; it's the direct outcome of the drumbeat's systematic transformation. This process is not reactive but intentional—grounded in the disciplined rhythm of review, iteration, and renewal. A high-performing, high-impact culture makes the right thing the easy thing to do. Greatness should always be the path of least resistance for every single member of the organization. This mindset forces leaders to consistently evaluate what must be improved, refined, or reimagined across the organization's management systems. It's how organizations ensure that their culture remains hungry to evolve.

In order to operationalize this cultural evolution, leaders must brutally prioritize: among their management systems, capability-building

JONATHAN ESCOBAR MARIN

Transparency kills confusion, and simultaneity kills politics. When the brutally important is built simultaneously by all, there's no space to hide, distort, or delay.

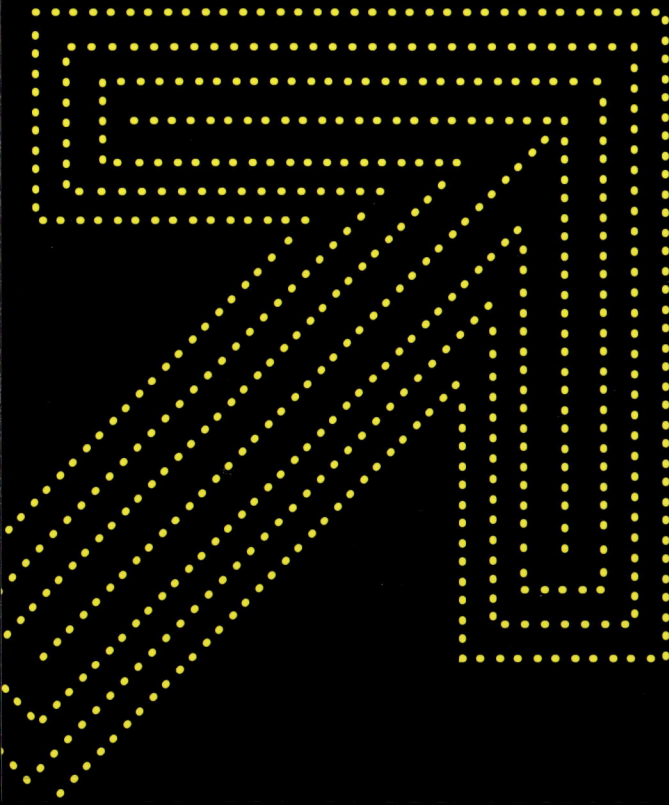

programs for leadership development, individual performance management, onboarding, succession planning, capacity planning—to name a few. The real challenge lies in identifying which systems require disproportionate attention and innovation to drive focus, multiply leadership impact, and amplify the hunger to win. This is where the drumbeat becomes essential to evolve the culture.

These systems must be transformed into enablers of focus, speed, agility, and impact. The drumbeat ensures that these systems are continuously refined to propel the organization forward, aligning every rhythm of cultural evolution with the vital objectives of the business we lead.

While every organization must define its own systems, in over two decades of practice, five areas consistently emerge as the most impactful to iterate and improve. These systems—carefully refined and relentlessly executed—become the foundation for building the capability infrastructure that keeps the culture not only alive, but also evolving through the drumbeat: stronger, sharper, and more aligned with every cycle.

Leadership Development

The most important investment you can make is in leaders who can make everyone around them better. Companies grow through great leaders and die because of poor ones. It is crucial to cultivate leaders who understand that their work is not to create PowerPoint slides and give pep talks, but to build an organization where new leaders arise—leaders who can drive the teams toward achieving the company's brutal focus areas.

The drumbeat revolutionizes leadership development by creating a dynamic system where leaders emerge through impact, not through programs. It ensures that leadership isn't just concentrated at the top—it's also distributed, multiplied, and embedded across the organization, creating an ecosystem where everyone grows by delivering impact and learning from execution.

The most important investment you can make is in leaders who can make everyone around them better. Companies grow through great leaders and die because of poor ones.

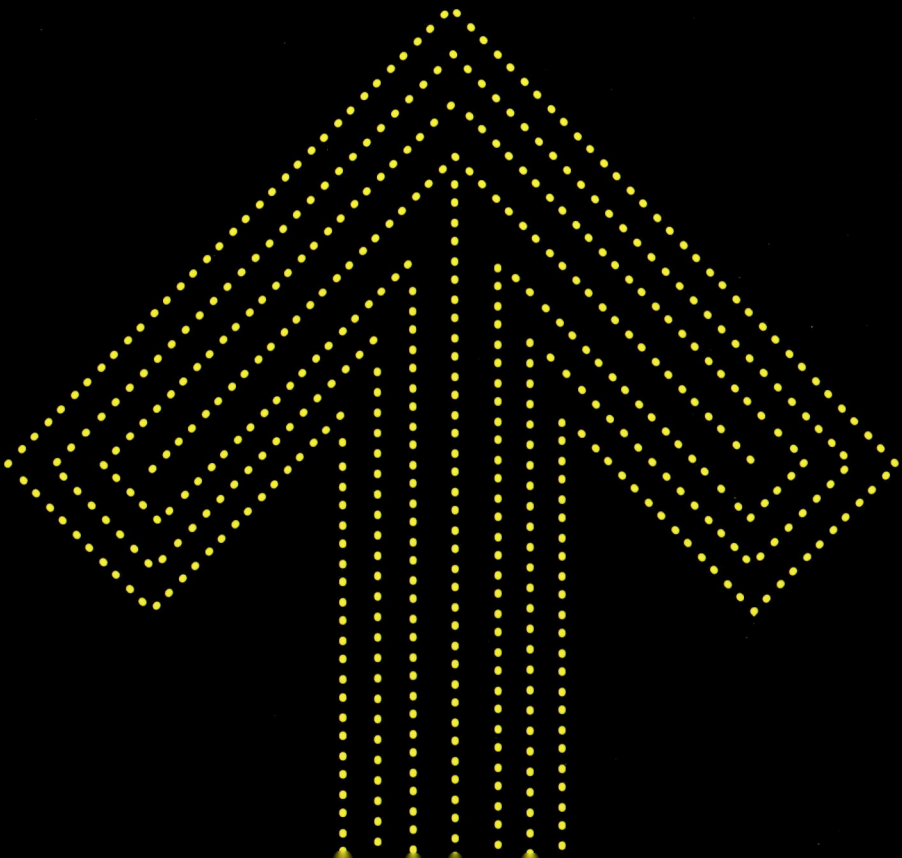

This system operates on three critical dimensions:

1. **Real-Time Impact Validation:** Weekly synchros provide immediate feedback on a leader's ability to drive outcomes and empower teams.

2. **Strategic Thinking Development:** Quarterly Wall refinements test and strengthen leaders' ability to make brutal choices under pressure.

3. **Cross-Boundary Excellence:** Leading cross-functional missions develops the ability to orchestrate complex transformations.

The system demands leaders who are not only executors, but also system thinkers—capable of connecting strategy, operations, and culture while navigating ambiguity with confidence. Traditional leadership programs are replaced by immersive challenges where leaders must deliver measurable impact through others.

Development metrics shift from completion of training modules to tangible outcomes: How many new leaders have emerged? How effectively do they deliver on critical missions? How successfully do they multiply leadership in others? This creates what we call *the leadership drumbeat*—a rhythm of talent capable of making brutal choices, driving cross-functional execution, delivering transformative impact, and evolving at the pace that markets require.

This leadership drumbeat inherently surfaces hidden talent by giving everyone equal opportunity to lead missions, breaking traditional development biases. When someone demonstrates exceptional mission delivery and team self-organization capabilities, they earn the right to lead increasingly complex missions—creating a meritocratic leadership pipeline driven by proven impact rather than tenure or politics.

Leadership development becomes a powerful rhythm—one that scales across silos and ensures that the organization is constantly creating leaders who align with its evolving North Star metrics.

Performance Management

Make sure that performance is managed by establishing individual development systems that measure what truly matters and really help individuals to grow, in a culture of focus, ownership, fast execution, an obsession with impact, and continuous evolution.

The Wall and weekly synchros create a revolutionary performance management system that eliminates subjectivity and delayed feedback. Performance becomes immediately visible through three dimensions:

1. Mission impact: clear accountability for delivering specific outcomes within timeboxes

2. Leadership multiplication: ability to thrive in high-impact cross-functional teams

3. Learning velocity: speed and effectiveness in evolving execution based on results

This system rewards "pilots" over "reporters"—those who proactively drive outcomes rather than document activities. Performance conversations shift from annual reviews to continuous outcome-focused dialogues that build capabilities in real time.

The system must be deeply personal while maintaining brutal objectivity. Leaders need to understand what drives high performance while creating systems that reward autonomy, mastery, and purpose—the psychological drivers of motivation that we learned with Daniel Pink's insights.[2] When individuals see direct links between their work and strategic missions, they naturally align with what we call *unambiguous ownership*—where performance expectations and measurement are crystal clear.

This clarity eliminates political maneuvering and focuses energy on actual value creation. The drumbeat ensures performance management becomes a forward-looking exercise focused on future impact rather than past activities.

Sales and Operations Planning

Integrating sales and operations planning (S&OP) is indispensable in ensuring that supply chain and production capabilities are perfectly aligned with the missions on the Wall that will accelerate growth and transform the supply systems. This seamless integration prevents the common disconnect between business ambition and operational capability by ensuring both sides co-create achievable missions and maintain continuous dialogue through weekly synchros.

S&OP is where brutal focus is synchronized with delivery capacity. It is the system that ensures the organization's supply chain, production capabilities, market demands, and ambitions on the Wall remain in harmony, even as external conditions shift with increasing speed and unpredictability. In a world where turbulence is the norm, S&OP serves as the critical calibrator between the ambitions we set on the Wall and the impeccable service we must maintain while fulfilling those ambitions—especially those that significantly alter our supply processes. Teams in the S&OP cycles develop what we call *operational brain with strategic heart*—where daily decisions about capacity, inventory, and resource allocation directly support strategic priorities rather than just functional efficiency, eliminating the traditional gap between strategic intent and operational execution.

The drumbeat elevates S&OP from a functional planning process to a strategic enabler. It transforms S&OP into a living, dynamic system that responds to disruptions and aligns seamlessly with the organization's most critical missions—those brutally focused and visible on the Wall. S&OP also becomes a key driver of agility. By anchoring operational decisions in the rhythm of the drumbeat, organizations can pivot quickly when disruptions arise—whether from supply chain constraints, demand surges, or geopolitical shifts. This ensures that operations are not only reactive, but also proactive, maintaining consistent alignment with the company's missions on the Wall.

In this system, decisions are no longer made in silos with fragmented data or competing priorities. Instead, S&OP unites every product and service supply stakeholder with the rhythm of the business, enabling rapid adjustments, cross-functional collaboration, and real-time responses to both transformative missions and external market demands or disruptions.

Onboarding

Streamlining the onboarding process ensures that new hires are immediately immersed in and energized by the company's cultural rhythm and the drivers from day one: the strategic choices, the boundary-spanning empowerment, the execution mindset, and the winning DNA that make impact and learning an unrelenting drive.

Onboarding is not a formality; it is the foundation for raising the next generation of leaders. The drumbeat transforms onboarding from an HR process into an impact accelerator through the following:

1. Immediate mission integration—new hires join cross-functional teams within their first week

2. Real-time learning through weekly synchros and direct exposure to strategic execution

3. Clear ownership of specific outcomes that contribute to broader missions

4. Active mentorship from guides who help navigate organizational dynamics

This approach eliminates the traditional "observation period" and immediately embeds new talent into the organization's rhythm of execution and learning.

From day one, new employees are immersed in the Wall and Stop Wall, understanding how their role directly contributes to strategic priorities. This requires more than orientation; it demands active engagement through real-world scenarios that demonstrate principles in action. Leaders guide new hires through mission execution and synchros, instilling a culture of impact over activity.

The process includes rigorous feedback loops at thirty, sixty, and ninety days to evaluate whether new hires are demonstrating the hunger to win and delivering initial outcomes. Onboarding becomes about integrating individuals into a high-performance ecosystem rather than filling seats.

Succession Planning

Succession requires proactively identifying and developing future leaders who can advance the company's focus on its critical strategic choices and its culture. Succession planning is about more than filling roles; it is about ensuring the organization's leadership pipeline is always ready to meet the challenges of tomorrow. The drumbeat reinvents succession planning by creating the following:

1. Real-time leadership auditions: through mission ownership and delivery

2. Cross-functional capabilities: through team leadership roles

3. Strategic thinking: through Wall refinement participation

4. Change management skills: through continuous iteration cycles

This dynamic approach replaces traditional succession planning's focus on theoretical potential with proven impact delivery. It surfaces unexpected successors who demonstrate exceptional execution capabilities rather than just strong presentation skills or political acumen.

The system identifies not only high performers, but also high-potential disruptors—individuals who challenge the status quo and demonstrate hunger to lead transformative missions. Key questions emerge: Who has delivered exceptional results on the Wall? Who shows resilience in ambiguity? Who consistently takes ownership of outcomes?

The weekly synchros and quarterly Wall renewal provide top leaders with constant visibility into who can truly drive results. This ensures succession decisions are based on demonstrated impact rather than projected potential. During Wall refinement sessions, leaders evaluate not only mission progress, but also the readiness of emerging leaders to take on bigger challenges.

Building this readiness requires exposing potential successors to cross-functional missions where they gain experience navigating complexity. The result is a leadership pipeline that evolves in lockstep with strategy, ensuring transitions are seamless and aligned with long-term objectives that shape tomorrow.

Succession planning must also address future readiness. Leaders should be rotated across missions that expose them to emerging challenges—such as leading digital transformation or navigating market entry in ambiguous environments. This ensures that the next generation of leaders is prepared to drive the organization forward, whatever the future holds.

By embedding succession planning into the drumbeat, organizations create a leadership pipeline that evolves in lockstep with their strategy, making sure that transitions are seamless and aligned with the company's long-term objectives.

The final piece of the puzzle is the alignment of must-have capabilities and management systems with the company's brutally important priorities. This requires a dynamic and evolving company Wall that clearly outlines the prioritized missions and ensures that every system and capability is geared toward achieving them.

The drumbeat's impact on culture transformation and business performance is powerfully illustrated by Enna Kursukangas, country manager for Finland at Vend. Kursukangas's experience provides a vivid illustration of how the principles discussed previously translate into real-world practice. She says, "Business will always necessitate transformation. As we learn and progress, we continually uncover new potential within our team and leadership. This is the cultural power of the drumbeat.

"The drumbeat is how it places business results at the core of our conversations about culture, with behavior and mindset serving to deliver those results," she continues. "Cultural transformation is not a separate initiative."[3]

Kursukangas's testimony underscores the practical application of the drumbeat to drive the rhythm of the organization, demonstrating how it fosters continuous improvement, aligns cultural transformation with business objectives, and drives tangible results. Creating a disciplined drumbeat makes a dynamic, adaptive organization capable of meeting and exceeding ambitious goals even in challenging circumstances.

This ability to build, learn, and evolve continuously is not a modern business imperative; it was presciently identified decades ago by psychologist Herbert Gerjuoy. Gerjuoy—quoted by the futurist Alvin Toffler in his seminal work *Future Shock* (1970)—anticipated the core principles that the drumbeat embodies today: "Tomorrow's illiterate will not be the man who can't read; he will be the man who has not learned how to learn."[4]

Gerjuoy's insight perfectly captures the essence of the disciplined drumbeat. In today's rapidly changing business landscape, the capacity to learn, unlearn, and relearn is not just an advantage; it's also a necessity for survival and success. The drumbeat cultivates this exact skill set, enabling organizations to stay agile, innovative, and ahead of the curve.

EVOLVE OR EVAPORATE, BUT NEVER LOSE YOUR SOUL

At the heart of every disciplined drumbeat lies a deeper truth: Evolution is nonnegotiable, but it must always be consistent with the essence of who you are—not as written in presentations, but as recognized and valued by those who matter most: your customers. Without this careful balance, the rhythm of change can deteriorate into mere decadence.

Evolution without fidelity to your core identity is a recipe for irrelevance. To thrive, you must stretch, learn, and innovate, but never stray

Tomorrow's illiterate will not be the man who can't read; he will be the man who has not learned how to learn."

—Herbert Gerjuoy

from what customers identify as uniquely you, and that has nothing to do with the features of your products, services, or systems, because those are the things that precisely need to evolve. This principle isn't just intuitive; it's also validated by compelling data and rigorous research, demonstrating that organizations maintaining their foundational identity while evolving consistently outperform those that don't.

Jim Collins and Jerry Porras demonstrated that enduring companies maintain an unwavering core ideology while simultaneously driving progress and transformation. In their seminal work *Built to Last*, they found that successful companies preserve their fundamental purpose and values even as their business strategies and operating practices evolve with time.[5] This phenomenon, which they termed "preserve the core/stimulate progress," was evident in companies like Hewlett-Packard, which maintained its commitment to technical contribution and respect for the individual (the "HP Way") while evolving from an electronic instruments company to a major computing corporation. Their subsequent *Harvard Business Review* article further refined this concept, noting that effective core ideologies consist of both core values and core purpose—the former being essential and timeless tenets, while the latter represents the organization's fundamental reason for existence beyond just making money.[6] This research was later supported by Collins's longitudinal study of corporate transitions from good to great companies, where he found that successful transformations preserved core values while changing practices and strategies to thrive in dynamic markets.[7]

The pattern is unmistakable. Enduring market leaders don't succeed merely because of their current market position; they thrive because they honor their soul, as defined by their customers' deepest connections with their brand. This connection is captured in a simple yet powerful equation: 1 customer = 1 fan. Organizations that truly understand this principle don't just serve customers—they create passionate advocates who feel a profound connection to their brand's essence. The goal isn't transaction but transformation—turning every interaction into an opportunity to convert customers into devoted fans who recognize and value your authentic core.

Take Nokia and BlackBerry's cautionary tales: They mistook their temporary technological advantage for their true identity. Their customers didn't love them for their keyboards or operating systems; they loved them for enabling better communication and productivity. When Apple offered a superior way to deliver these same values, customers moved on because Apple better served what they truly valued.

Apple's essence isn't about technology; it's about empowering those who think differently, challenging the status quo, and creating tools that enable creativity and self-expression. Their mission is to make complex technology feel magically simple and personal—a value their customers consistently recognize and reward.

Similarly, Nike's soul isn't and will never be about shoes or apparel; it's about honoring the pursuit of greatness in athletes and inspiring people to push their limits, about the feeling of athletic achievement and personal empowerment that their customers experience. Every innovation they pursue must enhance this core value, and when this has failed to happen, their customers have rapidly recognized it and will continue to do so.

NVIDIA's essence isn't about graphics cards or chips; it's about accelerating the future of computing to solve the world's most challenging problems. It's about enabling the Leonardo da Vincis of our time by giving them the tools to create and innovate, whether it's through AI agents, AI robotics, AI autonomous driving, or scientific discovery. Every breakthrough NVIDIA pursues must honor this mission of empowering creators, scientists, and innovators to push the boundaries of what's possible—a value their customers and partners deeply resonate with.

The crucial distinction is this: Your organizational soul isn't what you claim it to be; it's what your customers have grown to love and expect from you. When you successfully convert customers into fans—achieving that 1 customer = 1 fan transformation—you've discovered your true

JONATHAN ESCOBAR MARIN

1 CUSTOMER

=

1 FAN

essence. Companies that died "keeping their soul" often preserved the wrong thing: internal or industry traditions, outdated technologies, or comfortable business models rather than the deeper value their customers actually cherished.

This disciplined approach to evolution—rooted in the core values your customers cherish—feeds directly into the drumbeat. It powers the organizational beat, driving progress and amplifying what matters most to your market. The soul of your company isn't found in decks—it's alive in the moments when customers say, "This is why I choose you."

Back to these iconic brands.

Apple's continued success depends on multiple factors, including technological evolution while honoring its commitment to "Think Different," along with maintaining its ecosystem advantages, supply chain excellence, and customer loyalty. By combining intuitive design with emotional connection, Apple has achieved industry-leading brand loyalty metrics—achieving the number one ranking in Brand Keys Loyalty Leaders 2024, which assessed 1,465 brands in 142 categories.[8]

Nike's path to sustaining market leadership will depend on revolutionizing athletic wear without wavering from its mission to empower athletes. With Nike as one of the world's most valuable apparel brands in 2024, its comeback and lasting greatness will depend on its ability to maintain this connection to its soul.[9]

NVIDIA has cemented itself as an indispensable partner in advancing humanity's greatest challenges, from climate modeling to autonomous vehicles. As long as NVIDIA continues to pair its relentless technological evolution with its mission to provide the tools for solving the world's toughest problems, its relevance and impact will endure.

The message is clear: Sustainable market leadership belongs to those who master the art of evolution without sacrificing their organizational soul. Evolve, but never lose the soul that turns customers into fans. This 1 customer = 1 fan philosophy isn't just a metric—it's the ultimate validation that you're honoring your essence while evolving your capabilities. This balance is the drumbeat of enduring success. This isn't just about sentiment or brand nostalgia; it's also a documented driver of lasting business success. This is not merely about survival; it's about thriving through authentic transformation. The organizations that will dominate tomorrow are those that boldly innovate while honoring the DNA that made them great in the first place.

NEVER A VICTIM, NEVER IN DENIAL

One of the most transformative principles I had the honor of learning from Nitin Paranjpe, during the time we worked together when he was Unilever's chief people and transformation officer, is encapsulated in the powerful mantra "never a victim, never in denial." This guiding philosophy has been a cornerstone for me and countless leaders, fostering the right mindset to navigate the inevitable challenges that arise throughout the transformative cycle of the drumbeat.

IF YOU SEE THE PROBLEM, YOU OWN THE PROBLEM.

Nitin consistently emphasized the critical importance of not externalizing problems but owning them. Integrating this approach within the drumbeat cycle means taking full responsibility for our circumstances, refusing to see ourselves as passive victims of external conditions. Instead, we transform into active agents, fully capable of driving change and fostering growth.

Throughout business cycles, many of us expect the world to align with our expectations. However, reality often diverges from these expectations, ensnaring us in the trap of a victim mindset—a mindset we've all found ourselves in at various times in our careers.

Reorganizations, pandemics, acquisitions, mergers, geoeconomic challenges, unfair competition, political games—all these factors can

EVOLVE, BUT NEVER LOSE THE SOUL THAT TURNS CUSTOMERS INTO FANS.

trigger initial reactions of anger and frustration. We take these circumstances and decisions personally, perceiving ourselves as victims of corporate decisions, shareholder interests, political power plays, or competitors' unethical practices.

But when we adopt the "never a victim, never in denial" mantra from the outset, our response transforms. Instead of succumbing to self-pity and resentment, we focus on forging ahead and finding new ways to contribute positively. We use the next cycle of the drumbeat to channel our energy into what is vitally important, enriched by past learnings and the opportunities presented by current circumstances.

When Jeff Bezos sat down with ABC News in 2013 to talk about his motives for acquiring the *Washington Post*, he said, "What we need to do is always lean into the future. . . . When the world changes around you and when it changes against you—so that what used to be a tailwind is now a headwind—you have to lean into that and figure out what to do because complaining is not a strategy."[10]

Taking ownership of our circumstances, no matter how challenging, empowers us. It shifts our focus from what is beyond our control to what we can influence. This shift is not just about surviving difficult situations, but also thriving despite them.

"Never a victim, never in denial" is more than a mantra; it's a powerful mindset that can be integrated into the drumbeat. It reminds us that the power to shape our business outcomes lies within us, regardless of external circumstances. By owning our responses and refusing to adopt a victim mentality, we unlock our true potential and pave the way for a more resilient and empowered future within our organizations.

THE DRUMBEAT IS FAIR

Without human growth, there is no business growth. One of the keys to enabling individuals and teams to perform at their peak is a fair and nonmanipulative talent review process. A high-performing, high-impact culture creates clear growth paths for talent that delivers results and demonstrates the right behaviors. Moving away from subjective

What we need to do is always lean into the future . . . When the world changes around you and when it changes against you—so that what used to be a tailwind is now a headwind—you have to lean into that and figure out what to do because complaining is not a strategy."

—Jeff Bezos

assessments, dubious talent reviews, or isolated performance snapshots, the drumbeat ensures maximum fairness, transparency, and accountability in evaluating and leveraging talent. It provides a consistent system that is the same for all, allowing leaders to see how their associates perform and evolve under equal conditions.

A Unified Talent System

When properly utilized by leaders and internal talent specialists, the drumbeat becomes a unified talent system. It offers the opportunity to see talent perform within the fairest and most common system imaginable. Everyone receives the same information about the missions for the next quarter simultaneously. Teams are staffed under equal conditions, with the same time, model, and accompaniment to build their missions. Feedback is given in the same way, at the same time, and with the same principles, and everyone gets equal guidance and support from leaders. This ensures that all talent working on the critical missions is aligned from the outset.

To be specific, once per quarter, the entire organization is informed simultaneously about the missions and the team leaders for each mission. Within this system, every team leader has one week to staff their teams, adhering to the same rules to ensure fair and transparent resource allocation. Once the teams are staffed, each team member has the same amount of time to understand their mission and what is expected of them. Over the next two weeks, the team together develops their specific execution plans, with every team member having equal opportunities to contribute and make an impact. This level playing field is crucial for fostering a culture of fairness and collaboration.

Central to the Wall refinement cycle in the drumbeat is the feedback meetup—an electrifying, open forum where every contributor, from team members to mission leaders, gathers with a shared purpose and equal access to the same information, echoing Jensen Huang's vision of collective clarity. In this dynamic session, the 1:1:1 formula takes center stage: Team leaders unveil the specific mission they own, the dedicated team they've assembled, and their bold execution plans. Top executives step in with candid, constructive guidance, while the floor opens to all—inviting spot-on insights, fresh perspectives, and alerts to untapped synergies or collaboration opportunities. This isn't just feedback; it's a crucible where every voice strengthens the plan, ignites innovation, and propels the mission forward together.

Likewise, beyond the once-per-quarter Wall refinement and feedback meetup, the weekly synchro provides the most frequent and powerful opportunity to witness talent in action. In these sessions, individuals demonstrate not only their execution capabilities, but also their ability to think strategically, communicate clearly, and pivot swiftly to meet challenges. This weekly rhythm creates around forty-five moments of truth per year where talent truly reveals itself—far more telling than any annual review or assessment center.

By placing everyone on the same system, with equal time allocated and the same opportunity to own their missions, organizations can clearly see who is making a difference. The design of the drumbeat rhythm, with its different moments of truth like the Wall refinement, the feedback session, and the weekly synchros, highlights those who demonstrate the willingness, attitude, energy, and business acumen to deliver results.

Surfacing Mediocrity

The drumbeat eliminates the possibility of mediocrity hiding behind polished presentations and narratives. It brings relentless discipline, focus, simultaneity, and transparency to every corner of the organization, dismantling the illusions that mediocrity depends on to thrive. It ensures that no executive, leader, team, or initiative can hide behind the comfort of appearances, forcing everyone to confront reality and deliver real impact.

Mediocrity seeps in when leadership shifts to PowerPoint painters—those to whom the truth and pace of the drumbeat bring discomfort. These narrative architects, masters of the beautiful slide but enemies of brutal transparency, thrive on crafting polished stories instead of driving the Wall's brutally important priorities. But under the cadence of the drumbeat, these individuals are quickly exposed. The drumbeat's relentless demand for outcome-oriented, brutally transparent execution makes it impossible for PowerPoint karaokes to masquerade as meaningful progress.

In a forward-looking system where all execution plans are in a simple, pragmatic one-pager and presented, without exception, in a sharp, outcome-oriented, and transparent manner, the drumbeat strips away the layers of unnecessary complexity that mediocrity hides behind. It becomes evident who is contributing meaningfully and who is not. This clarity is amplified during the Wall refinement process, where leaders iteratively review every mission, every timebox, and every priority to ensure alignment with the North Star metrics. The Wall becomes the organization's unblinking eye—constantly refined in sync with evolving realities—while the Stop Wall reinforces brutal focus by eliminating distractions and activities that are not the top ones to create value.

The cadence and consistency of the synchros ensure that no green dot can hide a red reality. If a red reality is concealed during one week, the relentless cadence of the drumbeat will inevitably unearth it—and when it does, it is celebrated and confronted, never ignored or excused. Synchros become arenas of truth, where theatrical performances and comfortable nods evaporate under the sharp discipline of the drumbeat. Through simultaneity, this transparency extends across the entire organization, ensuring that all leaders and teams see the same realities at the same time. By bringing the right people together in Wall-across-silos refinement sessions, dissent is cultivated, silos are eliminated, and alignment is forged. Failed execution from those who didn't deliver what is needed cannot be repackaged as "learning experiences" in PowerPoint victories.

Beware: Mediocrity doesn't announce its arrival with fanfare; it creeps in under the guise of pragmatism and flexibility, cloaked in comforting habits that no one dares to question. It tempts with the illusion of safety, whispering that the status quo is "good enough." It thrives in the comfortable lull of unchallenged decisions and the collective agreement to avoid hard truths. It manifests in misaligned priorities disguised as strategic pivots, in ambiguous targets that make everyone comfortable but drive no real impact, and in the weight of unnecessary processes. But the drumbeat prevents this entirely. Its transparency and simultaneity create synchronized accountability, forcing every individual and team to align with the North Star metrics and the missions on the Wall. During each refinement cycle, leaders challenge what to Keep, Improve, Start, or Stop, ensuring priorities remain brutally focused and that entropy never takes hold. This discipline eliminates the disconnect between genuine impact and theatrical busywork.

While some may continue seeking recognition through narratives and PowerPoint slides, the drumbeat reveals their hollowness. It systematically shines a harsh, unflinching light on gray areas and duplications, leaving no room for excuses or wasted effort. It lays bare the hidden agendas of those who prioritize personal brands and individual bonuses above collective outcomes, revealing the corrosive impact of self-interest on the organization's rhythm and focus. It ensures that no one can dance the dance of mediocrity, whispering, "Don't disrupt our peace." Instead, the drumbeat amplifies the instinct of those who see the disconnect and demand real change, giving them a platform on which to act and holding others accountable to the same standard.

Beware that most people don't want to be part of the drumbeat; they just want to be part of the recognition. But the drumbeat is where you figure out who is worth being recognized. The drumbeat makes recognition impossible to fake. Its relentless cadence demands results, not appearances, and forces everyone to operate in alignment, with no room for ambiguity or comfort-driven complacency. Those who deliver with clear bets, initiatives, and a defined glidepath stand out unmistakably, while those who choose activity over impact are unmasked. Simultaneous transparency ensures that the contributions of every team are visible and evaluated in real time, leaving no space for superficial efforts to hide.

The Wall, supported by each team's execution plan, provides clear visibility into each team's progress and BIG choices—or their absence.

It eliminates the gravitational pull of mediocrity through regular cycles of refinement and renewal, where leaders confront this critical question: "Do our current missions align with the pace of change and our long-term aspirations?" This iteration process constantly redefines priorities, ensuring that resources are directed toward impact and that the organization operates with agility and precision. Instead of falling into the defense of bureaucratic peace, the drumbeat transforms the Wall into a mechanism for accountability and focus, forcing all the organization to be brutally focused on the must-win battles and cut the rest.

This transparency ensures that only those who truly add value are recognized and rewarded. By maintaining the drumbeat's relentless rhythm, the organization not only prevents mediocrity, but also ensures it never takes root. Simultaneity and transparency kill any chance of confusion or politics, guaranteeing that the organization's rhythm remains focused, aligned, and relentless in its pursuit of impact. Mediocrity's gravitational pull is overpowered by the drumbeat's discipline, building a culture where high impact and high performance thrive—a culture unshaken by ambiguity, distraction, or the haunting regret of what might have been.

Empowering New Leaders to Show Up

By ensuring that everyone has the same access to information and opportunities and by enforcing proven principles—like the idea that one person should only lead one team and participate in a maximum of two teams—the drumbeat empowers new talent to show up across the organization. It promotes a culture of fairness, where contributions are judged based on merit and impact rather than politics or manipulation. This equitable environment fosters trust and motivation, driving individuals to perform at their best and collaborate effectively.

Every time we have introduced this principle to leadership teams in a new organization, there has been initial resistance. Leaders have consistently told us, without exception, that in their company, it would

JONATHAN ESCOBAR MARIN

Most people don't want to be part of the drumbeat; they just want to be part of the recognition. But the drumbeat is where you figure out who is worth being recognized.

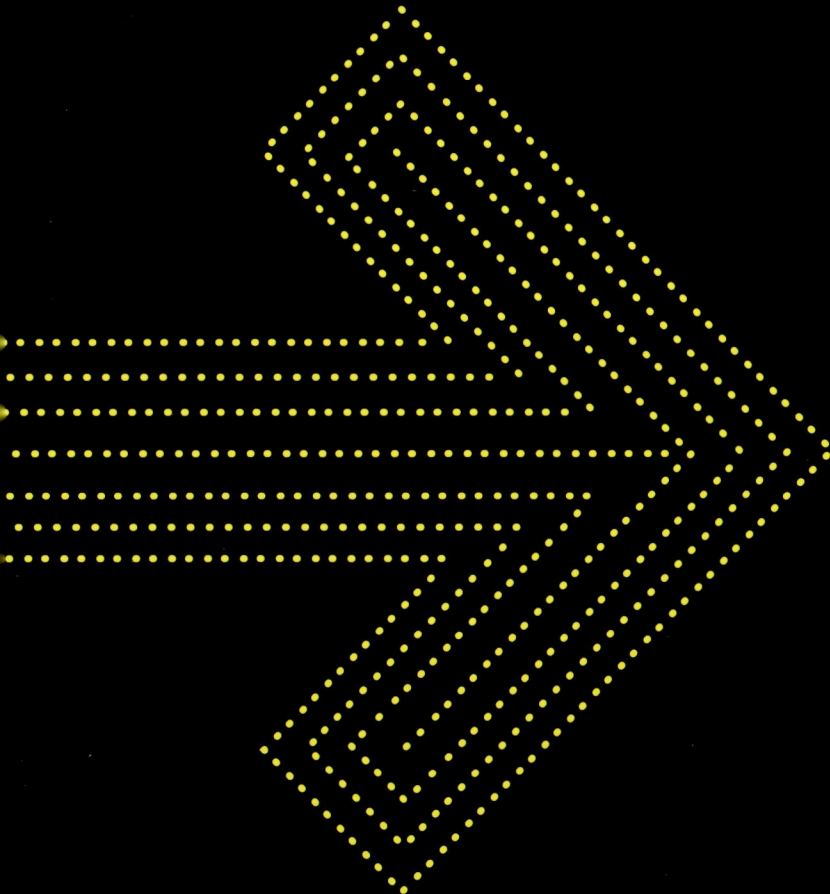

be impossible to match this principle. They argue that their business is too complex, their organizational structure too entrenched, or the number of leaders below their level capable of leading brutally important missions is too limited for this approach to work. And yet, despite this skepticism, the results speak for themselves. Across more than 320 organizations, after over six quarters of iteration, we have seen over 90 percent adherence to this principle.

This adherence has unlocked something extraordinary: the unparalleled power of the drumbeat to surface new talent, to give possibilities to those willing to deliver, and to challenge the outdated idea that leadership is reserved for a select few. By limiting team leadership to one mission at a time and participation to a maximum of two teams, organizations create space for others to step forward—often individuals who previously went unnoticed but who have the drive, ideas, and commitment to make an impact.

What does this mean for you as a leader? It means embracing discomfort and challenging the status quo. It means recognizing that the systems you've inherited may inadvertently suppress potential and create bottlenecks at the top. The principle of one person leading one team and being a member of no more than two is not a constraint; it's a liberation. It enables your organization to run on merit and outcomes, not hierarchy and history.

This approach drives a deeper connection between opportunity and capability. It forces organizations to confront the reality that too often talent is underused or hidden by overly complex structures. When implemented, this principle doesn't just add incremental value; it also transforms the organization. It creates a leadership pipeline where none existed, surfaces new possibilities, and ensures that the right people are empowered to lead at the right time.

Right Talent, Right Team, Right Time

One of the unique aspects of the drumbeat is its evolving and dynamic nature. As the business landscape shifts, so do the priorities expressed in clear missions. This requires a dynamic, flexible, and adaptive approach to talent management that continuously opens opportunities for talent to thrive. By continuously reviewing and adjusting team compositions and execution plans, organizations can spot new minds and hearts that can respond swiftly to emerging challenges and opportunities. The drumbeat's regular cycles of feedback, refinement, and iteration also allow for the continuous reevaluation of talent, ensuring that the right talent is on the right team at the right time. Likewise, as entropy makes skills and knowledge obsolete faster than ever, the drumbeat ensures continuous talent upskilling to maintain organizational vitality.

Fostering Talent Density: A New Meritocracy

The drumbeat inherently promotes a culture of meritocracy built on the power of exceptional talent working together. This approach aligns with what leading high-impact organizations like Netflix have proven works. As Netflix's culture demonstrates, "What makes a fantastic workplace isn't a great office or free meals and massages; it's the people."

The drumbeat, like Netflix's proven model, develops a culture where organizations and teams operate more like a professional sports team than a family. While families offer unconditional love, professional sports teams focus on performance, impact, and picking the person who deserves it more for every position. At Netflix, they validate this through their *keeper test*—asking "if X wanted to leave, would I fight to keep them?"[11] This reflects a fundamental truth that "a high performer in any role is many times more effective than the average employee."

Netflix's culture, as with the cultures in different organizations we have seen thrive under a powerful drumbeat, also emphasizes the importance of personal responsibility and self-reflection among employees. Every individual is expected to act like an owner of their career and performance. Employees are encouraged to assess their value and alignment with the company's strategic ambitions and standards by regularly reflecting on their contributions, their passion for the work, and their ability to deliver exceptional results.

The drumbeat's transparent processes and equal opportunities for contribution create an environment that attracts and inspires lasting commitment from exceptional talent. These individuals are, as Netflix describes their own team members, "great at what they do and even better at working together."[12] This isn't just about individual achievement; it's also about creating an environment where talented people can thrive, lifting themselves, each other, and their work higher and higher.

This focus on talent density doesn't merely drive performance—it fundamentally reshapes the work environment. When talented people work well together, trusting each other's intentions and respecting their differences, it makes everyone more successful. The result is a culture that naturally attracts and retains top talent through maintaining consistently high-performance standards and clear meritocratic principles.

THE VITAL FORCE

The drumbeat serves as the vital force that propels your organization's beat forward, acting as more than just a driver but as a meta-driver that orchestrates your organizational rhythm. Like a conductor's baton, it coordinates all other drivers to create your company's distinctive beat. It bridges the boldness of your aspirations with the discipline of execution and evolution, ensuring that every beat drives growth, learning, and leadership empowerment. It embodies a philosophy of continuous challenge and improvement through quarterly reevaluations of every mission and goal, always chasing faster, stronger, leaner, better, and more focused, while staying true to what customers deeply value. Reset. Restart. Refocus. But always be guided by what your customers value and your long-term aspirations. This rhythm keeps the organization both grounded and forward-looking.

Central to the drumbeat of successful organizations is learning and evolution. Teams and leaders engage in reflective analysis and conversations by deciding to Keep, Improve, Start, or Stop to focus on impact.

These conversations, grounded in firsthand observations from the *gemba* (where real work happens), enable leaders to make informed decisions and drive continuous improvement. The drumbeat emphasizes the importance of being present in the workplace, getting direct customer feedback about what makes the products and services of the organization uniquely valuable to them, echoing Taiichi Ohno's philosophy of prioritizing facts over distant data. The drumbeat also facilitates a synchronized evolution across the organization through simultaneity and transparency.

SUCCESS ISN'T A LUCKY TUNE; IT'S DISCIPLINE'S DRUMBEAT.

Success isn't a lucky tune; it's discipline's drumbeat. It involves regular refinement of strategic tools like the Wall and the Stop Wall, ensuring alignment of North Star metrics, missions, talent allocation, and time-boxes with current realities and future aspirations. This process fosters a culture of brutal focus, where leaders commit to start less and impact more, continuously cutting unnecessary activities to maintain strategic clarity while strengthening what customers recognize as the organization's unique value.

The drumbeat encourages ownership of challenges and viewing them as opportunities for growth rather than insurmountable obstacles. This mindset shift to "never a victim, never in denial" empowers individuals and teams to step up proactively to changing circumstances, turning potential setbacks into stepping stones for success.

The drumbeat transcends mere organizational rhythm; it's a catalyst for continuous innovation and transformation. It embodies Satya Nadella's insight he shared with all Microsoft employees in his motivational email on his first day as their CEO on February 4, 2014: "Our industry does not respect tradition—it only respects innovation."[13]

JONATHAN ESCOBAR MARIN

Reset. Restart. Refocus. But always be guided by what your customers value and your long-term aspirations.

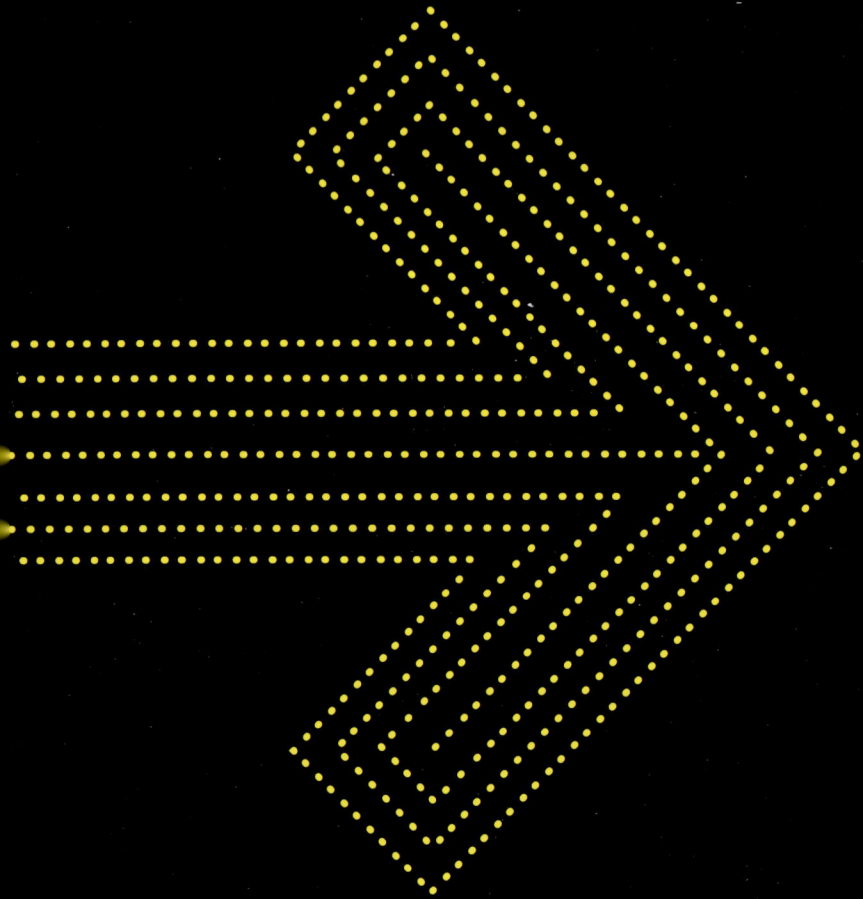

This principle, relevant a decade ago, has only intensified across all sectors. Today, we can affirm that no industry will survive on tradition alone; yet the most powerful innovations are those that enhance rather than abandon what customers truly value about us. Success comes through innovation, renewal, and continuous transformation that amplifies—rather than dilutes—the essential connection customers have with our organizations.

The choice between evolution and the comfort of great last-quarter results becomes starker as entropy accelerates. The drumbeat ensures you're actively choosing evolution by instituting regular cycles of renewal and reinvention. A disciplined drumbeat instills this ethos of perpetual cultural evolution, creating a dynamic learning feedback loop that enhances both individual capabilities and the management systems that define the culture of an organization. It ensures the right talent is strategically positioned, fostering a meritocracy where impact, not politics, drives recognition. By synchronizing cultural evolution with the strategic choices expressed on the Wall, the drumbeat sustains an unshakable focus on critical objectives—whether their impact is immediate, mid-term, or long-term. It's not about what you delivered last quarter; to be where you want to be tomorrow, in one quarter, or in five years, you must remain brutally focused today.

This approach doesn't just respond to change; it also anticipates and propels it forward. Through each cycle, the disciplined drumbeat forges organizational culture into an innovation engine, continuously challenging the status quo and pushing boundaries. It's not about preserving what worked yesterday but about creating what will work tomorrow.

In doing so, it equips organizations to not only navigate, but to also lead in an ever-evolving business landscape, turning the relentless pace of change from a threat into a powerful advantage for transformative growth and sustained success.

The power of a consistent drumbeat is crucial to drive transformation while conducting all drivers in a symphony of impact. This rhythmic approach entails continuous adjustment, swift course corrections, and

"

Our industry does not respect tradition—it only respects innovation."

—Satya Nadella

TO BE WHERE YOU WANT TO BE TOMORROW, IN ONE QUARTER OR IN FIVE YEARS, YOU MUST REMAIN BRUTALLY FOCUSED TODAY.

the ability to capitalize on unexpected successes, all while reinforcing rather than diluting the essential value proposition that customers have grown to love and expect.

Jussi Lystimäki, CEO of Swappie, brings exceptional expertise to integrating transformative ways of working within already dynamic, fast-paced, and technologically sophisticated organizations. His implementation journey with me and my team occurred in two pivotal contexts: first as an executive member of Adevinta's global markets leadership team, and subsequently during his tenure as CEO of Nordic Marketplaces Finland at Schibsted. This dual-context experience offers invaluable insights for leaders committed to driving authentic organizational transformation. Based on these experiences, he offers me valuable insights into how the drumbeat functions as a transformative force in organizations: "The drumbeat . . . is key in our ever-changing environment. We need to constantly monitor and reshape our ambitions, adjusting to shifts in the external context. We also need to evolve our team's composition. A team that was effective at one stage of our journey towards a mission might need adjustments later—perhaps even a change in leadership—as circumstances evolve; sometimes they start being more functional teams, then they need to shift to being more multidisciplinary and so on.

"Without this consistent rhythm, we'd lose touch with the pulse of our situation. It's crucial to maintain this cadence; it's not something we set once and leave untouched for a year. This drumbeat keeps us dynamic, fast, responsive, and always moving forward."[14]

Lystimäki's experiences perfectly illustrate the transformative power of a consistent drumbeat. It enables organizations to stay nimble, adjusting strategies and teams as needed, while maintaining a clear focus on overarching objectives. This approach ensures that companies can respond effectively to both challenges and opportunities, fostering a culture of continuous improvement and anticipation.

Cycle fast. Learn hard. Transform relentlessly. Keep winning. The drumbeat serves as a powerful tool for maintaining alignment, driving

JONATHAN ESCOBAR MARIN

The drumbeat is not about preserving what worked yesterday but about creating what will work tomorrow.

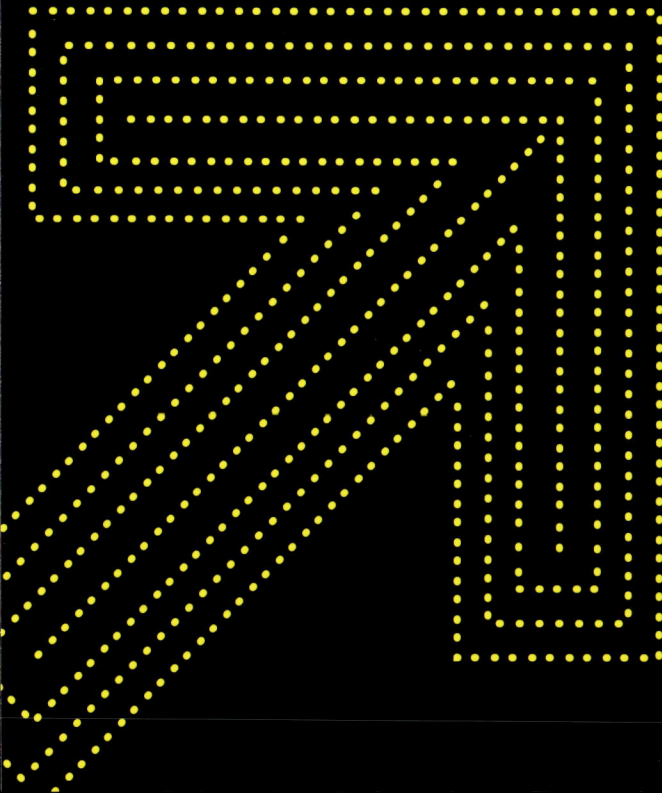

progress, and fostering a proactive mindset throughout the organization. It fosters regular reflection and adjustment, ensuring that the company remains on course despite the turbulent waters of today's business environment.

And ultimately, these principles apply across all organizational contexts, industries, and cultural environments. Remember that what we're discussing is common sense applied with uncommon discipline. The secret is there is no secret.

> When you are capable of translating a strategy containing your long-term vision and your purpose into a Wall of missions with committed targets, dates, and staffing, you create brutal focus.

> When those missions are broken down into bets, initiatives, and glidepaths that are owned across the silos and hierarchies, you create distributed leadership.

> When talent is in the pilot seat to execute seamlessly and leaders are there to unlock, you get impact over activity.

> When you build the capability to sync everyone around a disciplined drumbeat, you shape a high-impact organization. And you do this over and over again, by stepping your culture up, with a disciplined drumbeat.

This cultural evolution compounds over time, turning today's disciplined evolution into tomorrow's sustainable competitive advantages. Leaders who master the drumbeat become conductors of their business and culture, shaping tomorrow through each disciplined beat.

CYCLE FAST. LEARN HARD. TRANSFORM RELENTLESSLY. KEEP WINNING.

What Is Needed

Answer these questions to beat tomorrow—or watch others lead while you lag. Every honest response separates those who drive the future from those who will chase it.

- ↗ Do you want to keep believing that you created the perfect strategy that doesn't need adjustments as you learn?

- ↗ Are you clear on what to Keep, Improve, Start, and Stop for the next quarter?

- ↗ Are you creating an environment where mediocrity has nowhere to hide, or are polished presentations masking underperformance?

- ↗ Is your leadership still disconnected from the *gemba* and real-world execution?

- ↗ Do you want to maintain a talent review process driven by politics or subjective evaluations (often masked in scientific approaches) rather than fairness?

- ↗ Is your talent density strong enough to win?

- ↗ Are you letting past victories create complacency?

- ↗ Do you have the strategic discipline to maintain your focus through disruptions?

- ↗ Are your market needs, brand building, functional enablement, and talent decisions unified in one single source of truth, or scattered across silos?

- ↗ Do you want your individual performance appraisals to keep tracking project completion instead of real measurable impact?

WHAT IS NEEDED

COURAGEOUS
BEATS
FEARFUL.

Beyond the four drivers of success, we've experienced a handful of mental traps that sabotage organizations, and that prevent them from embracing the disciplined actions required to lead and shape tomorrow. These pitfalls are not obstacles encountered during execution; they are mindsets and behaviors that block progress before it even begins.

We've seen these five pitfalls time and again:

1. The Mirage of the Ideal Moment, where leaders wait endlessly for the "perfect time" to act

2. The Fallacy of Assessments, where organizations mistake analysis for progress and delay meaningful change

3. The Delusion of Uniqueness, where companies convince themselves they are too different for proven principles to work

4. The Flawed Pilot Project Approach, where timid, fragmented experiments fail to achieve systemic change

5. The Artifacts Shortcut, where organizations adopt the surface symbols of success without committing to the principles behind them

These pitfalls are not external challenges but internal limitations: excuses, hesitations, and superficial efforts that separate the visionaries from the bureaucrats, the leaders from the managers, the disruptors from the disrupted. As we dissect each one, prepare to confront uncomfortable truths. This is not about incremental improvement; it's about unleashing a tidal wave of transformation that will sweep away the old and usher in a new era of unprecedented performance.

In the relentless pursuit of excellence, there is no room for half measures or lukewarm commitments. The market doesn't reward good intentions; it bows only to exceptional results. As we dive into these pitfalls, steel yourself to challenge your assumptions, test your resolve, and, ultimately, redefine what you believe is possible for your organization.

The path ahead is not for the faint of heart. It demands courage, discipline, brutal focus, and an unwavering commitment to superior results. For those bold enough to embrace this challenge, the rewards are nothing short of extraordinary. Are you ready to leave the comfort of the familiar behind and lead into the arena of true transformation?

THE 5 MOST-COMMON PITFALLS

1. The Mirage of the Ideal Moment

A widespread phenomenon in many organizations is leaders who habitually defer crucial decisions under the pretext that "the timing isn't right." This evasion is often a manifestation of political motivations or personal agendas overshadowing organizational priorities. The pursuit of an elusive "perfect moment" for initiating change is nothing more than a self-deception; it fosters stagnation and missed opportunities in a world characterized by FATE-driven ceaseless evolution.

- Isn't it the perfect time to stop wasting time on PowerPoint karaoke sessions that don't provide radical clarity on what we need to deliver, when, and who's going to take responsibility?
- Isn't it the perfect time to stop having off-sites full of great intentions but lacking execution afterward?
- Isn't it the perfect time to multiply leaders capable of owning wildly important priorities in the organization?
- Isn't it the perfect time to dismantle the kingdom of silos?
- Isn't it the perfect time to stop long business reviews where we mostly look at lagging metrics in the rearview mirror that we cannot change?
- Isn't it the perfect time to speed up decision-making from one month to one week on average?
- Isn't it the perfect time to make brutal focus a company habit?
- Isn't it the perfect time to discover high potentials and unearth mediocrity?
- Isn't it the perfect time to create a hungry culture where every day feels like day one?

Leaders who fall into this "perfect moment" trap unwittingly stifle their organization's dynamism and potential for growth. By allowing their fears—or the fears of others—to cloud their judgment, they create a chronic delay in decision-making that paralyzes progress. In doing so, they risk driving their organizations toward obsolescence.

To illustrate this point, let's consider the insights from two of our leaders introduced earlier. Judith Viader reflects on the cost of indecision: "I feel that all the time we spent discussing if it was the best time to shape the way of working was a waste of time."[1] Jerome du Chaffaut expresses regret over delayed action: "It took me six months to decide, and I regret those six lost months. I finally made the decision with COVID upon us."[2] These testimonials underscore a timeless wisdom, eloquently captured in this anonymous proverb: "The best time to plant a tree was twenty years ago. The second-best time is now."

Transformation is not about waiting for the stars to align; it's about making bold choices, even in uncertainty.

2. The Fallacy of Assessments

Countless organizations worldwide rely heavily on expensive and time-consuming assessments as the benchmark for their readiness to achieve world-class status, placing undue trust in these evaluations as a definitive measure of progress. However, this blind dependence, part of a multibillion-dollar global industry, often obscures a crucial truth: True progress lies in the willingness to lead change and consistently drive high performance. Assessments and change road maps are business drugs; they make us feel like we're moving without taking a step.

The role of leadership is not to wait for assessments but to harness latent potential and transform it into superlative results. Look at leaders like Steve Jobs (Apple), Jeff Bezos (Amazon), A. G. Lafley (Procter & Gamble), Howard Schultz (Starbucks), Sam Walton (Walmart), or Zhang Ruimin (Haier) among many others; did they sit back and wait for an assessment before building or evolving their company cultures? No, these transformative leaders didn't commission extensive cultural

The best time to plant a tree was twenty years ago. The second-best time is now."

—Anonymous proverb

Assessments and change road maps are business drugs; they make us feel like we're moving without taking a step.

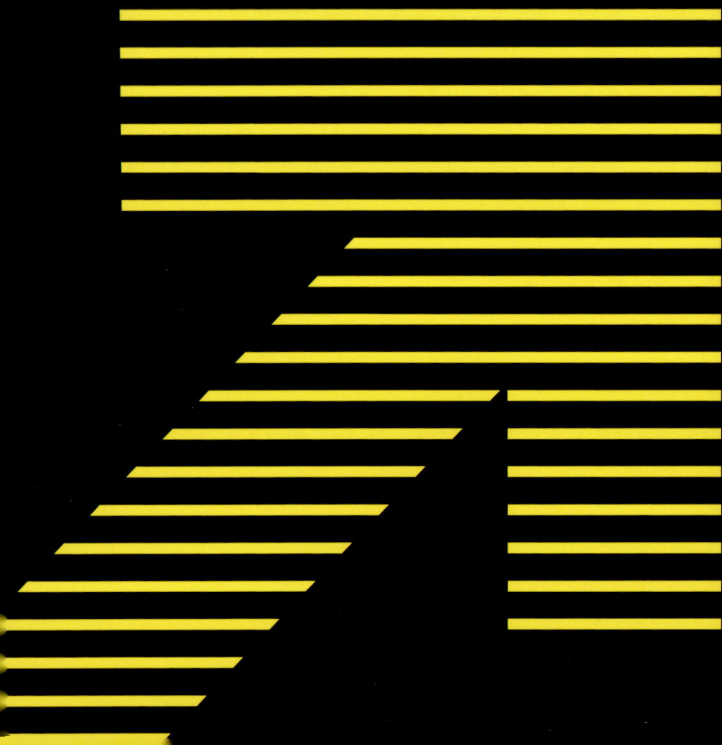

assessments before driving change. Instead, they had clear visions of the cultures they wanted to build and poured all of their energy into making them a reality, relentlessly driving their organizations toward those visions through daily actions and decisions. They understood that culture reveals itself through execution, not through analysis.

Back in the early twentieth century, Kurt Lewin was already aware of the greatest advantage of change. According to Charles W. Tolman, in his book *Problems of Theoretical Psychology*, Lewin said, "If you truly want to understand something, try to change it."[3]

The opportunity for dramatic improvement often lies right under our noses, yet for some reason, it does not enter our consciousness. This phenomenon is not limited to business enterprises. In professional sports, teams frequently transform from losing to winning almost overnight with the same roster but under the guidance of a different coach and without making change wait for weeks of assessments. Some call it the X factor, others the spark. I personally call it leadership; it's about creating immediate impact through action. Great coaches don't spend months assessing; they observe, decide, act, learn, and adjust. They create winning cultures through daily practices and real-time learning, not through weeks-to-make reports. Whatever its name may be, it is real and accessible to anyone who dares to tap into it—although few do.

This principle of immediate action over endless analysis applies equally to organizational transformation. In the journey to evolve culture and ways of working in an organization, excessively dedicating resources to assessments is not only fruitless, but also expensive—not merely in monetary terms but in the time, energy, and focus it drains from your people. Every hour spent analyzing the past is an hour not spent building the future. Every dollar invested in assessment reports is a dollar not invested in actual transformation. The true cost isn't just financial; it's also the opportunity cost of delayed action and lost momentum. Think about the countless hours spent in interviews, reporting, analyzing, and debating the current situation before even starting the change. And what is the result? A report? A diagnosis? A snapshot of the past that risks misguiding the future? Some might

"

If you truly want to understand something, try to change it."

—Kurt Lewin

argue, "But assessments focus the change!" And to that we would respond, "Or they misfocus it."

Consider this: If an elite, high-performing sports team spent three months assessing their current situation without playing a single game, would they know where to improve? Of course not. They form the team to win what they want, to improve where they want, and to play how they want, and the feedback they need emerges from action, not analysis. Likewise, if you want to know where your organization stands culturally or operationally—where the bottlenecks are, where to invest, where to divest, where collaboration is breaking down—don't waste three months diagnosing. Spend those three months actively moving the organization in the direction you aspire to take it, and by the end of that time, you'll know exactly where to focus and what to tweak. Progress reveals the truth far better than any assessment ever could. Transformation isn't about diagnosing the past; it's about relentlessly forging tomorrow with disciplined grit.

As Dan Millman's version of Socrates said, "The secret of change is focusing all your energy not on fighting the old, but on building the new."[4] The real work begins when you take a vivid vision of the working culture you aspire to create and translate it into meaningful change: new routines, new behaviors, new habits, new conversations, new mindset, practiced, seen, corrected, evolved every day. The assessment mindset is a comfort zone that keeps organizations trapped in analysis while competitors drive forward through action. Real transformation happens in the daily choices and behaviors of teams, not in the pages of assessment reports. Not in workshops, not in sterile meeting rooms, but in the trenches of daily business.

3. The Delusion of Uniqueness

Over the years, I've heard countless variations of the same theme: "We're different because we're not a multinational" or "because we're too complex" or "because we're in a unique sector" or "because

PROGRESS REVEALS THE TRUTH FAR BETTER THAN ANY ASSESSMENT EVER COULD.

we're a family-owned company" or "This won't work here because [our national culture] is so different" or "because our industry is too regulated" or "because we're much smaller." In essence, these all boil down to one core belief: "We're too different from the more than three hundred examples you've shown us. Our uniqueness makes us immune to universal principles of success."

Beware of this alluring and deceptive call of exceptionalism, a deceptive fantasy that tempts organizations into a false sense of security. It whispers enticingly in their ears, convincing them of their unparalleled uniqueness and immunity to the proven business drivers we've discussed. This dangerous mindset lurks in the shadows of nearly every corporate entity, blinding them to potential opportunities for growth, innovation, and transformation. The reality is that these excuses are just that—excuses.

We've encountered and overcome every single one of these objections in organizations ranging from multinational giants to family-owned businesses, the largest cooperatives in the world, heavily regulated industries like pharmaceuticals or banking, and even companies in a complete turnaround in low-margin businesses. We've successfully implemented our strategies in tech companies, proving that even in fast-paced, innovative environments, there's room for evolution, or, as they perceived, revolution. We have helped businesses embrace the drivers in North America, South America, Africa, Asia, and Europe, addressing cultural differences and unique market challenges in each region. We've achieved impact in companies of all sizes, from small growing businesses to well-established global corporations. We've worked with companies experiencing rapid growth and those facing losses. In every single case, the four drivers of success create meaningful change and accelerate impact.

Rather than threatening an organization's distinctiveness or undermining its unique qualities, the universally applicable drivers can actually strengthen its strengths. They have the power to amplify innate abilities and increase success rates in which these distinctive attributes thrive.

"

The secret of change is focusing all your energy not on fighting the old, but on building the new."

—Dan Millman

Consider the principle of *genchi genbutsu* ("go and see for yourself"), which is fundamental to Toyota's success.[5] This principle is universally applicable yet can be tailored to fit the unique contexts of different organizations.

Every business is unique, and when the leaders at the top have the right mindset and courage to lead change, that uniqueness becomes a launching pad. Dr. John Kotter, a renowned expert on leadership and change, emphasizes that successful transformations are often driven by leaders who understand the balance between maintaining core values and embracing new strategies.[6] By embracing time-tested strategies while leveraging individual strengths, companies can strike a balance between conformity and originality—creating a synergy that drives unparalleled success and impact. The key is not to see universal principles as constraints but as enablers of your unique vision. By integrating proven strategies with their distinctive strengths, leaders can navigate the complexities of today's business landscape with agility and foresight, ensuring sustained growth and innovation. Saying, "That won't work here; we're different" is the perfect excuse to stay the same.

4. The Flawed Pilot Project Approach

The allure of the pilot project approach is often a shimmering mirage in the vast desert of organizational change. It seduces leaders with the illusion of safety, control, and "measured progress." It whispers promises of risk-free transformation, luring organizations into believing that small, isolated experiments will deliver meaningful results. But, like an oasis that vanishes upon closer inspection, pilot projects frequently fail to achieve the deep, systemic change organizations need. They deliver shallow results that barely scratch the surface of what is possible, leaving behind a trail of wasted time, energy, and opportunity.

Organizational transformation cannot be treated as a timid dip of one's toe into unknown waters. Instead, it demands complete immersion and unwavering commitment from every member of the organization.

One fundamental flaw is the assumption that what works on a pilot project will seamlessly translate to larger, more complex systems. In reality, scaling a way of working often introduces entirely new variables—such as increased interdependencies, resource constraints, and resistance from other parts of the organization—that were absent in the controlled, isolated environment of the pilot. This false equivalence between "small" and "big" creates a dangerous disconnect between the pilot's outcomes and the broader organizational reality.

Pilot projects also have a tendency to isolate change within a specific part of the organization, creating a cultural silo. When we establish new ways of working, we are not implementing processes; we are building a shared language and rhythm for the entire organization. Imagine an organization where one team speaks one language, and another team speaks something entirely different—it would result in miscommunication, inefficiency, and chaos. The same happens when one part of the organization adopts a new rhythm while the rest clings to the old. It's like an orchestra where half the musicians ignore the conductor; what results is cacophony, not harmony.

Pilot projects perpetuate this fragmentation. Pilot projects are often framed as a cautious "let's see if it works" experiment. And, unfortunately, they create division, not alignment. Instead of uniting an organization, they highlight misalignment.

Pilot projects, instead of inspiring teams, often invite sabotage. The reality is this: Those who feel threatened by the speed, intensity, or transparency of a new way of working often seize the opportunity to undermine the pilot, whispering, "See? It doesn't work."

But the most glaring failure of pilot projects lies in what they reveal about leadership. A pilot project signals hesitation. It signals doubt. It says, "We're not fully convinced, so let's test this in a corner of the organization and see what happens." This lack of belief communicates an even more damaging message to the organization: that change is negotiable, optional, and expendable. And if leadership is not fully committed, why should anyone else be? This cautious approach often fails because it lacks the critical mass needed for true transformational change. It's like trying to start a blazing fire with just a single matchstick; there may be an initial spark, but without enough fuel, it will quickly fizzle out, leaving nothing but cold ashes of unfulfilled potential.

True transformation is not a cautious experiment; it is a bold declaration. It is a decisive act of leadership that says, "This is where we are going, and we are going together." Genuine transformation demands more than tentative steps. It requires unwavering commitment from all levels of the organization, from top executives to new hires. It's about believing in a vision and having the courage to make bold moves that push boundaries and challenge norms. Transformation requires leaders to reject the timid safety of the pilot project and embrace the courage to go all in. Transformation is not about proving something works; it's about making it work.

A true leader doesn't test the waters—they chart the course and dive in with their teams. Leaders who rely on pilot projects fail to understand that transformation is not about finding "what works in one area"; it's about creating the conditions where the entire organization can thrive. Change cannot be achieved piecemeal because transformation relies on creating a collective momentum that propels the organization forward. It's about building a unified rhythm across all teams, departments, and levels of the organization—a drumbeat so strong and consistent that it shapes the beat of the company's future.

Bold moves are not reckless; they are necessary. Leaders must have the courage to challenge entrenched norms, disrupt comfortable routines, and push their organization beyond its perceived limits. They must create an environment where hesitation is replaced by action, fear by belief, and fragmentation by unity.

Pilot projects may feel like a safe bet, but they are a betrayal of an organization's potential. They are a compromise when what is needed is conviction. Real transformation happens only when leaders and teams commit fully—heart, mind, and resources—to a new way of working. Anything less is a concession to mediocrity.

TRANSFORMATION IS NOT ABOUT PROVING SOMETHING WORKS; IT'S ABOUT MAKING IT WORK.

So, to those who still cling to the pilot project approach, I ask this: What are you waiting for? Are you leading your organization boldly toward tomorrow, or are you content to linger on the sidelines, watching the opportunity for transformation slip away?

5. The Artifacts Shortcut

Organizations must exercise caution when they find themselves tempted to merely adopt the outward symbols of success, without truly understanding and embracing their core essence. It's a common pitfall to believe that implementing surface-level changes, such as erecting a wall of achievements or scheduling weekly synchros, will miraculously transform the organization into a thriving entity. But as we've seen throughout this book, these artifacts, when disconnected from the principles behind the four drivers—brutal focus, distributed leadership, impact over activity, and a disciplined drumbeat—are just illusions of progress.

Many times, I've joined board discussions where someone proudly announces, "All that you've told us is great, but we already work like this: We have a Wall, we work cross-functionally, we have a PMO (project management office) to manage projects, and we even have weekly synchros. Maybe not so 'disciplined and well done' as you described, but we have them." My response is always, "Great! Then let's dive into it so we can build from there. Can you show me the updated Wall for this week?" And that's when the unraveling begins.

"Well," they reply, "I hope it's updated. Maybe it's not as clear as you explained. We also put so many different things on it."

"No problem," I say. "It's a first step. So, who's leading the missions on the Wall?" The response is, "We, the board, and some people on our teams, but always the same people." My internal thought: Oh my God, game over.

The same pattern repeats itself when I hear, "We have synchros too; we've been doing them for years." I ask, "Great! How often?" The reply is, "Well, normally every two to three weeks, it depends, but we haven't been very disciplined lately." Then they mention, "We also have a PMO." I ask, "Who's leading those projects?" The response is, "Well, the PMO and their team leads most of them." My follow-up is, "Okay, okay. And is the PMO framing the most important outcomes for the organization in the short, medium, and long term?" The hesitant response is, "Well, I think we have mostly projects there, but yes, the strategic ones are there too."

This is where I press harder: "Can you show me a single source of truth with the most important priorities for the organization right now?" The silence that follows is telling. "We have it, but we'd need to ask each department for their updates."

"Can you show me the confidence levels for this week in delivering these wildly important goals?" The answer is, "No, I don't think we track that. We might have the business review from last quarter."

I push further: "Can you show me the talent map for all the people working on these missions?" The answer is, "No, HR might have that somewhere." It gets worse: "Can we ensure that one person isn't assigned to five teams at once?" The answer is, "I don't know; we'd have to check with HR."

Finally, I ask, "When's your next synchronization, and can I join?" The response is, "Yes, but I'm not sure when it will happen since I think they have paused now—and we, as leaders, don't always attend."

These conversations expose a hard truth: Many organizations believe they are operating with clarity and discipline when, in reality, they are drowning in fragmented and disconnected artifacts. This isn't a system of brutal focus or a disciplined drumbeat; it's a theater of busyness masquerading as progress. That theater of busyness fills egos and calendars. The truth of focus, ownership, and impact fills real-world results.

Artifacts alone won't create change. In the theater of busyness, they are nothing more than wearing a doctor's white coat without having endured the grueling years of medical school and medical practice. Yes, it might present an impressive facade, but in reality, it won't heal any real

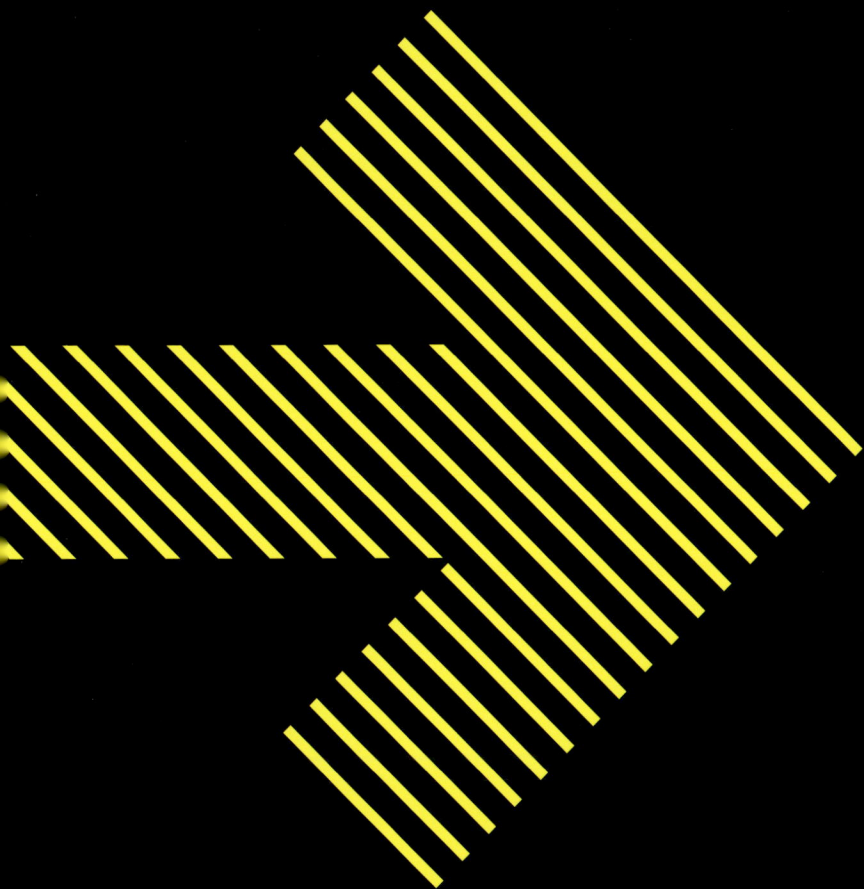

JONATHAN ESCOBAR MARIN

The theater of busyness fills egos and calendars. The truth of focus, ownership, and impact fills real-world results.

ailments. Real transformation demands far more than these cosmetic alterations. It requires embedding the principles behind the four drivers into every level of the organization, and building systems that convert strategy into tangible outcomes.

True organizational metamorphosis necessitates a deep dive into the very marrow of an organization's way of working and culture. It calls for challenging long-held behaviors that have become so ingrained they're almost second nature. It requires reshaping mindsets that have been cemented over time and fostering new habits that align with the vision of success.

Transformation isn't about copying the artifacts of successful organizations, it's about comprehending and implementing the fundamental principles and drivers that guide their success. It's about going through the work of shaping these drivers from the principles, putting them into practice, and evolving, scaling, expanding them through action. Change is a journey of discovery, of unlearning and relearning, of breaking down and rebuilding.

Artifacts alone are not the answer. Merely implementing rituals and visible elements isn't enough to effect lasting change. This is akin to implementing the keeper test to have the same culture as Netflix, or to implement QBRs for OKRs but with the same mindset and behaviors when metrics were called "KPIs" and QBRs "business reviews." Artifacts without ownership, alignment, and discipline are just hollow rituals, disconnected from the brutal focus and seamless execution needed to achieve strategic outcomes.

Action reveals truths that artifacts never will. The path toward lasting change can be daunting, but it's the only one that leads to genuine transformation. It's not an easy path, but it's the only one that promises real growth and enduring success.

Let's return to the experience of Jussi Lystimäki, whose earlier insights on the drumbeat apply powerfully to this discussion of authentic transformation. Having worked with our team to lead major strategic shifts and inspire a culture of agility and innovation, Mr. Lystimäki

JONATHAN ESCOBAR MARIN

Change is a journey of discovery, of unlearning and relearning, of breaking down and rebuilding.

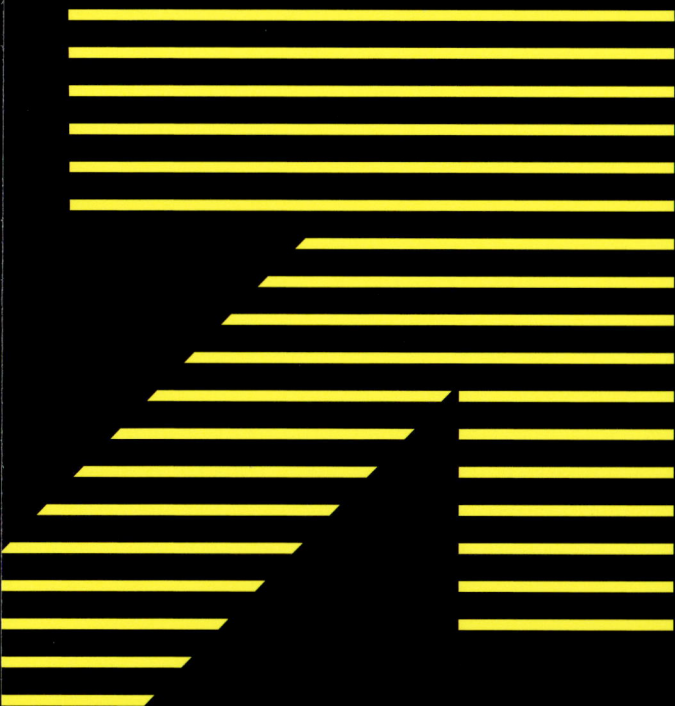

shares his personal learnings and experiences from his transformation journeys: "A successful transformation requires patience and iteration, never shortcuts or deterministic road maps," he tells me. "First, things go slowly forward, maybe a bit backwards, until it truly accelerates. Then you need to change gears to drive it faster."[7]

His testimony reinforces a crucial truth: Organizations that focus on adopting the symbols of transformation without the substance inevitably fail. The real work isn't in erecting a Wall or scheduling meetings—it's in the patient, often uncomfortable journey of authentic change. As Lystimäki suggests, meaningful transformation isn't linear or predictable—there's no shortcut that can replace the genuine work of embedding new principles into every aspect of organizational life. While artifacts might provide the illusion of quick progress, only a sustained commitment to the principles behind them can create lasting transformation that drives real results.

LEADERSHIP HABITS

In a world defined by FATE (fragmentation, ambiguity, turbulence, and entropy), avoiding leadership pitfalls is necessary to prevent change from starting but insufficient to make change thrive. We must actively foster the habits that drive strategy into reality, reality into learnings, learnings into impact, and impact into evolution, renewal, and growth. Just as brutal focus shapes priorities, distributed leadership multiplies impact, impact accelerates learning, and the drumbeat drives evolution and collective elevation, leadership habits are the force multipliers that turn these drivers into unstoppable organizational momentum.

Leadership habits aren't formed in isolation; they must beat in harmony with your organization's transformative rhythm. The power of habits extends beyond individual actions; they become the living pulse of organizational culture. When leaders consistently demonstrate these habits, they create the psychological safety and collective and individual clarity needed for teams to thrive in uncertainty. These habits aren't just behaviors; they're also the neural pathways of high-performing, high-impact organizations.

Habits are automated behavioral patterns that become embedded in the brain's efficiency-seeking mechanisms, ensuring that we don't expend unnecessary focus on routine tasks.[8] By establishing and relying on these leadership habits, the brain can focus its resources on novel or complex challenges. In essence, we free up our talents' minds from nonvaluable tasks, such as chasing approvals through hierarchical layers, preparing PowerPoint karaokes for status updates, defending past activities instead of focusing on future impact, wrestling with the scheduling of meetings, or wondering when and how to escalate obstacles. By establishing these habits through the drumbeat, teams can focus their energy on what truly matters: owning ambitious missions, making BIG choices, driving seamless execution, learning fast from results, and continuously evolving their impact. This allows them to focus solely on the business challenges, prioritizing, executing, anticipating obstacles, and making decisions.

At its core, the process of habit formation revolves around the development of neural pathways. Think of it like creating a shortcut on a computer; rather than going through a long process every time you want to perform a task, the shortcut allows for quick and efficient access. Similarly, when we repeat an action or behavior often enough, the brain starts to process that behavior through a more direct neural route. This shortcut is facilitated by a loop: A cue triggers a craving, which motivates a response, which delivers a reward. This pattern is the backbone of every habit.[9] Over time, as this loop is reinforced, the connection between the cue and the routine strengthens, making the behavior more automatic.

This automation is crucial for daily functioning. Imagine if every daily task, from brushing your teeth to driving to work, required active thought and decision-making. We'd be overwhelmed and exhausted in no time! Habits, in essence, free up our cognitive bandwidth, allowing us to focus on tasks that require more attention and critical thinking. Moreover, positive habits can have a transformative impact on individuals and organizations alike. They create systems of behavior that operate below the level of conscious awareness, paving the way for consistency, efficiency, and growth, all while conserving our cognitive resources for the wildly important tasks and decisions that arise.[10]

Let's look at some proven leadership habits that reinforce the four drivers of success and form high-impact teams.

Habit 1: Connect Relentlessly with the "Why"

Leaders must ignite teams by relentlessly connecting them with the "why" behind their mission and make them viscerally understand the importance of their impact—or the lack thereof. They need to vividly articulate the reasons why the team's mission is crucial to the company's success and illuminate the interdependence that exists with other teams' missions. It is essential to ensure that the team internalizes the relevance of its execution in delivering the expected result, fostering an unwavering commitment to a common purpose.

Habit 2: Shape Reality with Radical Clarity

Leaders must forge radical clarity and crystallize understanding about the outcomes to be delivered. To do this, they must transform each communication into a catalyst for action, presenting teams with precise missions, anchored by clear targets, that are time bound and free of ambiguity. During weekly synchros, they must sharpen the team's focus and projection on the mission's target, their bets, initiatives, and key actions, building unequivocal clarity about their confidence and commitment to them.

Habit 3: Enable Ruthless Prioritization to Make an Impact

It is key to empower teams to prioritize with fierce intention. Success demands one specific mission that is crystal clear, measurable, and time bound; one specific team that is cross-functional, cross-hierarchy, and fully empowered; and one specific execution that is unmissable, ruthlessly prioritized, and impact-driven. To achieve this specific execution, leaders must guide teams without micromanaging, ensuring at all times that they have unwavering clarity about their 3-3-3 BIG choices: the three quantified bets, the three initiatives to achieve each bet, and the three most important outcomes of the glidepath per initiative for the following weeks. The goal is to ensure that teams maintain laser focus on what is truly crucial to unleash the outcome of their missions.

Habit 4: Make the Drumbeat Clearly Heard

Leaders must ensure that the drumbeat sounds loud and clear, starting with a compelling and continuous pulse of communication that orchestrates the quarterly key moments of truth: when teams can expect the reviewed Wall and the feedback meetup each quarter, and how the weekly synchros will unfold in the next cycle, liberating teams from uncertainty about when things will happen, who will be there, and what is expected.

Leaders must hammer the culture into every move, driving a relentless rhythm of focus and impact through every synchro and Wall reset. The unambiguous communication through the drumbeat must clarify not only when things happen, but also the standards by which they happen: what inputs to bring, what outputs to expect, who will be there, and their roles. Making these rhythmic collaboration points consistently alive in internal communication channels reduces cognitive load, while regular reinforcement of each checkpoint's purpose and timing helps team members embed both the practical value and deeper meaning of these rituals. When teams operate within this clear structure, it establishes predictable patterns that become automatic mental schemas, reduces decision fatigue by eliminating recurring scheduling decisions, creates stable reference points for navigating complexity, and channels mental bandwidth from cross-silo coordination toward higher-value activities like innovation, impact creation, and meaningful collaboration—a shift that proves especially valuable in organizations where traditional governance and reporting structures often consume disproportionate mental energy.

Habit 5: Forge a Tribe Identity

A tribe feeling is kindled by authentically embedding a shared sense of purpose and culture within teams, unleashing them to use and take ownership of powerful communication resources, motivating them to organically advocate for their way of working beyond the organization. To achieve this, leaders must equip teams with tailored, accessible, and dynamic communication assets and opportunities that enable them to inspire others with the core values and principles that fuel their way of working, sparking genuine pride and a sense of belonging in what they do and how they do it. Pride and ownership are the bedrock of a high-impact culture.

Habit 6: Energize with Your Words

Energizing with words is vital, especially in the valleys of disappointment that every team traverses during the quarter. Leaders should challenge themselves before meeting with each team: *Do I want to communicate like an automated phone recording, or do I want to ignite a wild desire to act, as a true leader would?* Reflecting on the last communication and before the next one is crucial to embody the type of leader we choose to be.

Habit 7: Foster a Relationship of Proximity

Fostering proximity means being accessible without micromanaging, creating periodic anchors that remind the team that they have a safe space, at a defined time, to receive help and guidance and to unlock obstacles or decisions. Offering these safe spaces liberates the team from the need to seek out the leader, focusing their attention and reinforcing their stability and psychological security; they know you're there, when they can count on you, and they know you won't micromanage because you'll help them discover answers on their own and lead with more autonomy and confidence.

Habit 8: Inspire Ambition to Exceed Resources

Leaders must instill a founder's attitude in their teams, ensuring that their ambition and eagerness surpass their current resources. To do this, each week they should inspire each team to improve or pioneer new ways of approaching challenges, sharing practical improvements or mindsets that can be applied immediately, focusing on what they should do, change, or catalyze to rise above circumstances and victimhood. Provoking them with questions like, *What would you do if the survival of your company depended on achieving something in a week and not in a month?* helps to cement the principle of never playing the victim and always taking responsibility with a high sense of urgency.

Habit 9: Lead by Example

Leadership is service, period. Your drumbeat powers your cultural beat—miss a beat, and you lose the rhythm. Leading by example is the embodiment of role-modeling through the drumbeat, where leaders themselves demonstrate the discipline and commitment they expect from their teams. Missing once is an accident. Missing twice is a choice. Missing three times is sabotage. When you lead, you elevate—you forge leaders out of your team members. You grow by growing people through your example and service, not with pep talks on a stage once per quarter. Service means being intentionally present in the drumbeat, in the rhythm of progress. When teams execute and need guidance, alignment, energy, and unlocking—those are the drumbeat's moments of truth. Remember, teams are too busy to listen to your speeches; they just see your behaviors in the drumbeat.

Teams trust leaders who consistently walk the talk, nothing else.

Missing **ONCE** is an ACCIDENT
Missing **TWICE** is a CHOICE
Missing **THREE** times is SABOTAGE

Image 5.0: Leadership is service—demanding consistent example, not intentions.
© 2025, Jonathan Escobar Marin

Habit 10: Close the Loop, Boost the Trust

Demonstrating leadership credibility requires swift decision-making and obstacle removal with committed time frames. In essence, closing the loop and building trust means showing teams the quick response time and velocity expected from them by resolving obstacles or making decisions within a week's time. This involves crystal clear communication with the teams, ensuring they have complete clarity on the direction and decisions, allowing them to focus on the next steps with full confidence and without any doubts. When leaders consistently deliver their commitments on time, teams naturally accelerate their own delivery cycles.

JONATHAN ESCOBAR MARIN

TEAMS ARE TOO BUSY TO LISTEN TO YOUR SPEECHES; THEY JUST SEE YOUR BEHAVIORS IN THE DRUMBEAT

Habit 11: Cut the Crap

Transforming complexity into simplicity is a fundamental leadership habit. Leaders should ruthlessly simplify and eliminate the unnecessary by working with teams to reduce or stop the excess of meetings, projects, initiatives, reports, or presentations, and communicate in unambiguous terms about what should be stopped or postponed, keeping the teams' cognitive focus on what truly drives impact.

True courage in leadership isn't found in starting new initiatives, but in the bold act of elimination—daring to say no to deeply ingrained practices, halting seemingly unstoppable processes, and challenging "we've always done it this way" thinking. It's about having the fierce courage to cut through what seems untouchable, to brave the uncomfortable questions of "what will happen if we stop this?" It's about recognizing that every yes to the nonessential is a no to something potentially transformative and having the fortitude to create space for what truly deserves our energy and focus. Real leadership means having the bravery to stop what everyone assumes must continue, making room for what could genuinely revolutionize the game.

Habit 12: Stop Ambiguity

Leaders should shatter ambiguity by crystallizing expectations, explicitly communicating the behaviors and achievements that will be recognized and rewarded, and establishing complete mental security for all team members about what is expected and what is not regarding their behaviors, attitude, mindset, and performance. Precision in these expectations forges the foundation for high impact and high performance.

Habit 13: Embrace Recognition

Making recognition a habit means celebrating the expected behaviors at an individual or team level, day by day, week by week, without waiting for the perfect moment or the quarterly formal awards event. It's essential that the recognition catalyzes not only the recognized individuals, empowering them to further amplify their actions, but also ignites the rest of the organization, setting the standard expected of everyone. Recognition becomes the fuel that propels collective elevation.

Habit 14: Stop the Undesirable Before It Normalizes

Stopping undesired behaviors before they become normalized is crucial. Performance debt is like technical debt: The longer you wait to address it, the more costly it becomes. Building a high-impact, high-performing culture requires paying down this debt consistently and proactively. Taking swift, decisive action when standards aren't met preserves cultural integrity and signals unwavering commitment to the impact customers expect; for this, leaders need to act decisively against poor performance or attitudes that fall below clearly stated expectations to prevent them from becoming the new standard. This habit cultivates a culture where the people we want on our teams feel inspired to contribute their best and be part of a coherent, high-performing environment.

After reading this section, examine your habits and reflect: Are they the product of innumerable little moments of cowardice, fears, and hints of comfort—or of your bold courage and innovative reasoning to create an unbeatable organization with a rhythm of unmissable execution? Let this question guide your transformation before we wrap up with a few final thoughts.

THE BEAT OF YOUR LEGACY

It's breathtaking how unfocused, unled, impact-less, slow, and unevolving many companies are, and they think nothing of it. Your opportunity as a leader is to reset these four dimensions because now you are aware of them, and many leaders like you have done it. Beware, without stopping for a minute, that the path to a culture of high performance, high

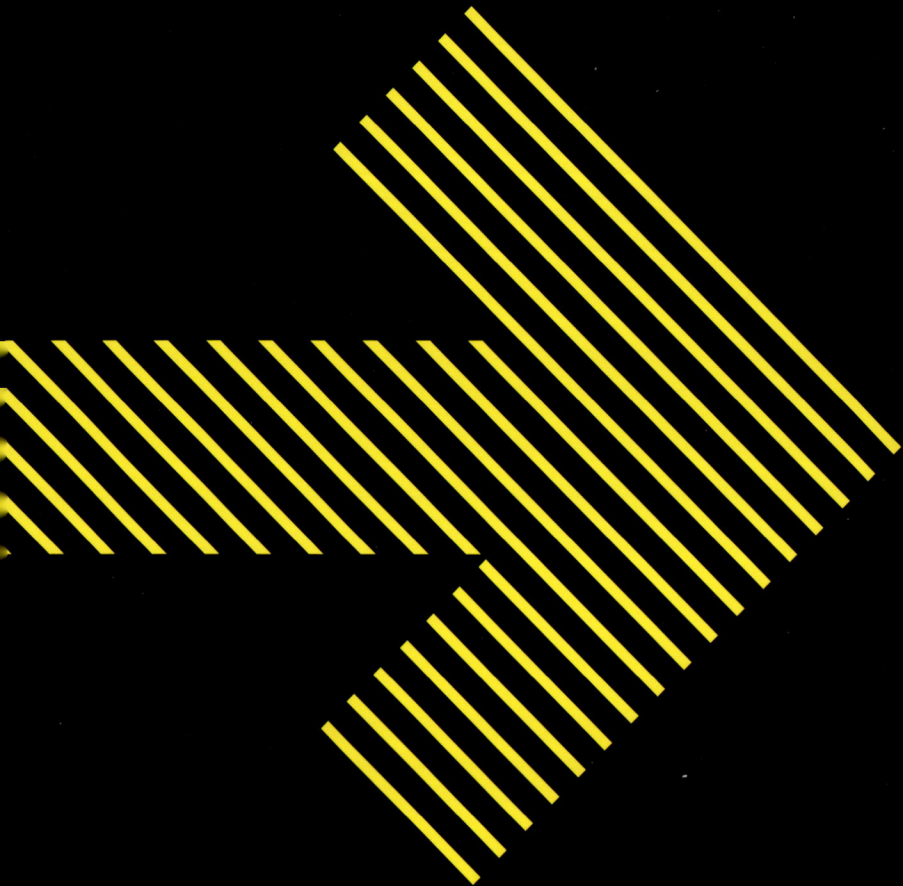

JONATHAN ESCOBAR MARIN

Performance debt is like technical debt:

The longer you wait to address it, the more costly it becomes. Building a high-impact, high-performing culture requires paying down this debt consistently and proactively.

impact isn't a sprint; it's a marathon without a finish line—one where the success of the collective depends on each individual's commitment to growing up to victory.

This journey of cultural shift demands unwavering commitment, and the courage to challenge the status quo. It's about creating an environment where performance, impact, and care coexist, where high standards and human development reinforce each other rather than compete. The path involves running with narrowing focus, developing more leaders, generating greater impact, achieving higher velocity, and continuously evolving standards—all while ensuring that everyone has equal opportunity to contribute, learn from failures, and grow.

True leadership means investing in people's growth while maintaining clear performance expectations. It's about creating an impact-based culture where support and accountability go hand in hand. Those who demonstrate commitment through their actions naturally receive more support to grow and opportunities to advance, while those who choose not to engage with the common good and shared mission naturally self-select their path. In high-performing, high-impact organizations, people can focus on their impact and have confidence that if they deliver it, great things will happen for both the company and themselves personally.

This journey will push our organizations forward, at a completely different speed, pace, and level. It will be uncomfortable, even painful at times. But that discomfort is the price of progress. Not everyone will have the stamina or the will to keep up, and that's to be expected. The process reveals not just individual performers, but also builders—those who elevate their peers while pursuing collective victory. This isn't about going alone or together; it's about creating a high-impact community where individual excellence catalyzes collective achievement.

Driving this change isn't easy. It pushes people out of their comfort zones and inevitably faces resistance. Some may even vote with their feet. But remember, the leader's job isn't to be popular; it's to change the status quo for the common good. That is defined by customers, employees, and society. For those who want to make everyone happy,

JONATHAN ESCOBAR MARIN

In high-performing, high-impact organizations, people can focus on their impact and have confidence that if they deliver it, great things will happen for both the company and themselves.

running an ice cream shop is the best option—and an important one. Leadership, however, isn't about pleasing everyone; it's about doing what's right for all, even when it's hard for some.

In a world often preoccupied with feel-good initiatives and aggregated employee satisfaction scores (which measure those who drain the energy and motivation of others too), we must recognize that true organizational vitality emerges from a deeper understanding of human potential. Just as we opened this book acknowledging that unpredictability is the only stability, we must embrace that human excellence thrives not in comfort, but in purposeful challenge. The modern workplace cannot become a refuge for mediocrity, nor can it be a grinding machine that treats humans as replaceable cogs. Instead, we must forge environments where performance, impact for customers, and humanity reinforce each other—where the pursuit of building great products and services that solve unsolved problems for others becomes the ultimate form of human care.

This is not about choosing between employee well-being and business results. Rather, it's about understanding that in an age where AI, humanoid robots, and AI agents increasingly handle human tasks, human work must evolve toward its highest expression.

The brutal focus we champion, the distributed leadership we cultivate, the impact-driven seamless execution we demand, and the disciplined drumbeat we forge—these are not just business imperatives; they are also human imperatives in an era that demands we move faster and think bigger than ever before. They represent the path to uniquely human and meaningful work in an age where AI, as an amplifier, augments our capabilities, freeing us to focus on what makes us distinctively human.

Leaders must become the energy catalysts of human-alive organizations, not by demanding mechanical performance, but by creating cultures where meaningful impact through great products and services is the natural outcome of engaged, supported, and purposeful teams. Sustainable superior success comes not from choosing between people and performance, but from creating systems where both flourish together.

The high-performing, high-impact cultures we have built with leaders across the globe aren't just about business results; they're also about redefining work itself for a new era, because work is the most powerful force on the planet to lead positive impact at scale.

Your legacy isn't what you leave behind. Your legacy is the beat that will continue evolving all around it. It's the rhythm that will outlast your individual contribution—the one that will continue after you've stopped playing. It's the beat that will keep inspiring others to keep going. It's the enduring pulse that will drive progress, a sound that will grow louder as others join in, ensuring it echoes far beyond your own time.

This is why your legacy isn't measured in quarters or years; it's in the beat of the culture that continues to focus, elevate, accelerate, and transform long after you're gone. The true measure of a leader's heritage is not in the temporary victories you achieve, but in the lasting rhythm you create—a beat that transforms possibilities into priorities, potential into performance, activity into impact, and challenges into advancement.

Your legacy is a culture where humans can contribute their uniquely human capabilities: creativity, emotional intelligence, complex problem-solving, and innovative thinking—all while maintaining the scrappy entrepreneurial spirit that drives true innovation. In this way, we elevate our workforces to their highest potential, embracing AI as an amplifier of human capability rather than a replacement, and protecting them from the only real threat: the loss of purpose and meaning in their work.

Take your vision of a high-performing, high-impact culture and breathe life into it with relentless urgency. Transform potential into results, focusing harder, empowering better, moving faster, and aiming higher every single day. Create an environment where caring for people means helping them achieve their highest potential through growth that sparks creativity, not enabling complacency.

JONATHAN ESCOBAR MARIN

Create an environment where performance, impact, and care coexist, where high standards and human development reinforce each other rather than compete.

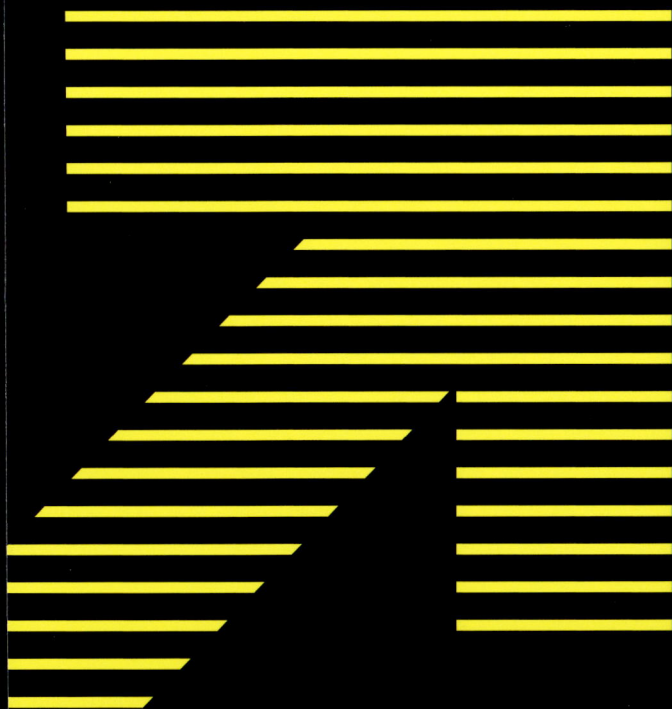

For those who want to make everyone happy, running an ice cream shop is the best option—and an important one. Leadership, however, isn't about pleasing everyone; it's about doing what's right for all, even when it's hard for some.

Mediocrity and high performance stand before us as equal possibilities in this new world. What separates them is not chance, but choice. As leaders, we need to swing the balance—not just for our organizations, but also for the future of human work.

Transform potential into results by focusing harder, empowering better, moving faster, and aiming higher every single day.

JONATHAN ESCOBAR MARIN

→ **WORK IS THE MOST POWERFUL FORCE ON THE PLANET TO LEAD POSITIVE IMPACT AT SCALE.**

Your legacy isn't what you leave behind. Your legacy is the beat that will continue evolving all around it.

JONATHAN ESCOBAR MARIN

NOTES

INTRODUCTION

1. Peter Bartram, *IT and Corporate Transformation* (Business Intelligence, 1995).
2. Andreas Joehle, in discussion with the author.

CHAPTER 1

1. Jerome du Chaffaut, in discussion with the author.
2. Mark Ritson, "Mark Ritson: Starbucks and Nestlé Must Focus on Three Key Areas to Avoid a Bitter Brew," *Marketing Week*, May 8, 2018, https://www.marketingweek.com/mark-ritson-starbucks-and-nestle.
3. Rajat Gupta and Jim Wendler, "Leading Change: An Interview with the CEO of P&G," *McKinsey Quarterly*, July 2005, https://leadway.org/PDF/Leading%20Change%20-%20An%20Interview%20with%20the%20CEO%20of%20P&G.pdf.
4. Paul Chandler and John Sweller, "Cognitive Load Theory and the Format of Instruction," *Cognition and Instruction* 8, no. 4 (December 1991): 293–332, https://doi.org/10.1207/s1532690xci0804_2.
5. John R. Rizzo, Robert J. House, and Sidney I. Lirtzman, "Role Conflict and Ambiguity in Complex Organizations," *Administrative Science Quarterly* 15 (1970): 150–63.
6. Justin Apsey, in discussion with the author.
7. Steve Jobs, "Apple's World Wide Developers Conference 1997 with Steve Jobs," superapple4ever, posted on June 5, 2011, YouTube video, 1:10:50, https://www.youtube.com/watch?v=GnO7D5UaDig&t=1s.
8. Gupta and Wendler, "Leading Change."
9. Gupta and Wendler, "Leading Change."

10. Robert B. Duncan, "The Ambidextrous Organization: Designing Dual Structures for Innovation," in Ralph H. Kilmann, Louis R. Pondy, and Dennis Patrick Slevin, eds., *The Management of Organization Design: Strategies and Implementation* (North Holland, 1976), 167–88; James G. March, "Exploration and Exploitation in Organizational Learning," *Organization Science* 2, no .1 (1991): 71–87, https://psycnet.apa.org/doi/10.1287/orsc.2.1.71.

11. Charles A. O'Reilly III and Michael L. Tushman, "Organizational Ambidexterity: Past, Present, and Future," *Academy of Management Perspectives* 27, no. 4 (2013): 25, https://doi.org/10.5465/amp.2013.0025.

12. Julian Birkinshaw and Cristina Gibson, "Building Ambidexterity into an Organization," *MIT Sloan Management Review*, July 15, 2004, https://sloanreview.mit.edu/article/building-ambidexterity-into-an-organization/.

13. Wendy K. Smith and Marianne W. Lewis, "Toward a Theory of Paradox: A Dynamic Equilibrium Model of Organizing," *Academy of Management Review* 36, no. 2 (2011): 381–403, https://psycnet.apa.org/doi/10.5465/AMR.2011.59330958.

14. Regina Kuzmina, in discussion with the author.

15. Jay Yarow, "Jony Ive: This Is the Most Important Thing I Learned from Steve Jobs," *Business Insider*, October 10, 2014, https://www.businessinsider.com/jony-ive-this-is-the-most-important-thing-i-learned-from-steve-jobs-2014-10.

CHAPTER 2

1. Rajat Gupta and Jim Wendler, "Leading Change: An Interview with the CEO of P&G," *McKinsey Quarterly*, July 2005, https://leadway.org/PDF/Leading%20Change%20-%20An%20Interview%20with%20the%20CEO%20of%20P&G.pdf.

2. Rosa Carabel, in discussion with the author.

3. George A. Miller, "The Magical Number Seven, Plus or Minus Two: Some Limits on Our Capacity for Processing Information," *Psychological Review* 63, no. 2 (1956): 81–97, https://psycnet.apa.org/doi/10.1037/h0043158.

4. John Sweller, "Cognitive Load During Problem Solving: Effects on Learning," *Cognitive Science* 12, no. 2 (1988): 257–85, https://doi .org/10.1207/s15516709cog1202_4.

5. Edwin A. Locke and Gary P. Latham, "Building a Practically Useful Theory of Goal Setting and Task Motivation: A 35-Year Odyssey," *American Psychologist* 57, no. 9 (2002): 705–17, https://doi .org/10.1037//0003-066x.57.9.705.

6. Robert S. Kaplan and David P. Norton, "The Balanced Scorecard: Measures That Drive Performance," *Harvard Business Review* (1992): 71–79, https://hbr.org/1992/01/the-balanced-scorecard-measures -that-drive-performance-2.

7. Henri Tajfel and John Turner, "An Integrative Theory of Intergroup Conflict," in W. G. Austin and S. Worchel, eds., *The Social Psychology of Intergroup Relations* (Brooks/Cole, 1979), 33–37.

8. Daniel J. Beal, Robin R. Cohen, Michael J. Burke, and Christy L. McLendon, "Cohesion and Performance in Groups: A Meta-Analytic Clarification of Construct Relations," *Journal of Applied Psychology* 88, no. 6 (2003): 989–1004, https://doi.org/10.1037/0021-9010.88.6.989.

9. Pol Codina, in discussion with the author.

10. Melissa A. Valentine, Amanda L. Pratt, Rebecca Hinds, and Michael S. Bernstein, "The Algorithm and the Org Chart: How Algorithms Can Conflict with Organizational Structures," *Proceedings of the ACM on Human–Computer Interaction* 8 (2024): article 364.

11. Amy Edmondson, "Psychological Safety and Learning Behavior in Work Teams," *Administrative Science Quarterly* 44, no. 2 (June 1999): 350–83, https://doi.org/10.2307/2666999.

12. J. Richard Hackman and Greg R. Oldham, "Motivation through the Design of Work: Test of a Theory," *Organizational Behavior and Human Performance* 16, no. 2 (1976): 250–79, https://psycnet.apa.org/ doi/10.1016/0030-5073(76)90016-7; Edward L. Deci and Richard M. Ryan, *Intrinsic Motivation and Self-Determination in Human Behavior* (Springer eBooks, 1985), https://doi.org/10.1007/978-1-4899-2271-7.

13. Patrick Lencioni, *The Five Dysfunctions of a Team: A Leadership Fable*, 20th anniversary ed. (Wiley, 2010).

14. Peter Senge, *The Fifth Discipline* (Currency, 1990).

15. Larry Huston and Nabil Sakkab, "Connect and Develop: Inside Procter & Gamble's New Model for Innovation," *Harvard Business Review*, March 2006.

16. A. G. Lafley, "A Fortune 50/500 View of Freelancing," *Medium* (blog), December 29, 2021, https://medium.com/@leadingtowin/a-fortune-50 -500-view-of-freelancing-cc5a4a93bf47.

17. Alfonso Gómez, in discussion with the author.

18. Gómez, in discussion with the author.

19. Justin Apsey, in discussion with the author.

20. Brian Tracy, *Great Little Book on the Gift of Self-Confidence* (Career Press, Inc., 1997).

21. Noel M. Tichy, *The Leadership Engine* (Collins Business Essentials, 1998), http://archive.org/details/leadershipengine00tich_0.

22. Carabel, in discussion with the author.

23. Carabel, in discussion with the author.

24. Christine Doig-Cardet, in discussion with the author.

25. Doig-Cardet, in discussion with the author.

CHAPTER 3

1. K. Anders Ericsson, Ralf T. Krampe, and Clemens Tesch-Romer, "The Role of Deliberate Practice in the Acquisition of Expert Performance," *Psychological Review* 100, no. 3 (1993): 363–406, https://psycnet.apa .org/doi/10.1037/0033-295X.100.3.363.

2. Carol S. Dweck, *Mindset: The New Psychology of Success* (Random House, 2006).

3. Leena Rao, "Facebook's Zuckerberg: If I Were Starting a Company Now, I Would Have Stayed in Boston," *TechCrunch* (blog), October 30, 2011, https://techcrunch.com/2011/10/30/facebooks-zuckerberg-if-i-were -starting-a-company-now-i-would-have-stayed-in-boston/.

4. Judith Viader, in discussion with the author.

5. Jeff Bezos, "Transcript for Jeff Bezos: Amazon and Blue Origin | Lex Fridman Podcast #405," Lex Fridman, https://lexfridman.com/jeff -bezos-transcript/.

6. Takehiko Harada, *Management Lessons from Taiichi Ohno: What Every Leader Can Learn from the Man Who Invented the Toyota Production System* (McGraw-Hill, 2015).

7. Placid Jover, in discussion with the author.

8. Jover, in discussion with the author.

9. Jensen Huang, "A Conversation with NVIDIA's Jensen Huang," Stripe, posted on May 21, 2024, YouTube video, 1:04:49, https://www.youtube.com/watch?v=8Pfa8kPjUio.

10. "Video: Steve Jobs One-on-One, the '95 Interview," *ComputerWorld*, October 27, 2011, https://www.computerworld.com/article/1534762/video-steve-jobs-one-on-one-the-95-interview.html.

11. Arantxa García, in discussion with the author.

CHAPTER 4

1. "Microsoft's CEO on the Power of Being a Learn-It-All," Next Big Idea Club, https://nextbigideaclub.com/magazine/conversation-microsofts-ceo-on-the-power-of-being-a-learn-it-all/17851/.

2. Daniel H. Pink, *Drive: The Surprising Truth about What Motivates Us* (Riverhead Books, 2011), https://www.danpink.com/books/drive.

3. Enna Kursukangas, in discussion with the author.

4. Alvin Toffler's interview with Herbert Gerjuoy. *Future Shock* reissue (Bantam, 1984).

5. Jim Collins and Jerry I. Porras, *Built to Last: Successful Habits of Visionary Companies* (Harper Business, 1994).

6. Jim Collins and Jerry I. Porras, "Building Your Company's Vision," *Harvard Business Review* 74 (1996): 65–77.

7. Jim Collins, *Good to Great: Why Some Companies Make the Leap . . . and Others Don't* (Harper Business, 2001).

8. "Brand Keys Loyalty Leaders 2024," Brand Keys, September 9, 2024, https://brandkeys.com/wp-content/uploads/2024/09/PRESS-RELEASE-2024-Loyalty-Leaders.pdf.

9. Annie Brown, "Apparel 50 2024," Brand Finance, https://brandirectory.com/reports/apparel.

10. "Jeff Bezos Says Washington Post Could Take a Page from Amazon," ABC News, September 24, 2013, https://abcnews.go.com/Technology/jeff-bezos-washington-post-page-amazon/story?id=20364644.

11. Eleanor Pringle, "Netflix Wants Managers to Ask Themselves Whether They Would Rehire Their Current Employees—and Fire Them, If the Answer Is No," *Fortune*, June 25, 2024, https://fortune.com/2024/06/25/netflix-managers-keeper-test-rehire-or-fire-staff/.

12. "Netflix Culture—the Best Work of Our Lives," Netflix, accessed March 15, 2025, https://jobs.netflix.com/culture.

13. "Satya Nadella Email to Employees on First Day as CEO," Microsoft, February 4, 2014, https://news.microsoft.com/2014/02/04/satya -nadella-email-to-employees-on-first-day-as-ceo/.

14. Jussi Lystimäki, in discussion with the author.

WHAT IS NEEDED

1. Judith Viader, in discussion with the author.

2. Jerome du Chaffaut, in discussion with the author.

3. Charles W. Tolman, *Problems of Theoretical Psychology* (Captus Press, 1996).

4. Dan Millman, *Way of the Peaceful Warrior: A Basically True Story* (J.P. Tarcher; Distributed by Houghton Mifflin, 1980).

5. Joe Clifford, "What Is Genchi Genbutsu? Toyota Production System Guide," *Toyota UK Magazine*, July 25, 2024, https://mag.toyota.co.uk/ genchi-genbutsu/.

6. Jennifer Pinter, "Transforming Organizations: Lessons from John Kotter's Change Model," Kapta, accessed April 15, 2025, https://kapta .com/resources/key-account-management-blog/transforming -organizations-lessons-from-john-kotters-change-model.

7. Jussi Lystimäki, in discussion with the author.

8. Ann M. Graybiel, "Habits, Rituals, and the Evaluative Brain," *Annual Review of Neuroscience* 31, no. 1 (2008): 359–87, https://doi. org/10.1146/annurev.neuro.29.051605.112851.

9. James Clear, *Atomic Habits: An Easy and Proven Way to Build Good Habits and Break Bad Ones* (Penguin Random House, 2018).

10. Charles Duhigg, *The Power of Habit: Why We Do What We Do in Life and Business* (Random House, 2014).

INDEX

A

accessibility, optimizing, 150

accountability
across all organizational levels, 161
distributed leadership and, 108, 120, 126
pilot mindset, 191–96

action plans, 55

Advanced Customer Decoding, 145–48

agentic AI, 1–2, 121, 183–85

Agile theater, 52–53, 188–89

agility, beating turbulence with, 16–20

Allen, Brandt, 15, 17

ambiguity
distributed leadership, beating with, 12–15, 27
as enemy of execution, 136
overview, 4, 6
stopping, 310

ambition, 72, 75–76, 307

analysis paralysis, combating, 88–91, 180–83

annual recurring revenue (ARR), 72, 75–76

anticipating threats and opportunities, 16–19

antifragility, 19

Apple, 255, 257

Apsey, Justin, 64–67, 133, 135

ARR (annual recurring revenue), 72, 75–76

artifacts shortcut, 297–302

artificial intelligence (AI)
AI³, 186
cross-functional teams powered by, 13–15
as impact partner, 183–87
layering on outdated structures, 15
O-shaped talent model, 120–27
unpredictability in business and, 1–6

assessments, fallacy of, 284–89, 290

augmented mediocrity (RAM), 72, 75–76

autonomy, 126

B

BBVA Switzerland, 131

behavioral segmentation, 146, 148–52

bets
creating initiatives, 151–53

overview, 136, 139–40
segmentation unleashing, 150–51
Bezos, Jeff, 183, 184, 260, 261, 284
BIG choices
creating initiatives from bets, 151–53
enabling ruthless prioritization, 304–5
evolving from initiatives to glidepath, 153–55
overview, 136, 139–40, 142
segmentation unleashing big bets, 150–51
Birkinshaw, Julian, 80
BlackBerry, 255
brutal focus
analytical paralysis, overcoming, 88–91
beating FATE with, 9–11, 27
building, 49–52
cross-silos compass, 91–98
cutting the crap, 67–79
organizational ambidexterity, 79–88
overview, 8, 34
power of strategy, 43–48
reflection questions, 101
the Wall, 52–67
Buffett, Warren, 222
Built to Last (Collins & Porras), 254
busyness, 65–67

C

Carabel, Rosa, 110, 156–60
Chaffaut, Jerome du, 49, 51, 284
challenges, overcoming, 258–61
clarity, commitment to, 63–64

closing loop and boosting trust, 308–9
Codina, Pol, 118, 120
cognitive load theory, 63, 113
cognitive psychology, 113
collaboration sessions, 126–27
collective intelligence, 13, 133, 135
collective learning, 207, 209
collective ownership, 161
Collins, Jim, 254
communication
about the Stop Wall, 69
closing loop and boosting trust, 308
commitment to clarity and simplicity, 63–64
distributed leadership and, 112
in effective teams, 126–27
energizing with words, 306
making drumbeat clearly heard, 305–6
radical clarity, shaping reality with, 304
radical transparency, 69, 71
unambiguous, 305–6
competitive advantage, 170
complacency, fighting against, 233
"connect and develop" strategy, 127
connecting relentlessly with "why," 304
continuous innovation, 23–26
continuous learning, 127
continuous reevaluation of talent, 269
core ideology, 254–57, 293
cross-functional teams, 107–13, 123, 161. *See also* distributed leadership
cross-silos compass, 91–98
culture

drumbeat as, 31–35
shaping with every beat, 241–44
Customer Compass, 147–48
customers. *See also* segmentation
ambiguity caused by preferences,
12
retention, improving, 117
turbulence caused by preferences,
15–16
cutting the crap
courage to say no, 76–79
as leadership habit, 310
overview, 67–68
Pareto principle and, 68, 70
resource management and, 72,
75–76
the Stop Wall, 69

D

Danone, 210, 213
"day one" mentality, 10
decision-making speed, 172, 176–78,
180–83
decisive action, prioritizing over
analysis paralysis, 88–91
deliberate practice, 168
Delusion of Uniqueness, 282, 289–93
demographic segmentation, 147, 150
deprioritization, ruthless, 10
development life cycles, 20
digital campaigns, 152, 154
disciplined drumbeat
beating FATE with, 20–26, 27
evolution consistent with essence,
254–58
evolution of, 224–29
gemba, 229–30
general discussion, 221–24

Keep, Improve, Start, and Stop,
230–33
leadership development, 244–47
leading to beat, 28–38
making drumbeat clearly heard,
305–6
onboarding, 249–50
overview, 8, 34
performance management,
247–48
refining the Wall, 233–34
reflection questions, 280
renewing the Stop Wall, 234–36
sales and operations planning,
248–49
shaping culture with every beat,
241–44
succession planning, 250–53
synchronized evolution, 236–41
talent review process, 262–70
victim mindset, avoiding, 258–61
as vital force, 270–80
distributed leadership. *See also* one
specific execution; one specific
team
beating FATE with, 12–15, 27
benefits of, 107–12
breaking free from siloed thinking,
105–7
leaders building new leaders,
155–63
1:1:1 Formula, 112–13
one specific mission, 113–17
overview, 8, 34
transparency and, 241
Doig-Cardet, Christine, 160–61
drumbeat, disciplined. *See* disciplined
drumbeat
duality of exploration and
exploitation. *See* organizational
ambidexterity

Duncan, Robert, 79
Dweck, Carol, 168

E

Edmondson, Amy, 126
electric vehicle (EV) company, 85–88
employee engagement, brutal focus
    and, 63–64
empowering new leaders, 266–69
energizing with words, 306
engagement events, 44, 47
entropy, 4, 6, 20–26, 27
Ericsson, Anders, 168
Eroski, 110, 156–60
essence, drumbeat evolution
    consistent with, 254–58
evolution of drumbeat
    gemba, 229–30
    Keep, Improve, Start, and Stop,
        230–33
    leadership development, 244–47
    onboarding, 249–50
    overview, 224–29
    performance management,
        247–48
    refining the Wall, 233–34
    renewing the Stop Wall, 234–36
    sales and operations planning,
        248–49
    shaping culture with every beat,
        241–44
    succession planning, 250–53
    synchronized evolution, 236–41
exceptionalism, delusion of, 289–93
execution, 44–49, 117. *See also* one
    specific execution
exploitation, 79–85, 87–88
exploration, 79–85, 87–88

F

Fallacy of Assessments, 282, 284–89
FAST approach, 118, 120
Fatal Five, 58, 62–63
FATE
    beating with leadership rhythm, 27
    brutal focus and, 9–11
    disciplined drumbeat and, 20–26
    distributed leadership and, 12–15
    four forces of, 4, 6
    impact over activity and, 15–20
fear of failure, 170
feedback meetup, 263
Fernandez, Fernando, 72
5 pitfalls
    Delusion of Uniqueness, 282,
        289–93
    Fallacy of Assessments, 282,
        284–89
    Flawed Pilot Project Approach,
        282, 293–97
    Mirage of the Ideal Moment, 281,
        283–84
    overview, 281–83
    Artifacts Shortcut, 282, 297–302
Flawed Pilot Project Approach, 282,
    293–97
fragmentation, 4, 6, 9–11, 27
Frit Ravich, 178, 180
Future Shock (Toffler), 252

G

García, Arantxa, 210, 213
gemba, 229–30
genchi genbutsu ("go and see for
    yourself"), 293
geographic segmentation, 146–47,
    149, 150

Gerjuoy, Herbert, 252, 253
Gibson, Cristina, 80
glidepath, 136, 139–40, 153–55, 188
Gómez, Alfonso, 131, 133, 134
ground-level intelligence, 13
growth mindset, 23–26, 168

H

habits, leadership
    ambiguity, stopping, 310
    ambition, inspiring, 307
    closing loop and boosting trust,
        308–9
    connecting relentlessly with "why,"
        304
    cutting the crap, 310
    energizing with words, 306
    leading by example, 307–8
    making drumbeat clearly heard,
        305–6
    overview, 302–4
    proximity, fostering, 306–7
    radical clarity, shaping reality with,
        304
    recognition, embracing, 310–11
    ruthless prioritization, enabling,
        304–5
    tribe identity, forging, 306
    undesirable behaviors, stopping
        before normalized, 311
Hackman, J. Richard, 126
hesitation, overcoming, 88–91
Hewlett-Packard, 254
hierarchy, organizational, 108, 123,
        124–25
high-performing teams,
        characteristics of, 123, 126–27
Huang, Jensen, 207–9

I

ideal moment, mirage of, 283–84
impact over activity
    AI as impact partner, 183–87
    analysis paralysis, combating,
        180–83
    beating FATE with, 15–20, 27
    exposure of waste with speed,
        202–6
    at Frit Ravich, 178, 180
    iteration over romanticization,
        209–17
    overview, 8, 34
    paranoid obsession on outcomes,
        187–90
    pilot mindset, 190–96
    reflection questions, 217
    speed in decision-making, 172,
        176–78
    synchrony over chaos, 196–201
    transparency over secrecy, 206–9
    unseen execution in private, 202
    winning mindset, 167–72
industry boundaries, dissolution of,
        12
initiatives
    creating from bets, 151–53
    evolving to glidepath, 153–55
    overview, 136, 139–40
innovation
    continuous, 23–26
    distributed leadership and, 112
    organizational ambidexterity and,
        79–85
    Six P framework, 148
iteration, 209–17
Ive, Jony, 98, 100

J

Jackson, Phil, 128, 132
job characteristics model, 126
Jobs, Steve, 67, 68, 209–10, 284
Joehle, Andreas, 28
Journal of Applied Psychology, 118
Jover, Placid, 190, 194–96

K

keeper test, 270
Keep, Improve, Start, and Stop
    principles, 230–33
Kotter, John, 293
Kursukangas, Enna, 252
Kuzmina, Regina, 94, 96–97

L

Lafley, A. G., 63, 76, 108, 110, 111,
    127, 284
leadership. *See also* leadership
    habits; leadership pitfalls
    as conductor of drumbeat, 224
    development, 244–47
    empowering new leaders to show
        up, 266–69
    leaders building new leaders,
        155–63
    leading by example, 307–8
    leading to beat, 28–38
    succession planning, 250–53
leadership drumbeat, 246–47
The Leadership Engine (Tichy), 156
leadership habits
    ambiguity, stopping, 310
    ambition, inspiring, 307

closing loop and boosting trust,
        308–9
    connecting relentlessly with "why,"
        304
    cutting the crap, 310
    energizing with words, 306
    leading by example, 307–8
    making drumbeat clearly heard,
        305–6
    overview, 302–4
    proximity, fostering, 306–7
    radical clarity, shaping reality with,
        304
    recognition, embracing, 310–11
    ruthless prioritization, enabling,
        304–5
    tribe identity, forging, 306
    undesirable behaviors, stopping
        before normalized, 311
leadership pitfalls
    Delusion of Uniqueness, 289–93
    Fallacy of Assessments, 284–89
    Flawed Pilot Project Approach,
        293–97
    Mirage of the Ideal Moment,
        283–84
    overview, 281–83
    Artifacts Shortcut, 297–302
learning culture, 23–26
learning organizations, 127
learning, speed of, 172, 175
legacy, 311–19, 321
Lencioni, Patrick, 126
Lewin, Kurt, 287, 288
Lewis, Marianne, 80
loyalty program, 151, 154
Lystimäki, Jussi, 276, 278, 300, 302

M

March, James, 79
mediocrity, surfacing, 263–66
meritocracy, culture of, 269–70
metamorphosis, age of, 1–6
microsegmentation, 9–11
Microsoft, 233, 273
milestones, setting, 153–55
Miller, George A., 113
Millman, Dan, 289, 292
Mirage of the Ideal Moment, 281,
    283–84
mission
    clarity of, 62
    connecting relentlessly with "why,"
       304
    one specific, 113–17
    with well-defined targets, 58
multiplying leaders, 13–15
Murdoch, Rupert, 206

N

Nadella, Satya, 233, 273, 274
Netflix, 269–70
"never victim, never in denial," 258–61
Nike, 255, 257
Nokia, 255
noncritical goals and activities,
    eliminating, 67–79
North Star metrics
    brutal focus, building, 49–50
    one specific mission, 113–17
    the Wall, 58–62, 64–65
not-do list, 76
NVIDIA, 207–9, 255, 257–58

O

off-site extravaganzas, 44, 47
Ohno, Taiichi, 185, 229
Oldham, Greg, 126
onboarding, 249–50
once-per-quarter Wall refinement,
    262–63
1:1:1 Formula. *See also* one specific
       execution; one specific team
    one specific mission, 113–17
    overview, 113
    the Wall refinement cycle, 263
one specific execution
    Advanced Customer Decoding,
       145–48
    from big bets to initiatives, 151–53
    BIG choices, 136, 139–40
    Customer Compass, 147–48
    general discussion, 136–45
    from initiatives to glidepath,
       153–55
    1:1:1 Formula, 113
    segmentation unleashing big bets,
       150–51
    Six P framework, 148–50
one specific mission, 113–17
one specific team
    characteristics of high-performing
       teams, 123, 126–27
    enabling open talent pools, 128–30
    1:1:1 Formula, 113
    O-shaped talent model, 120–27
    overview, 118
    power of open-talent pools, 127,
       131–35
open talent pools, enabling, 128–30
organizational ambidexterity
    electric vehicle company, 85–88
    general discussion, 79–85
    the Wall and, 62

O-shaped talent model
    characteristics of high-performing
      teams, 123, 126–27
    enabling open talent pools, 128–30
    general discussion, 120–27
    power of open-talent pools, 127,
      131–35
outcomes, paranoid obsession on,
    187–90
ownership
    BIG choices, 140
    distributed leadership and, 108,
      126
    pilots, 191–96
    unambiguous, 247
owning problems, 258–61

P

packaging, in Six P framework, 149
Paranjpe, Nitin, 72, 258
paranoid obsession on outcomes,
    187–90
Pareto principle, 67–69, 70, 136, 139
pay-per-value systems, 4
PepsiCo, 118, 120
perfect moment, waiting for, 283–84,
    285
performance debt, 311, 312
performance, distributed leadership
    and, 118, 120
performance management, 247–48
performance review, 127
physical AI, 1–2, 121
pilot project approach, flaws in,
    293–97
pilots, 190–96, 210, 213, 247
Pink, Daniel, 247
Artifacts Shortcut, 282, 297–302

pitfalls, leadership. *See* leadership
    pitfalls
pivoting, 16–19
place, in Six P framework, 150
Plan-Do-Check-Act thinking, 54–55
Porras, Jerry, 254
PowerPoint slides, 44, 47, 114, 116,
    264–65
precision marketing, 149
price, in Six P framework, 150
prioritization, enabling ruthless,
    304–5
Problems of Theoretical Psychology
    (Tolman), 287
problems, owning, 258–61
Procter & Gamble (P&G), 54–55, 63,
    76, 127
product, in Six P framework, 148
promotion, in Six P framework, 149
proposition, in Six P framework, 149
proximity, fostering, 306–7
psychographic segmentation, 146,
    149, 150
psychological safety, 126

R

radical clarity, shaping reality with,
    304
radical transparency, 112, 156
RAM (augmented mediocrity), 72,
    75–76
recognition, embracing, 310–11
reporting, shifting to piloting from,
    190–96
resilience, 19
resource management, 72, 75–76,
    307
respect within teams, 126

rewiring organization, 13–15

RFM (recency, frequency, monetary value) analysis, 146, 151

rhythm of change

beating FATE with, 27

brutal focus, 9–11

disciplined drumbeat, 20–26

distributed leadership, 12–15

finding, 6–27

impact over activity, 15–20

leading to beat, 28–38

Ritson, Mark, 55

romanticization, 209–17

Ruimin, Zhang, 284

ruthless prioritization, enabling, 304–5

S

sales and operations planning (S&OP), 248–49

Schultz, Howard, 284

secrecy, prioritizing transparency over, 206–9

segmentation

Advanced Customer Decoding, 145–48

BIG choices, 150–55

Customer Compass, 147–48

overview, 142–45

Six P framework, 148–50

self-determination theory, 126

self-organized teams, 127

Senge, Peter, 127

Shingo, Shigeo, 204

silos

breaking free with distributed leadership, 105–7

the Wall as cross-silos compass, 91–98

simplicity, commitment to, 63–64

simultaneity, 236–41

Six P framework, 148–50

Smith, Wendy, 80

social identity theory, 118

speed in decision-making, 16–19, 172, 176–78, 180–83

Spotify, 160

the Stop Wall, 69, 97, 234–36

strategy. See also brutal focus

five primary dysfunctions of, 58, 62–63

power of, 43–48

the Wall, 52–67

succession planning, 250–53

sustainability campaigns, 152–53, 155

Swappie, 276

Sweller, John, 63, 113

swift, data-informed decision-making, 19–20

synchronized evolution, 236–41

synchros

and iteration, 210, 213

maintaining communication, 126

overview, 112, 176

Artifacts Shortcut, 297–98

radical clarity, shaping reality with, 306

results of, 202, 203

speed in decision-making, 183

surfacing mediocrity, 264

synchrony over chaos, 196–201

transparency and, 206–7

in unified talent system, 263

waste exposed by, 205–6

T

Tajfel, Henri, 118

talent allocation

    brutal focus and, 50–52

    enabling open talent pools, 128–30

    the Wall and, 62

talent review process

    continuous reevaluation of talent, 269

    culture of meritocracy, 269–70

    empowering new leaders to show up, 266–69

    overview, 262

    surfacing mediocrity, 263–66

    unified talent system, 262–63

teams. *See also* one specific team

    brutal focus, 50–52

    closing loop and boosting trust, 308

    cohesion, 118

    energizing with words, 306

    pilots, 190–96, 210, 213

    radical clarity, shaping reality with, 304

    recognition, embracing, 310–11

    synchros, 196–201

    the Wall and, 58–61

    the Wall as cross-silo compass, 91–98

technographic segmentation, 147, 148, 149, 150, 152

technology

    beating entropy with disciplined drumbeat, 20–26

    layering on outdated structures, 15

Teva Pharmaceuticals, 190, 194–96

Tichy, Noel M., 156

timeboxing, 58, 62–63

Toffler, Alvin, 252

Tolman, Charles W., 287

Toyota, 54–55

Tracy, Brian, 136, 138

transparency

    distributed leadership and, 120

    over secrecy, 206–9

    radical, 112, 156

    speed and, 204

    synchronized drumbeat evolution, 236–41

transparent chaos, 71

tribe identity, forging, 306

trust, boosting, 126, 308–9

T-shaped talent model, 120–21

turbulence

    in FATE, 4, 6

    impact over activity, beating with, 15–20, 27

Twain, Mark, 180, 181

U

unambiguous communication, 305–6

unambiguous ownership, 247

unambiguous talent allocation, 58, 62

undesirable behaviors, stopping before normalized, 311

unified talent system, 262–63

Unilever, 64–67, 94, 96–97

uniqueness, delusion of, 289–93

unpredictability, as only stability, 1–6

V

vagueness, eliminating, 63–64

velocity of change, 15–16

Vend, 252

Viader, Judith, 178, 180, 284

victim mindset, 258–61

viral products, 15–16
vital force, drumbeat as, 222, 270–80

W

the Wall
    commitment to clarity and
      simplicity, 63–64
    as cross-silos compass, 91–98
    distributed leadership and, 112
    organizational ambidexterity and,
      80, 83–84
    overcoming Fatal Five with, 58,
      62–63
    overview, 59–61
    Artifacts Shortcut, 297
    Plan-Do-Check-Act thinking, 54–55
    refining, 233–34, 262–64
    surfacing mediocrity, 263–66
    at Unilever, 64–67, 96–97

Walton, Sam, 284
waste, exposure of with speed,
    202–6
weekly synchros. *See* synchros
"why," connecting relentlessly with,
    304
winning mindset, 167–72
words, energizing with, 306

Z

Zuckerberg, Mark, 172, 174

ABOUT THE AUTHOR

JONATHAN ESCOBAR MARIN

Shaping work in the world's top firms

For over two decades, Jonathan Escobar Marin—entrepreneur, investor, CEO, and trusted advisor to global powerhouses—has been reshaping how the world's leading organizations connect strategy, execution, and results. He has played pivotal roles as a partner and execution expert to some of the most influential companies on the planet, building an extraordinary track record of over 320 successful transformations across thirty-two countries and five continents. Jonathan's expertise spans industries including FMCG, retail, pharmaceutical, and technology, where he has consistently empowered firms to outperform markets and dismantle organizational complacency.

After leaving school at sixteen to support his family, Jonathan reignited his educational and professional journey two years later, determined to make an impact. Early in his career, he embraced methods and strategies like Agile, Lean, MBO, OGSM, Big Rocks, and OKRs—not in their theoretical form, but with a laser focus on real-world application. By blending the most effective principles of these frameworks, he developed transformative operating systems that enable leaders, teams, and organizations to achieve and sustain peak performance, even in the most complex environments. A transformative career milestone at Procter & Gamble (P&G) and an international leadership role at the HARTMANN GROUP cemented his expertise in crafting ways of working that deliver top-line growth, bottom-line profitability, innovation impact, and employee engagement.

Under Jonathan's leadership, ActioGlobal has emerged as a global authority in building high-impact, high-performance cultures. Through copyrighted methods, operating systems, and proprietary technologies (including WWAALL® and DRUMBOT.ai), designed in collaboration with C-suites worldwide, ActioGlobal empowers organizations to lead with brutal focus, unleash leadership at every level, prioritize impact over activity, accelerate execution velocity, and continuously raise performance standards—effectively eliminating mediocrity and complacency. Global powerhouses including PepsiCo, Unilever, and Danone, alongside dozens of market leaders across FMCG, retail, pharma, digital, and tech sectors, have partnered with ActioGlobal to drive transformational growth, execute successful turnarounds, and catalyze cultural revolutions.

Beyond ActioGlobal, Jonathan's entrepreneurial vision fuels Actio.Ventures, his investment firm dedicated to nurturing startups poised to disrupt markets and redefine industries. His portfolio showcases companies pioneering innovation across energy, CPG, health care, and work technology sectors, delivering accelerated growth by solving unmet user and consumer needs. Strategic partnerships with Encomenda Capital Partners SGEIC, Nuclio Venture Builder, and select venture capital firms further amplify his investments' impact, addressing the demands of the world's most ambitious customers and consumers.

Jonathan's board positions at multiple growth-focused companies extend his influence in shaping high-performance business cultures. His unparalleled ability to transform organizations and inspire leaders has established him as a driving force behind some of the most ground-breaking business transformations of the twenty-first century.